Mending a Torn World

FAITH MEETS FAITH

An Orbis Series in Interreligious Dialogue
Paul F. Knitter & William R. Burrows, General Editors
Editorial Advisors
John Berthrong
Diana Eck
Karl-Josef Kuschel
Lamin Sanneh
George E. Tinker
Felix Wilfred

In the contemporary world, the many religions and spiritualities stand in need of greater communication and cooperation. More than ever before, they must speak to, learn from, and work with each other in order to maintain their vital identities and to contribute to fashioning a better world.

The FAITH MEETS FAITH Series seeks to promote interreligious dialogue by providing an open forum for exchange among followers of different religious paths. While the Series wants to encourage creative and bold responses to questions arising from contemporary appreciations of religious plurality, it also recognizes the multiplicity of basic perspectives concerning the methods and content of interreligious dialogue.

Although rooted in a Christian theological perspective, the Series does not limit itself to endorsing any single school of thought or approach. By making available to both the scholarly community and the general public works that represent a variety of religious and methodological viewpoints, FAITH MEETS FAITH seeks to foster an encounter among followers of the religions of the world on matters of common concern.

FAITH MEETS FAITH SERIES

Mending a Torn World

Women in Interreligious Dialogue

Maura O'Neill

ORBIS BOOKS
Maryknoll, New York 10545

Founded in 1970, Orbis Books endeavors to publish works that enlighten the mind, nourish the spirit, and challenge the conscience. The publishing arm of the Maryknoll Fathers and Brothers, Orbis seeks to explore the global dimensions of the Christian faith and mission, to invite dialogue with diverse cultures and religious traditions, and to serve the cause of reconciliation and peace. The books published reflect the opinions of their authors and are not meant to represent the official position of the Maryknoll Society. To obtain more information about Maryknoll and Orbis Books, please visit our website at www.maryknoll.org.

Manufactured in the United States of America.
Manuscript editing and typesetting by Joan Weber Laflamme.

Library of Congress Cataloging-in-Publication Data

O'Neill, Maura.
    Mending a torn world : women in interreligious dialogue / Maura O'Neill.
        p. cm. — (Faith meets faith series)
    Includes bibliographical references and index.
    ISBN-13: 978-1-57075-726-6
    1. Women and religion. 2. Religions—Relations. 3. Dialogue—Religious aspects.
I. Title.
    BL458.O53 2007
    201'.5082—dc22

                                                                2007013448

For Michael Harnett,
who mends my world

Contents

PART 2
PROPOSING SOME SOLUTIONS

Preface

In 1999 my husband and I traveled from our home in Southern California to South Africa to participate in the Parliament of World Religions. It was an exciting adventure, not just because of the location but because of the amazing variety of religions represented. The sight of Buddhist monks in saffron robes, Sikhs in white turbans, Hindu women in brightly colored saris, and Africans in tribal printed dashikis gave a sense of the great diversity of the world's beliefs. Despite these differences, however, the campus was filled with an air of understanding and cooperation since all those gathered understood that without these dispositions, world peace was a hopeless endeavor. On our return I was eager to share my experiences with my dear friend, an evangelical Christian very active in her church and its causes. Our friendship of twenty years was well grounded and had developed on the principle that our different ideologies, mine being that of a Roman Catholic feminist, only served to enrich and inform each other. Somehow, my friend's interest in participating in the interreligious dialogue project was not quite as enthusiastic as my own, and her response was curious and somewhat disappointing to me.

Since that time several major events such as those of 9/11, the Iraq war, the debate over legalization of gay marriage, and President Bush's faith-based initiative have served to highlight our differences and put a wedge in our relationship, which has caused me great sorrow. Too often our get-togethers, which were always filled with exciting news of travels and personal experiences, turned into heated disagreements about politics and religion. Her words remain in my mind to disturb my work and my thoughts throughout the days. They are particularly troublesome whenever I have the opportunity to engage in dialogue or to address a group of interfaith women. I try to imagine my friend's response to the discussions. What would she say about trying to find truth in all faiths, about respecting others' beliefs, and about interfaith cooperation on social issues, particularly the status of women?

As these thoughts and feelings run through me, I realize that the issues that come between my friend and me are really universal issues that affect all women. I have seen divisions turn into heated debates in my classes, at neighborhood meetings, and particularly in religious circles, where the role of women is growing increasingly ambiguous. It is becoming clear to me that those women engaged in interreligious dialogue often have more in common with one another than with many women of their own religion. Furthermore, when these women of different faiths come together, whom are they representing? Does the Christian, Jewish, or Muslim woman speak for all in her tradition? For the most part, the current dialogue occurs between the more liberal or progressive women who see themselves as battling the male establishment of their respective traditions. I have often thought that there is a great need for an intra-religious women's dialogue. But how is this possible? What would be the purpose? And what would be talked about? This book is an attempt to answer those questions. It is an effort to learn all sides of women's issues not only through an academic study but by dialogue with women on both ends of the ideological continuum. It is also an attempt to understand, grapple with, and reweave my relationship with my dear friend.

Acknowledgments

This work is the product of my collaboration with the many people whom I have been fortunate to have as teachers, colleagues, and friends over many years. I wish to thank my mentor, John Hick, for his challenges, guidance, and encouragement. I also thank my role models in women's dialogue, Ursula King and Riffat Hassan, who have graciously listened to my ideas. I am grateful to Allison Stokes, Rev. Marilyn Foster, Rev. Martha Forisha, Rev. Lesley Adams, Roxanne Gupta, Mary Skinner, and Nanci Rose-Ritter from the Women's Interfaith Institute for inviting me into their dialogue. Thank you also to those many friends and scholars who have read the pages, listened to my ideas, and offered advice and criticism, including Sr. Marion Defeis, Emily Snitow, Karen Torjesen, June O'Connor, Christa McNerney, Dani Falcioni, Debe Waddell, Betsy Wiggins, Zayn Kassam, Lina Gupta, Geeta Sikand, Dr. Shobhna Vohra, Vrushali (Sheila) Kene, Kay Lindahl, Mae Chu, Karma Lekshe Tsomo, Jeanne Sales, Christine Smith, Rabbi Hillel Cohn, and David and Barbara Evans.

I also thank Roberta and Howard Ahmanson for their friendship, inspiration, patience, and continuing generosity.

I owe a special thanks to my friend and colleague, Peggy Madden, who proofread on her sick leave from teaching, and to our friend James Kevin, who worked on his vacation. I am grateful also to the faculty and administration of Chaffey College for granting me the sabbatical leave to pursue my dream of writing.

Most especially, I am ever grateful to my husband, Michael Harnett, who listened patiently, criticized wisely, sacrificed greatly, and loved always.

Introduction

Our world is in dire need of peace. This fact is obvious when we see the increasing number of conflicts springing up throughout the world, creating prejudice and hatred for people we hardly know, much less understand. Furthermore, our leaders often frame these conflicts in religious terms, causing stereotyping of others' beliefs and a self-righteous conviction of one's own. As a result, people of different cultures and religions, whether they live far away or next door, are viewed as the enemy from whom we must be protected. Given this attitude, the long-range goal of world peace seems impossible indeed. In the midst of this fear, there are some hopeful people attempting to build understanding through interreligious dialogues. Several groups throughout the world are dedicated to this endeavor in the hopes of promoting world peace. However, I believe that these dialogues fall short of their goal and are, in many ways, ineffective for several reasons.

The first part of this book lays out the problems in the current dialogue as I see them. In the first chapter I suggest that these peace efforts, while very important, fail because dialogues are not inclusive enough. They have left out the more conservative voices in the traditions represented. Major rifts are occurring today not only between religions but inside religions as well. There is more divisiveness among the so-called conservative and liberal branches of the same religion than there is between those who engage in the current interreligious dialogues, since these participants are usually of the more liberal mindset. Unless we include those who are on the conservative side of the religious continuum, those engaged in dialogues cannot truly represent their faiths, and rifts will still be brewing among the conservative and liberal factions.

Another problem in the current dialogue is that women are still largely under-represented at the table, and women's issues, which are at the heart of so much controversy between conservatives and liberals, need far more attention than they have been given. The conclusion of this chapter makes a case for bringing together the conservative and liberal women in each religion for dialogues, both among themselves and with women in other religions. I believe that women's dialogue is better able to bridge the gap between religious factions because of its method and its content. Women's mode of interacting is more personal and their dialogue more practical. Also, the content of their conversation is the issues that most affect them and are also at the heart of much of the intra-religious controversy, issues such as the effect of the women's movement on the family and the role of women in the sacred traditions. Therefore, I believe that the problems faced by the current dialogue can best be solved by beginning with women's dialogue.

The second chapter defines some crucial terms bantered about in religious controversies that are used to label and stereotype the other. These terms include *conservative, fundamentalist, liberal, progressive,* and *feminist*. Once defined, these terms are applied to women's positions by placing them on a continuum. On the one end are those women who defend all the teachings of their traditions and on the other are those who wish to change the tradition to adapt to modern times. Defining where various women stand helps establish a common ground for mutual understanding and dialogue.

Chapters 3 and 4 then explain how each of five major world traditions—Judaism, Christianity, Islam, Hinduism, and Buddhism—has been represented by women on all segments of the continuum. People often form opinions about how other religions treat their women without really knowing the perspectives of the women themselves. Many express surprise when hearing that there are Islamic or evangelical Christian feminists or that modern women are turning to Orthodox Judaism. By presenting the diversity of women's voices, we can appreciate the need for and the possibility of dialogue among them. Such a meeting can enrich the greater dialogue, making it more inclusive and hence more effective.

The second part of the book poses some solutions to these problems by analyzing the motivation for dialogue among seemingly antagonistic groups and the methodology for a constructive meeting, and then suggesting some pertinent topics that need to be addressed. Chapter 5 examines some crucial social issues brought about by globalization that require the attention of diverse religious groups. In coming together, however, there are some obstacles discussed in this chapter that must to be dealt with in order for the dialogue to be productive. It is also essential to understand that dialogue is different from debate and that certain strategies, such as those presented in Chapter 6, can be used to improve understanding. Telling personal stories and practicing active listening are important means to overcoming stereotypes and are used more commonly among women than men. Chapter 7 discusses topics involving women throughout the world that are at the heart of differences within and among religions. Bringing these topics to the table of intra-religious and interreligious dialogue can help us understand the perspective of the other and thus clarify points of disagreement. Inevitably, understanding and clarification help soothe the wounds caused by animosity. Important topics to be covered are women's spirituality, attitudes toward social and religious changes in the modern world, and women's roles in the family and society. Finally, it is important to ask where women find the sources of authority that provide them with grounds for their beliefs and their behaviors. Where do they turn for direction and support in a chaotic world? These issues, which are at the heart of the differences between the opposing views, are essential for women's dialogue if mutual understanding is to be achieved.

Finally, the conclusion expresses some hope for the future. At the beginning of the project the thought of the two ends of the ideological continuum coming together seemed to be an impossible dream. But women's dialogue presents a method of dealing with opposing viewpoints. Furthermore, women share common subjects at the heart of many of the controversies. For these reasons it makes sense to bring together women who represent the various viewpoints, for it is in this coming together that there is hope for cooperation and understanding between the conservative and the progressive. I may be overly optimistic, but unless one tries, not much can be achieved. If women's dialogue can help increase mutual understanding, and if women then achieve a greater voice in the larger forum, such understanding might spread, thus laying the foundation for a more trusting environment in which peace becomes a possibility. Without small steps, no dream can be realized. It is my hope that these pages present some possibilities for such steps.

PART I

Understanding the Problem

1

Challenges
for a Fruitful Dialogue

THE CHALLENGE OF PEACE

What is this world coming to? This common cry is heard often today among people on both ends of the political and religious spectrums who blame society's ills on their opponents. Whether the problem is the war in Iraq or declining morals, liberals blame the conservatives, who, they claim, are narrow-minded and self-righteous, and the conservatives blame the liberals, saying they are wishy-washy and too soft on enemies. Particularly since the events of 9/11, the rift between these two groups has grown and continues to grow wider with each new government pronouncement and each new act of terror.

This animosity between the two ideological camps is more deeply solidified by the connection made between nationalism and religion. The world's governments have enlisted religious rhetoric to raise their issues to the level of the sacred and to give their national interests the stamp of divine authority. Accusations raised against enemies have also risen to the level of religion. George W. Bush and Tony Blair have justified invading Iraq by calling it a war between the forces of good and evil; Islamic leaders talk about defending themselves against infidels; and the Jews of Israel speak of their biblical right to the land given them by God. This use of religious concepts as methods of persuasion requires us to know about the religions of others in order to make sense of world events. It is imperative to understand the meaning of religious words as they are used in context in order to make clear judgments about the speeches we hear and the reports we read. What do these religions really teach regarding war, evil, and the treatment of enemies? Furthermore, we need to learn about these religions not just from books but by meeting and dialoguing with their practitioners, for only personal conversation can place an ideology in its human context.

There have been and continue to be attempts to bridge the religious divide and clarify the true nature of those religions used in political rhetoric. Interreligious dialogues are taking place on national and international levels. The Parliament of World Religions, a worldwide meeting of members of all traditions, met in Chicago in 1993, in South Africa in 1999, and in Barcelona in summer 2004. Other worldwide groups include the Global Dialogue Institute, which has made "significant progress in establishing dialogue as a valid and preferred approach to dealing with conflicts."[1] Many other such groups have sprung up throughout the world, even in particularly volatile areas such as Iran, where the members of the Institute for Interreligious Dialogue, a nongovernmental organization, believe that dialogue can foster peace, friendship, and spirituality among societies.[2] While these groups consist mostly of scholars and diplomats, there is also a growing number of local groups coming together not only for mutual understanding but also for more practical purposes such as promoting respect for neighbors and helping with social-service projects to better their communities. It is one thing to learn about a religion from books, quite another to engage in dialogue with the practitioners, and still another to work together toward a common goal. Regardless of their configuration or their purpose, each of these groups realizes that peace is dependent on the mutual understanding and acceptance of the diverse faith communities encountered in our shrinking world. In the words of Hans Küng, "Peace among the religions is a presupposition of peace among the nations."[3]

THE CHALLENGE OF INCLUDING CONSERVATIVE PERSPECTIVES

However, in the accounts of these interreligious dialogues, there are two deficiencies, which, in these troubled times, are becoming more and more glaring. First, those persons coming to the dialogue table, whether scholars of religion or interested neighbors, often share similar mindsets regarding the pluralistic framework within which they live out their beliefs. The people who dialogue often hold progressive views of the world, recognizing that it is shrinking and that our lives must adapt and change accordingly. In general, these participants do not represent the more conservative and traditional branches, which are becoming more and more visible and their leaders more and more vocal in the public forum. The problem is that these conservative voices are not speaking to or being heard by those in the interfaith forums. Some participants blame the conservatives for their absence, saying that they have "in most cases ignored interfaith councils"[4] Others, such as Peter Huff, believe that those already engaged in dialogue have not reached out to understand or to include these more conservative groups in their meetings. Regardless of the reason for their absence, it is clear in today's climate that the goals of mutual understanding and peaceful coexistence will never be realized if the dialogues do not become more inclusive. In Huff's words, "Interreligious dialogue will never fulfill its unique mission until it recognizes the fundamentalisms of the world as valued conversation partners."[5]

At first glance, many would consider this suggestion preposterous. I have heard people say that the conservatives only want to convert the nonbeliever, and therefore conversing with conservatives is impossible. I have heard others say that progressives are relativists going along with any proposition for the sake of peace and would sacrifice their principles to engage in dialogue. These attitudes seem to be fairly entrenched in the modern mindset and continue to be enforced by myriad talk shows, books, periodicals, and newspapers that spout half-truths and play on emotions. These publicity tools are shaping opinions of those on both ends of the ideological spectrum, and neither the conservatives nor liberals are free from the propaganda blitz, which only serves to widen the ideological chasm.

This book is dedicated to the proposition that, in the midst of all this animosity, a dialogue is still possible. For it to happen, however, we need a careful analysis of the issues that divide the religions among themselves. We also need to look at the methods used in successful dialogues and apply these to internal dialogues, for the opposing viewpoints within our own religious groups are as estranged as those among other religions. In short, there needs to be a serious intra-religious dialogue. It is in this dialogue that various conflicting factions within religions can better understand one another so that when Jews, Christians, Muslims, Hindus, and Buddhists come to the dialogue table, they will be speaking with and for the many branches of their traditions and not only for the liberal sectors.

THE CHALLENGE OF HEARING WOMEN AND THEIR ISSUES

The second deficiency in today's dialogue is the shortage of women participants and the dearth of women's issues as subjects of conversations. While there have been scattered meetings of religious women throughout the world, their presence and their concerns in the large global interfaith organizations are sparse or marginal. Modern psychological and philosophical studies reveal that gender is an important factor in the way religions are lived and experienced. Women view their world and their beliefs differently than men do. In the words of popular author and organizer Joan Chittister, "Women see things differently, do things differently, and are affected by things differently than men. This is a crucial factor for us to consider at this point in our history when religion has assumed [such a] . . . prominent role in domestic politics and international relations."[6] Not only have women's roles in religion been different from those of men, but also they have been defined and controlled by the male power structure. It is important to find out from the women themselves how they see their religious identity and what they wish their roles to be. Majella Franzmann, in her study of women and religion, claims that "once women are allowed to speak about their own space, rather than have male religious professionals speak for them from the male-dominated space, an entirely other world of experience may be identified."[7] Therefore, unless women's voices are heard, the conversation among religions will be one-sided and the attempts at understanding one another's traditions will be deficient. At the 1999 Parliament of World Religions in South Africa, many of us assembled after a week of sessions to discuss the noticeable dearth of women's voices. And, while I did not attend the 2004 meeting in Barcelona, many of my colleagues noticed the same problem. They told of coming together as a group formally to report the absence of the full range of women's voices that would have balanced the parliament's dialogue. They realized, as we did in 1999, that religious and spiritual dialogue would be irrelevant if a rainbow of women's voices, the poor and the disenfranchised as well as the scholars and the leaders, were not heard. Viewed in this light the absence of women's voices severely weakens the goal of interreligious dialogue, namely, mutual understanding and world peace.

BEGINNING WITH WOMEN'S DIALOGUE

Besides the need to be included in the larger forums, women need also to dialogue among themselves. The case was made for women to come together in my first book, *Women Speaking, Women Listening*, which presented a methodology and rationale for women's dialogue. However, the need has become greater in recent years because the growing fundamentalist or conservative movements within all traditions have their greatest effect on women. Most often these movements focus on issues of sexuality and the family, each of which has a direct bearing on women's identity. In some cases these conservative ideas are viewed as oppressive to women, while in others they are spawned and supported by women, but in either case women's issues are central to the movements. As noted by Anne Davison, a worker with the World Council of Churches, "The issues of women, their social and religious roles, the perceptions of women's sexuality and bodily functions, the question of women's human rights are in themselves divisive issues"[8] within religions as well as among religions. Given the need to bring conservative factions into the dialogue and given the fact that women and women's issues are at the heart of the debates between conservatives and liberals, it seems logical that a place to start to bring together these disparate and opposing spectrums of believers is in women's dialogue. One of the intentions of this work is to demonstrate that the content and nature of women's dialogue is the ideal place to start the long journey of understanding the diverse factions of religious followers both within each tradition and across traditions.

While it may appear that such a dialogue is exclusive, that is, leaving out men, I believe that women's dialogue is a vital supplement to, rather than a replacement for, the current work in the field of interfaith relations. I am convinced that women are better able than men to bridge the wide abyss of misunderstanding that plagues our world. I am aware of the feminist debates that try to fathom how and why women are different from men in their means of relating. Whether there is some essential difference, whether men and women are conditioned differently, or whether there is really only a perceived difference have been and will continue to be heated academic controversies. However, our purpose here is not to philosophize on the whys and wherefores but rather to acknowledge that expressing emotions and communicating on a personal level are more commonly seen in women than in men and are important tools to a successful dialogue. These skills, coupled with the experience of being marginalized, would indicate that dialogues conducted by women, for women, and about women's issues are essential for mutual understanding, and, therefore, a good starting point for the meeting of conservative and liberal world views.

2

The Problem of Definitions

An important factor for a successful dialogue is clarifying the definitions for some of the basic terms that are bandied about in this ideological conflict. Terms such as *conservative, fundamentalist, evangelical, liberal, progressive,* and *feminist* are used often to label opponents. But they are also used to self-identify, which indicates that all of these terms have both positive and negative connotations. For the sake of discussion, it is important to look at how these terms can simply describe a contextual position without carrying the baggage of ideologies.

CONSERVATIVE AND TRADITIONAL

Looking at its root, the word *conservative* means one who wishes to conserve, and a religious conservative would be one who seeks to maintain the practices that have traditionally been associated with her or his belief system. We could alternately apply the word *traditionalist* to the same individual. A conservative or traditionalist, therefore, would be against making changes in a religion to adapt to our modern world. The question here is, How far back does a practice have to go to be called a tradition? In Roman Catholicism, for example, a conservative might want to maintain priestly celibacy even though that practice did not become standardized until the eleventh century.

The advances made in science, medicine, sanitary practices, human and civil rights, and our knowledge of history and anthropology have drastically changed our lifestyles. No longer do we have to worry about the pork we eat causing trichinosis or a woman's menses causing her to be polluted; exorcisms are not the usual way of dealing with mental illness; and women are allowed to vote and participate in the public arena. Another significant factor is the theory of evolution by a process of natural selection. These changes have affected the way many people interpret their traditions. A reform Jew will eat pork; a modern Hindu woman will interact socially and pray at the temple during her menstruation; and modern

Christians believe in evolution, that psychiatry is a viable science, and that women can be capable ministers. On the other hand, not all religious people see the value in modern findings, particularly if they contradict what appears in the original revelation. Many Jews do not eat pork; in many cultures menstruating women have a dangerous power; and some Christian churches still do not allow women to conduct a service. It is also evident by the many legal battles occurring in several states that creationism—or intelligent design—is believed by many Christians in the United States. For the sake of consistency, therefore, the word *conservative* will be used here to describe the groups of religious people who believe that modern research in various fields of knowledge may threaten the integrity of the belief system and, therefore, that changes in the religion to accommodate modernity are to be resisted.

FUNDAMENTALISM

A fundamentalist by definition is one who adheres to the fundamentals of a movement. However, according to three Canadian scholars, the word takes on specific connotations at this time in history. "Fundamentalist movements profess to be upholding some kind of orthodoxy or right practice and regard themselves as instrumental in preserving the tradition from erosion. . . . [They] tend toward self-separation or exclusivity, as well as prescriptive distinctions that mark adherents from outsiders."[1] Once again the tradition that is being preserved here refers to a specific interpretation of the long history of beliefs and practices particularly within Judaism, Christianity, and Islam.

Within Christianity, there is a very specific tradition of fundamentalism, which many Christians want to distinguish from contemporary evangelicalism. This tradition, which began in the mid-nineteenth century, developed into a movement named for a set of essays called *The Fundamentals: A Testimony of Truth*, which reasserted the fundamental creed of evangelical Christianity in response to a growing liberal theology.[2] Fundamentalist subcultures separated themselves from other evangelicals by their adherence to a more literalist view of scripture, strict adherence to a core set of doctrines, an anti-ecumenical attitude, and a strong reaction to changes in social mores, especially feminism and the "perceived decline in womanhood."[3] However, in the latter part of the twentieth century segments of evangelical Christianity reexamined scripture to discover that some of the narrow positions of the strict fundamentalists particularly with regard to women's roles "do not reflect an accurate interpretation of the texts."[4] The result of these conflicting interpretations is that, within the Christian communities, evangelicals today distinguish themselves from fundamentalists.

Jewish fundamentalism is often associated with the Jews in Israel, but it can also refer to the Orthodox sectors of Judaism, which adhere to a strict interpretation of the Torah, observing all the laws as they are written in the sacred text. Such communities exist in all countries and appear to be growing in numbers. This phenomenon needs to be understood and reckoned with by the more reformist movements within the Jewish tradition.

The label *fundamentalist* poses new problems, however, when used to refer to Muslims. The Western media have linked violence and terrorism to the term *Islamic fundamentalism*, thus creating much animosity and fear in their audience. However, a more careful study of Islam reveals that we cannot use the term in the same way that we use it for Christians. All Muslims view the Qur'an as the direct word of God, so the idea of textual inerrancy is held universally. Also the five pillars of Islam—the declaration of one God, the tax for the poor, prayer five times a day, fasting during the month of Ramadan, and the pilgrimage to Mecca—are requirements for all Muslims, or the fundamentals of the faith, if you will. Instead of using the word *fundamentalist,* Muslim historians and scholars refer to *revivalism.* Throughout the years of growth and change in Islam, there have been periodic attempts to return to the days of the Prophet Muhammad to revive the authentic practice, especially when particular circumstances are threatening to destroy Islam or to create undue hardship for its people. At these times Muslims believe that the answer to their problems is to return to the tenets of Islam as spelled out in the Shari'a (the Islamic law that is derived from God's word in the Qur'an). These attempts to defend and to live in an Islamic society are behind the current rift between Islam and the West, which, as history tells us, is not new but rather of very long standing. Throughout the history of Islam, at various times and places, from the crusades, to colonialism, to the influx of Western secularism, Muslims have viewed the West as a threat to Islam. To ward off the threat, revivalist movements have sprung up, which are characterized by making Islam a total way of life, rejecting the tenets of secularism and individualism, calling for a holy struggle or jihad against Western values, and reinforcing patriarchal family codes and the "proper place of women."[5] It is these revivalist movements that have become known in modern times as Islamic fundamentalism and sometimes take on extremist interpretations of the law and have, depending on the leader at the time, been very oppressive, especially to women. Therefore, ideas and practices such as jihad, Shari'a, and the veiling of women must necessarily be understood within a context so that their origins and mainstream meanings are not confused with extremist interpretations.

When speaking of fundamentalism, regardless of the tradition in which it appears, it is important to keep in mind that its adherents have committed themselves to the ideology for a purpose. On a practical level, the communal nature of fundamentalism contributes to its popularity because it satisfies some very human needs: the longing for security and well-being, the wish for a utopian society upholding human values, and the desire for strong bonds of solidarity. Participants in dialogue need to understand the motivations of fundamentalists in order to remain open and not allow, in the words of one scholar, "the visceral revulsion against fundamentalism to cloud their analysis of this human phenomenon."[6] In dialogue, fundamentalism can offer critical insights into the limitations of modernity and globalization. Peter Huff encourages the further study of fundamentalism as a particular kind of religious experience. Once those engaged in interreligious dialogue recognize such a study, then dialogue can serve to end what Huff calls the "theological cold war." To those skeptics who doubt that such a dialogue is possible, Jesuit scholar Arij A. Roest Crollius replies, "Dialogue with Fundamentalists is not impossible. Especially the first forms of Interreligious Dialogue . . . (collaboration, agreeing to disagree, comparison of tenets) can often be practiced with fruit. After all, we live together in one village, global or not. A pragmatic approach can be helpful."[7]

From the above analysis it would appear that the term *fundamentalism* is ambiguous, having different connotations when referring to different religions. Because of this ambiguity and because of the negative connotations applied by the media and by others, the term *fundamentalism* will be avoided in this study and replaced by the more general term *conservative*. This term, which implies resistance to change or adaptation to the modern world, can be applied to several viewpoints distinguished by how resistant or how open they are to applying modern knowledge to the ancient traditions and revelations.

LIBERAL AND PROGRESSIVE

Turning now to the other end of the spectrum, we need to examine the terms *liberal* and *progressive*. *Liberal*, coming from the Latin *liber* meaning "free," refers to a mindset unfettered by convention or by tradition. A liberal, therefore would be open to new ideas and new information and find ways to apply these to what is already known or believed. However, in modern times the word *liberal* has acquired some more specific connotations. To many, it signifies an individualistic stance associated with a certain permissiveness. In other words, a person can do what she or he wills, because, as many of my students often claim, "it's a free country." This form of liberalism ignores the sense of community basic to most religions as well as to our human condition. If an individual is to live in a community, religious or otherwise, she or he must exercise responsibilities such as respecting the rights of others and contributing to the common welfare. While freedom is a good thing, freedom to do what one wants without the accompanying communal responsibilities, whether to one's family, civic community, or religion, is a dangerous idea by anyone's standards and not the one referred to in this study. Hence, because it bears the connotation of freedom without the accompanying responsibility, *liberal* will be avoided here.

The term *progressive* is perhaps a better one to be used here because it carries the positive sense of liberal without its negative baggage. Like liberals, progressives look favorably on most of the changes brought about by the latest discoveries and increases in knowledge. They apply the study of history and the social, physical, and life sciences to sacred texts, to religious traditions, and to religious experiences. The results of this endeavor then determine the mode of being religious in today's world. It is important at this point to emphasize that this acceptance of modern research does not of necessity turn the religious progressive into an unbeliever. An atheist or an agnostic is in a separate category and, while she or he may possibly contribute to our dialogue, nonbelievers lie outside the parameters of the present study. We are speaking here of the believer who uses modern textual criticisms rather that literalism to determine the divine will, who believes that the religious organizations must be relevant to today's world, and who looks favorably on most of the social changes of modernity. For example, the progressive will use historical criticism of scripture and modern psychological studies to make decisions on the morality of homosexuality instead of using a natural-law or biblical argument condemning it as against God's design. The progressive will use the modern attitude toward gender equality to judge an all-male clergy as discriminatory. Note here that neither scripture nor tradition is ignored but merely understood in an historical context.

Later in our study stereotypes will be discussed, but let it suffice at this point to note that a religious progressive is not a relativist. That is, she or he does not accept any new idea that comes along because it is new. Moralities and belief systems are not all equal; there is a right and wrong, and truth does matter. Rightness or wrongness is determined by clear guidelines that have been carefully discerned from analyzing the basic tenets of faith. The content of these guidelines will be included in the further analysis of the dialogue between the two sides. Suffice it to say at this point that the religious progressive is, contrary to what many may think, a believer and one who has made a faith commitment.

FEMINIST

The next term to be considered is *feminist*. This word has been bandied about by so many political and religious factions that it has become loaded with connotations that make it difficult to utter without conjuring up various images, which, to some, are extremely negative and, to others, extremely positive. Just as beauty lies in the eye of the beholder so the meaning of the word *feminist* lies in the mind of the listener. Not on a few occasions have I had to proceed with caution in talking about feminism to my classes. It appears that many women who have dedicated themselves to being good wives and mothers, and who are fulfilled and happy in their role, view feminism as a condemnation of their chosen place in life. They think that to be a feminist is to renounce the value of family and go out of the home to seek a career for fame and fortune and, to use a cliché from the 1960s, to burn one's bra. These people view feminists as responsible for the breakup of the family, the rise of teen pregnancy, drug addiction, and abortion as birth control. Most threatening of all, however, is the image of the feminist as secular and godless.

Others hold more positive connotations to the term. To them, *feminism* means being liberated from the negative stereotypes that have been traditionally attached to women, such as mental and physical weakness, fickleness, and irrationality. To these people, sexism's rearing its ugly head in language, humor, and treatment in the work place or in the home is to be openly refuted and eliminated. They see feminism as a positive force that fights against wife abuse, unequal pay, and discrimination in all spheres.

To still others the word *feminist* conjures up the image of a middle-class white woman fighting the male power structure, while she herself is in a privileged position over women of color. More recently, the voices of Asian, Latina, and black women who understand their oppression as unique experiences have been calling for unique theologies and strategies for liberation. Black women in particular have challenged feminists in a large body of literature called womanist theology, deriving the term from Alice Walker's definition of womanism in her text *In Search of Our Mothers' Garden*. In her description of this theology, Linda Thomas explains that "feminist theology did not deal with the categories of race and economics in the development of its theological discourse."[8] Because it did not pay attention to the everyday realities of African Americans and other women of color, it does not speak to the oppression of all women. Womanist theology, on the other hand, is the positive affirmation of the gifts of black women and, says Thomas, is "an emergent voice which advocates a holistic God-talk for all the oppressed."[9]

These diverse understandings of the word *feminism* and the use of the more inclusive *womanist* will undoubtedly play a part in the dialogue between conservative and liberal women within religions. However, before the process begins, it is necessary to lay out some parameters on the use of the terms and their understanding. To begin, the positions that are spoken of in this study will refer to religious positions, and while these have been influenced and affected by secular feminism, those philosophies that are strictly political, social, or economic are not what are being considered in interreligious dialogue. It is important to note that there are women who identify themselves in one way or another as feminist or womanist in each of the five religions covered here. Within this context we can define the terms as the need to give women respect equal to that of men and of those in positions of power, and also the need to free women from those oppressive practices that have been detrimental to their fulfillment as women and as human beings. This said, it is understandable that these two criteria of feminism—respect and freedom from oppression—will be understood differently by different religious and cultural communities. For example, some might see respecting women as allowing time and freedom to work in the home unencumbered by other responsibilities such as jobs or religious obligations. They might see respect as protecting women from the evil that lurks in the marketplace or in the public arena, and hence they must cover themselves or stay at home. Others, on the other hand, might see respect carried out by allowing women to participate in full ministry or leadership of a particular tradition. They would allow women to be ministers or priests, to be board members of mosques, and to partake in the minyan (the group of ten needed for public prayer in Judaism). These different interpretations of respect and freedom from oppression will be the food for conversation that will be proposed further on in our analysis of intra-religious and interreligious dialogue.

THE CONTINUUM OF WOMEN'S POSITIONS

These various conflicting views of freedom are held by women themselves in each of the world's religions. These many positions can be best analyzed by placing them on a continuum from the most conservative to the most progressive viewpoints. It is important to note at the outset, however, that the one constant factor in all of the positions is faith in the tenets and practices of one's particular tradition, and it is this faith that distinguishes religious feminism from its secular counterpart, which generally views all religions as oppressive to women. The point of difference among religious viewpoints lies in how women relate to their traditions. Do they view their religion as liberating or oppressive? Do they believe their religion comes directly from the divine source or is a historic interpretation handed down by male authorities?

On the one end of the spectrum are the conservative or traditional women who believe that clear gender distinctions are an essential part of the very foundation of their religion. These distinctions are viewed not as restricting them but rather as the fulfillment of a divine will or of a natural order. These women see themselves as fully capable of achieving the saving or liberating goals of their religion, but they understand that their roles as laid out in sacred texts are those of supporters and helpers of men, who, in turn, provide them with leadership and protection. From the beginning of known history and continuing through to modern times, women have had distinct biological, psychological, and social characteristics that serve to determine their roles in the community. By being faithful to these roles, women are fulfilling themselves by following the natural order of the cosmos, which, depending on their religion, is either God's creation or a divine emanation.

In the centrist position on this spectrum are women who hold that the original revelation or insight is egalitarian, that is, that it holds women equal to men in dignity and in leadership. The oppression and subordination of women are cultural problems that arose later as the religion developed in history. When those men in the existing patriarchal societies institutionalized the original revelation or insight, they imposed on it their misogynistic views. These views left their mark in the translation of sacred texts and in the elimination of women from leadership and ritual. The results were that women's position in the religious structures gradually narrowed and declined such that their spiritual welfare and religious identity were totally in the hands of men. The women in this centrist position see their task as searching the sources of their tradition to return to the original revelation to find women's authentic experience. Jewish women who hold this position are engaging in the study of biblical texts to uncover women who held the position of prophets, such as Miriam and Deborah, but whose names are rarely included in the current rituals.[10] Christian women in this category believe that Jesus attempted to free his women followers from the patriarchal mores of his day. However, early in the history of Christianity, the dominant male power structure concluded that women, for a number of reasons, could not represent Jesus and therefore were to be barred from leadership in the churches. Likewise, Hindu scholars believe that the Vedas show evidence of women's sharing the performance of ritual with their husbands, a role later restricted by the Brahmins or male priests. Buddhist women are also looking at the discourses of the Buddha to discern the authenticity of his instructions on the subordination of nuns to male monks and his statements on the weakness and fickleness of women. Therefore, feminists in the center of the spectrum listen attentively to the exegesis of texts and history of religions to search out a practice that more closely resembles an authentic egalitarian tradition.

At the other end of our spectrum are those feminists who understand that, just as most ancient cultures were mainly misogynistic, so were the cultures that received the original revelation or insight. For this reason it is necessary to reexamine not only the sacred texts and history but also the very message itself. The essentials of the tradition must be sorted out from the accidents, or that which is attributed to culture, in order to determine how the practices based on the very foundations of the various belief systems can be faithfully carried out in the twenty-first century. An example of such a position is found in Rosemary Radford Ruether's *Sexism and God-Talk*. In this work dealing with Roman Catholicism, Ruether redefines the concepts of God as father, church as institution, and eucharist as Christ's body to present them as more egalitarian ideas instead of having inherently male connotations. Her work, like that of all feminists on this end of the spectrum, considers the progress made over time in racial and gender equality and in human rights as a good thing. If it is a good thing, then religion, the place where the divine will is systematically revealed, should and must reflect this progress. Ruether and her ilk are not rejecting revelation but merely attempting to understand it in light of the changing perceptions and understandings of humans, who are so slow to realize the true nature of things.

With more women writing in the field of religion and with the increasing polarization of conservatives and progressives in all traditions, a closer look at this gamut of positions is a necessary starting point for women's understanding of one another. What are the motivating forces behind these points of view? What can prompt some women to seek freedom from past patriarchal practices and others to look to them for self-identification and fulfillment? These are the questions to be addressed as we progress in our analysis.

3

Conflicting Viewpoints in Judaism, Christianity, and Islam

One of my Italian mother's favorite sayings is "there are always two sides to every story." This idea hit home with me when, at a meeting of John Hick's trialogue with Jews, Christians, and Muslims, a veiled American convert to Islam told us how freeing Islam is. She said that the American feminist movement was necessary because American women suffered far more oppression than Muslim women did. I was amazed to hear her story. At about the same time in the late 1980s, the *Los Angeles Times* published an article about three modern professional women who had turned to strict Jewish Orthodoxy. Again, I was perplexed, especially after I had read so much about the oppression of women in these religions. Since that time I have learned much about the variety of voices coming out of all of the world's religions and realize that there is no one feminism. There are not two but rather many sides to the story of women in these traditions. So I am less surprised today, as the American political and religious scene is picking up more and more right-wing voices, to hear from evangelical Christian women who are claiming a feminist identity. Also, my encounters with immigrant Buddhist and Hindu women make me very aware that there is a sense of self-identity within the male-dominated structure, which, to them, is not at all stifling. To begin to understand these women, it is important to hear their views in their own voices. Once this is done, their positions can be put in perspective by placing them alongside the many other women's viewpoints regarding their traditions. When the many voices are heard, we find that they lie on the continuum, described earlier, ranging from the most conservative to the most progressive. Studying all these positions makes clear the differences and conflicts that currently exist within religions. It also emphasizes the great need for a dialogue among the viewpoints.

JUDAISM

In the last few decades there have been more and more women studying, speaking, and writing about women's place in Judaism. These women represent views that fall on all points of the continuum ranging from the traditional Orthodox position, which adheres to the complete separation of the sexes in all religious roles and rituals, to the Reformists and Reconstructionists, who believe that all positions in Judaism should be opened to women. Regardless of their differences, these women have a common purpose. Leila Gal Berner writes, "We share a commitment to giving voice to Jewish women's spiritual concerns, and shaping a Judaism for the future that incorporates women's voices and life experiences as part of legitimate Jewish Tradition."[1] These voices are essential for the revitalization of the tradition without which, in the words of Pnina Nave Levinson, "Judaism will inevitably disappear."[2] We turn now to listen to women's voices within the various branches of Judaism to learn how each fits onto the continuum and how each contributes to assuring Judaism a vibrant future.

CONSERVATIVE POSITION

The most conservative position is that of the traditional Orthodox Jewish woman who believes that the original revelation is from God in its entirety and therefore immutable. There are several conservative Orthodox groups, including the Hasidim, but they all share the belief that men and women are essentially different and that this difference is part of God's plan. Each gender has its own role to play in the community, which is clearly set out in the Torah, Midrash, Talmud, and Halacha (Jewish law), and, in the event of discrepancies, in interpretations of the male rabbis. While all people are expected to love God and do good works, the living out of these mandates is done in two separate spheres, by men in the public sphere and women in the private sphere. Far from being a limitation however, Orthodox women understand their private role as unique and particularly suited to their God-given nature. As Wendy Wolfe Fine points out, their spirituality is also more private, and they are urged to develop an inner life of relationship with God following the words of Psalm 45, "The entire glory of the daughter of the king lies on the inside." Also, women's exemption from the male ritual practices is not understood as sexist exclusion but rather as a freedom to fulfill her familial duties without having the added burden of attending synagogue for public prayer. Wendy Wolfe Fine goes on to quote one Talmudic scholar on the subject:

The Talmud states that the exemption does not signify that men have greater worth than women, but rather both are equally sacred. Most authorities view these exemptions as an accepted part of Halachah. Others have attributed the exemption to inherent differences in men and women: women have the innate ability to reach spirituality, in contrast to men whose aggression inhibits this attainment and therefore necessitate their performance of additional commandments.[3]

It would appear from this interpretation that women are especially suited for a life of intimacy with God, particularly because they share God's nature by creating new life and by nurturing others. Woman has been called the soul of the family, which is the actual center of Jewish life, not the synagogue. It is she who is entrusted to pass on the tradition. Therefore, according to traditional Orthodox Judaism, the woman has a grave responsibility to assure the continuation of God's chosen people here on earth. Viewed in this light, the traditional Orthodox woman is hardly marginalized; rather, she stands at the center of the religion. She is ascribed a special identity, which in turn formulates her self-image.

The strength of this self-image is illustrated in a letter to the editor of *The Jewish Observer* in which one woman describes her reaction to some outside feminist influences in her community:

> How much more fulfilled we women would be if only we realized what a crucial role we play as wives and mothers. We are entrusted with taking care of a *Mishkan*, a holy sanctuary, and we are responsible to produce, to educate, and to inspire the next generation of *Ovdei Hashem* [servants of God].[4]

This statement is all the more powerful when we find that *mishkan*, sanctuary, or portable temple, was the word for the "first institutionalized mechanism for the presence of G-d on earth."[5] Therefore, this wife and mother considers herself the keeper of the holy temple that houses God; the divine presence itself dwells within her home.

In a study of modern women and Orthodoxy, sociologist Lynn Davidman interviewed single women at Bais Chana, a residential Lubavitch Hasidim institute that introduces young women to "traditional, Lubavitch-style Judaism through an intensive program of classes and everyday living."[6] At Bais Chana women live in a community where all aspects of their lives are shared and governed by the Halacha. At first glance, such an existence appears terribly restricting. However, what Davidman discovered when she joined the group for a short time was a sense of joy in community that surprised her. Her research found that women's purpose in joining the institute is to find a "clear articulation of their role as women, one that would place them in a center of nuclear families."[7] Given the sacredness of the family and the importance of the mother's role in Jewish Orthodoxy, these women were not just looking for love; rather, they were seeking a spiritual fulfillment that placed them in the midst of a larger community with a rich cultural tradition. This point of view was expressed clearly by a woman named Naomi, who said that "only in Judaism can a woman be a woman with all the dignity and respect she deserves."[8] Listening to these voices, one must respect these women for their quest for meaning, for their spirituality, and for their appreciation of the richness and beauty of an ancient tradition.

Moving along on the continuum of women's views, we encounter modern Orthodox women, who, while still adhering to the strict Jewish law, believe that its strictly male interpretations need to be supplemented with women's points of view. Within the last few decades Jewish women who have grown up in a more egalitarian environment have attempted to reconcile their secular experiences with their religious lives. In order to do this, women are coming together to search for ways in which Orthodoxy can best speak to them. One of the results has been the formation of the Jewish Orthodox Feminist Alliance (JOFA), whose mission is to "expand the spiritual, ritual, intellectual and political opportunities for women within the framework of *halakha*."[9] This organization has not shied away from the word *feminism* but has been willing to struggle with its use. Blu Greenberg, one of the JOFA's founding mothers, admits the word raises a red flag inside Orthodoxy. She notes that "half the Orthodox women who would be described by any objective standard as feminist shy away from the word in defining themselves." However, she and others understand that the feminist movement has been fine tuned so that it no longer signifies men as enemies or family as the locus of oppression. They have kept the designation and have done so, she says, with the explicit intention of keeping a "cognitive dissonance" within the tradition. By using the term, an Orthodox feminist can "define what she is, namely, a woman who believes in: the equal dignity of women within Orthodoxy; expanding the . . . opportunities for women to the fullest extent possible within *halakah*; the elimination of all injustice and suffering for Orthodox women arising out of hierarchical laws, such as Jewish divorce law (which puts power to end a marriage totally in the hands of the husband)."[10]

The women in this movement recognize inequalities within Orthodoxy and ask if they are really given by God. In their secular lives these women are equal and full citizens and would be outraged if their daughters were excluded from a school or a profession because of gender. Hence, the circumscribed and limited roles within their religion create a predicament for them because, according to Greenberg, they say that such roles "heighten dissonance in our thinking and hurt our spirits."[11]

There are two steps toward resolving such dissonance that Orthodox Jewish feminists have taken, which, though small in the larger arena, are very significant within their tradition; these are *tefillah* (public prayer) groups and the study of Talmud. First, while not all synagogues accept women's *tefillah* groups, several women in a recent study expressed their need to gather regularly to pray and sing together. One woman recalls that during these gatherings, even though some were hesitant at first to participate, "many grandmothers wept when they first looked into a Torah because they had not realized how deprived they felt."[12]

Perhaps the more revolutionary development within modern Orthodox Judaism is the growth in the number of women who are studying Talmud and Halacha. Jerusalem-based writer Rochelle Furstenberg reports that there is a generation of *talmidot hachamot,* women Talmudic authorities, emerging whose study of this vast and complex literature is producing a unique woman's approach to the texts. She quotes one woman scholar who claims that women are building a "new *midrash*, looking at the forgotten women of the Bible, confronting Dina's cry, Hagar's suffering, Potiphar's wife, and Lot's wife."[13]

Throughout Jewish history the study of sacred texts has been a deeply spiritual exercise equivalent to direct communication with God. Hence, most observant women do not view their study as a means to obtaining positions equal to men, but rather as a step in their spiritual development and part of an "unmediated channel to God."[14] For these women study is a prayer experience. Adena Berkowitz puts it best when she says that anyone who "has witnessed the face of a woman finally seeing what the inside of a Torah scroll looks like or reading from the Torah for the first time knows that that is a moment of transcendence."[15] Malka Bina, a pioneer in Orthodox women's study, says that "we see that the women involved are deeply and sincerely religious. [Women's classes] did not undermine their religiosity. Their desire to study emerges from their religiosity and strengthens it."[16]

In 1979 the Drisha Institute, a school for women to study Jewish texts, was established in New York City. Listening to some of the students' and teachers' voices gives us a sense of the commitment these women have to their tradition while at the same time working to ensure that it evolves in its perception of women and women's roles. Wendy Amsellem, a faculty member, writes:

> I feel a special connection to these texts and in trying to make sense of gender relations in early Babylonia, I better understand my place in the Judaism of today. . . . I could not continue in this mode [Orthodox Judaism] if I did not really believe that Jewish tradition and practice were evolving towards greater opportunities and equality

for women. I am committing my life to ensuring that women become increasingly a part of the text tradition that has sustained Judaism for millennia.[17]

Another woman, Melissa Nunes-Harwitt, who is a student, writes:

Rather than silencing us or insisting that we conform to one point of view, our teachers at Drisha encouraged us to share our diverse positions . . . and helped us begin the difficult task of hearing our own voices within Jewish tradition. For it is only when we can hear our voices in the present that we can learn to converse with our future and our past.[18]

What is important to note at this point is that these women who are devoted to studying Talmud and are committed to Orthodox Judaism recognize that there have been misogynistic interpretations of texts. Through their efforts, says one scholar, they are restructuring the concepts within the tradition. "These women are not willing to 'jump ship' because of what they see as the problems in Orthodoxy. Instead, they are demanding a rethinking of these issues within a Halachic framework.[19]

But what effect has such study had on Orthodox Judaism? Has it watered it down or made it less observant? These women teachers and students fervently believe that their work is strengthening the tradition, not weakening it. Blu Greenberg claims that Orthodox feminism is "a service to the community, a building up of faithfulness and commitment . . . [and] refreshing the tradition with women's new spiritual energy and revitalizing it with the ethical challenge of equality for women, thus bringing us one step closer to perfection of the world."[20]

CENTRIST POSITION

As we move along the continuum we encounter still another group of Jewish women speaking up. The women in the centrist position believe that the tradition as it was originally revealed was egalitarian. Problems of exclusion and oppression arose because the preservation of this tradition was in the hands of men influenced by the paternalistic and misogynistic society. Therefore, if women are to gain their true status within Judaism, they must recover the history and redeem it from its male interpreters. Susannah Heschel recounts that, due to the influence of feminism, Jewish women are asking questions about the role and status of women in Jewish history and in Jewish texts. "Recovery of women's history has been a dominant concern, as well as analysis of misogynous traditions embedded within Judaism's texts."[21] Investigations into the texts to uncover historical precedents for women leaders are changing the way

Jewish women see themselves, their roles, and their spiritual lives. For example, according to Heschel, Susan Ackerman has shown that women "functioned as ritual musicians and singers in the religious life of ancient Israel" in spite of the patriarchy and sexism in the Hebrew Bible.[22] The women around the midpoint of the continuum understand that the changes they are advocating are based in Jewish history and Jewish law and are not entirely new to the tradition.

This position is perhaps best represented by the women in Conservative Judaism. This form of Judaism, formally organized in 1913 by Dr. Solomon Schechter, was a reaction to the sweeping changes in the Reform Movement, which, it believed, went too far in rejecting the traditional authority. It saw the Orthodox movement, on the other hand, as standing still and rejecting any historical development. Thus Conservative Judaism stands between the Reform and the Orthodox in believing that the Halacha is normative and the laws of Shabbat (Jewish Sabbath), kashrut (keeping kosher), daily prayers, and observance of holidays and life-cycle events should all be followed. However, its commitment to Jewish law does not eliminate the importance of a rational faith; therefore, it recognizes the validity of historical development. Judaism, including the Halacha, say the followers of the Conservative branch, is constantly evolving to meet the needs of the Jewish people in varying circumstances. On a website describing Judaism and its branches, Lisa Katz defines Conservative Judaism's view of the law as capable of changing and adapting, "absorbing aspects of the predominant culture while remaining true to Judaism's values."[23]

Among the changes that Conservative Judaism has realized is the ordination of women rabbis, the first of which was Amy Eilberg in 1985. The debates and the studies that preceded this event included extensive delineation of what the Halacha permits and prohibits, for it was essential that such a monumentous change in the tradition be made within the boundaries of the Jewish law.[24] Other changes, such as women's participation in the minyan, their public reading of Torah, being called to Torah, and serving as a cantor were also made in keeping with an evolving Halacha. Furthermore, women in Conservative Judaism understand their tradition as possessing a spirit that is ethically as well as legally binding. The spirit of the Jewish law is justice and justice requires equal roles for women in the synagogue, claims one Jewish scholar, for "the woman of today is different from the second or even the nineteenth century.[25] Rabbi Judith Hauptman speaks of the changes being made for ethically compelling reasons such as giving women opportunities for leadership roles previously reserved for men. She goes on to say that "Talmudists like me know with precision that feminist changes, and others on the agenda like the ordination of gays as rabbis, are all doable within the framework of *halacha*."[26] Women's position in Conservative Judaism can perhaps best be summed up by Diana Villa when she writes:

I do thoroughly believe in a Halachic way of life, but that it can be adapted to our contemporary life style. The Torah itself, in Deuteronomy 17:8–12, grants license to the wise of each generation to reinterpret the law in accordance with its necessity, so that the commandments may truly be upheld.[27]

Thus we see that Jewish women who stand in the middle position on our continuum believe that the Jewish law, as God revealed it, can be adapted to our modern world and still retain its integrity.

PROGRESSIVE POSITION

Those women on the most progressive end of the continuum, Reform Judaism, have a different take on the tradition. They believe that misogyny has tainted not only the history of the tradition but the very revelation itself. As one feminist Helene Aylon puts it, "I have come to believe that Five Books of Moses are indeed the Five Books of Moses, not the Five Books of G-d."[28] As a result, these women advocate a revolution in Judaism that goes beyond changing the Halacha. Jewish feminist theologians are redefining the basic tenets of the tradition; they are going to the heart of the matter to create new understandings of such basic concepts as the nature of God, revelation, evil, and prayer. Progressive Jewish women are seeking not merely to include women in Jewish life but to create a new feminist Judaism.

One example of how such a transformation is under way is the feminist analysis of chosenness, a concept that lies at the heart of the Jewish identity. In the progressive feminists' view this concept, which sets Jews above non-Jews, also establishes hierarchical relationships within the community, such as that of men over women. Judith Plaskow, Drorah Setel, and others suggest that this idea of Jews being holier and more loved by God than the surrounding nations "is the chief expression of hierarchical distinction and . . . provides a warrant and a model for ranked differentiations within the community."[29] Plaskow believes that the idea of chosenness is linked with the idea of female sexuality being evil. Both ideas arose in the same historical period, and they bear a resemblance in that both stress difference, one between nations and the other between genders. Therefore, these feminists are calling for a search for new ways to think about difference that is not based on one group being over and above another. As a result of such thinking, new ways of being Jewish and of linking oneself with God and with others will emerge. Plaskow suggests that "what must replace chosenness, then, as the model for Jewish self-understanding is the far less dramatic *distinctness*"[30] This term can be understood not as hierarchical difference but rather in terms of Judaism being a distinct part of a whole. Drorah Setel agrees; she sees that a shift to a more relational way of viewing chosen is not to leave the tradition behind but rather to turn one's attention in a different direction.[31] Jewish identity can be retained without the connotations of superiority or elitism.

The practice of Jewish tradition is also being transformed by women such as E. M. Broner, who helped develop a Women's Passover using *The Women's Haggadah*[32] and Savina Teubal, who created a rite of passage, the *Sinchat Hochmah* (the Joy of Wisdom), to "celebrate the beginning of the last phase of life."[33] With these voices being heard, Susannah Heschel believes that "Judaism will undergo the most radical transformation it has faced since the Roman destruction of the Temple in Jerusalem in the year 70 C.E." Furthermore, there is no doubt in her mind that, instead of being weakened, "Judaism will emerge strengthened by feminism. . . . A revolution has occurred in the practice of Judaism . . . that will remain a permanent fixture of Jewish life."[34]

After viewing the immense diversity of Jewish women's understanding of their faith, one wonders if there can ever be a discussion among those on the various points of the continuum. The question of intrareligious dialogue, its possibilities and its practice, has become more poignant knowing these vast differences in Judaism, and will become even more so as we examine the continuum as it exists in the other religions.

CHRISTIANITY

A similar diversity of views is held by women in the Christian tradition. Just as Jewish women's perspectives deal with their relation to the Halacha, Christian women understand themselves and their faith in light of the Bible, both the Hebrew and the Christian scriptures. Throughout its history Christianity has been plagued with controversy over the authenticity and interpretation of the biblical text, which is the foundation of its revelation. In its earliest days there were debates over which stories to include and which to exclude in the canon of scripture, that is, the books accepted as divinely revealed works. Furthermore, the central doctrine of the incarnation, God taking on a human form in Jesus, gave rise to much speculation about the nature of this mystery. Such issues as the virgin birth, the hypostatic union (two natures in one divine Person), and the Trinity (three Persons in one God) were arrived at after many heated and sometimes violent debates. Besides these doctrinal problems, there were also problems of authority. Who had the right to speak for the Lord Jesus Christ in discerning truth from heresy? Who was able to interpret the Bible correctly and protect the illiterate masses from straying from the truth? Since the eleventh century, when the Eastern church separated from Rome over theological and political issues, there have been continual schisms and separations within Christianity over just these questions.

Luther, Calvin, Zwingli, and Wesley are just a few of those who set out to reform the church by giving the faithful what they saw as the correct meaning of the biblical texts and liberating Christianity from the power structures of pope and other bishops, whom they deemed corrupt.

And so the arguments continue into the present in spite of attempts at reconciliation. Today, however, the controversy over the interpretation and authority of the Bible is focused especially on issues of women, including their role in the family, their capacity as ministers and priests, and their sexual and reproductive natures. While much of Christian theology is done by men, a growing number of women is speaking out, either to other women, or, in the case of the more progressive voices, to the male hierarchies dominating many churches. These women's voices are coming out of the Protestant and Catholic circles, both of which contain the gamut of views from conservative to progressive on women. The main difference between these two segments of Christianity is the source of authority. For the Protestant denominations, particularly the evangelicals, the biblical text contains the essence of God's divine will and is referred to for all matters of governance and morality. The multiplication of denominations occurred because of the differences among groups regarding the interpretation of the texts. Catholics also see the Bible as authoritative, but the difference lies in their belief that God's message is continually unfolding and developing through the tradition of the church. Judgments on what is authentic in this unfolding of doctrine, according to Catholic tradition, are expressed through the teaching authority, the church's magisterium, which is a "progressive response to new concerns arising in the course of history in various ways: through issuing warnings, establishing norms, exercising discipline, etc."[35] Furthermore, different types of teachings hold different weights of authority. Contrary to popular belief, not everything the pope says is considered infallible by Catholics. In fact, the magisterium is often engaged in a dialectic with Catholic theologians on various dogmatic and moral issues, and letters often appear for clarification and reiteration rather than proclamation. Such a stance, which concerns itself with opposition, is perhaps the major reason Catholics who hold opposing views do not see themselves as leaving the church but simply challenging it. Given these two versions of Christianity and the fact that they both contain the gamut of viewpoints, it will be necessary to discuss them as parallels on the continuum. Many women in both Protestantism and Catholicism may be surprised to realize that they have much in common with their sisters across the divide.

CONSERVATIVE POSITION

On the farthest conservative end of the Christian continuum are the women who believe that God's original revelation, whether coming only from scripture or from scripture as interpreted by the church, tells us that men and women are both created in God's image but are essentially different with different gifts and have distinct and separate roles to play in creation. This revelation is authoritative and must not be altered by modern social trends that put the ego before the will of God. In the Protestant communities this position is held by some evangelical churches, which are represented by a group called the Council for Biblical Manhood and Womanhood (CBMW). In the Catholic world a group of women calling themselves Women for Faith and Family are representative of this position. Both of these organizations believe women should be helpers of their husbands, serving in a nurturing capacity, and should not hold a public ministerial office. The website for the CBMW publishes the views of several of its women members, all of whom agree that men and women are equal in the sight of God but have been given different roles. They believe that God gave men the role of head of the family and that women should submit to male authority. This view, termed *complementarian*, holds that "when rightly lived out, the complementary roles of men and women in the home and church bring freedom and joy to our lives, beauty to the church and world and most importantly, glory to God."[36] The articulation of this position is found in "The Danvers Statement," published in 1988. It includes among its affirmations the following:

> 2. Distinctions in masculine and feminine roles are ordained by God as part of the created order and should find an echo in every human heart (Gen 2:18, 21–24; 1 Cor 11:7–9; 1 Tim 2:12–14).
> 3. Adam's headship in marriage was established by God before the Fall, and was not a result of sin (Gen 2:16–18, 21–24, 3:1–13; 1 Cor 11:7–9). . . .
> 5. . . . Both Old and New Testaments also affirm the principle of male headship in the family and in the covenant community (Gen 2:18; Eph 5:21–33; Col 3:18–19; 1 Tim 2:11–15).
> 6. . . . In the family, husbands should forsake harsh or selfish leadership and grow in love and care for their wives; wives should forsake resistance to their husbands' authority and grow in willing, joyful submission to their husbands' leadership (Eph 5:21–33; Col 3:18–19; Tit 2:3–5; 1 Pet 3:1–7).[37]

While this position may appear to go against modern sensibilities, there are four important aspects of it that need to be understood. First, this attitude toward women differs from that held in the ancient world, whose cultures sometimes doubted the full humanity of women. It does so by proclaiming that women are equal in essence to men and equal before God. In a speech given at Bryn Mawr College in 2000, Rebecca Jones, a member of CBMW, stated that "the Bible is full of evidence of the ontological equality of men and women before the throne. They are both heirs of the covenant of grace accomplished by Jesus' death and resurrection (Gal. 3:28; 1 Peter 3:7)."[38] In other words, women are equally capable of holiness and rationality; both of these views were contested in some ancient ideologies such as those of Augustine and Thomas Aquinas. Augustine, in his treatise on the Trinity, "denies that women possess the image of God in themselves, [and they] are included . . . only under the headship of their husbands."[39] Thomas Aquinas believed that women's "defective nature, morally, mentally and physically, makes them non-normative humans, unable to represent the fullness of human nature."[40] Thus, while the modern conservative position holds to the hierarchically different roles of men and women, its adherence to women's ontological and spiritual equality represents a shift from tradition and gives evidence of the fact that conservatives, in spite of their objections, indeed have been influenced by the modern women's movement.

Second, these separate roles are always to be undertaken freely. The submission of the wife must be a voluntary choice, never forced. Critics of this position sometimes claim that it leads to wives being abused. However, when the Southern Baptist Convention added an article on the biblical standards for family life, it made sure to add that leadership must be of the servant kind and that any form of coercion on the husband's part would be considered a form of physical or emotional abuse.[41] When asked on CBMW's website what advice the group would give to a wife who was being physically or psychologically abused, its spokesperson, Kim Pennington, sent a lengthy and very clear response saying that the wife should consider separation, go for counseling, and seek support systems. On 29 November 2005 she wrote to me, "God does not call women to facilitate abusive behavior in the name of submission." She went on to refer to the pertinent Bible passage, Ephesians 5, explaining how husbands should lay down their lives for their wives.

The third important aspect of this position is that women's submission in conservative Christianity, as in Orthodox Judaism, is, above all else, a spiritual endeavor. In her defense of complementarianism, Kim Pennington explains that her reason for existence is to glorify God and live in fellowship with God through Jesus Christ. It is this relationship with Jesus that is her source of joy. For her, it is both satisfying and transcendent. There is a parallel here between what Catholic spiritual writers call union with God and what evangelicals are calling a personal relationship with Jesus. In other words, Kim Pennington's life is given meaning because in her family she finds Christ, and her familial duties become her spiritual prayer. In like manner, Dorothy Patterson, who converted to biblical complementarianism, says, "My commitment to marriage and home gained an added dimension—a divine contractual relationship reaching beyond my husband and me to include the Creator God Himself."[42] When listening to their voices, it becomes clear that, far from being restricting, the path these women have chosen has become the way for them to experience a deep and rewarding spiritual life.

The fourth aspect to be considered is that these writings take the form of a polemic, a defense against the more modern interpretations of the scriptures, especially within the evangelical community. Complementarians fear that other evangelicals are caving in to modern philosophies and straying from God's will as expressed in the Bible. The modern women's movement has encouraged women to seek careers and positions of power both in the secular world and in church communities. Such ambition, according to this conservative evangelical position, gives way to an arrogance and self-centeredness that not only leads women away from God, but eventually leads the way to society's worst ills. Carolyn McCulley blames feminists for marginalizing men through anger, thus sending a message that they are irresponsible and giving them ways to shirk their responsibilities for the children they create. In this way the feminist movement is the cause of such atrocities as "pornography, child abuse, public murders of estranged wives, fatherless children, and sexually transmitted diseases to name a few."[43] A similar polemical stance is held by a conservative Christian group based in Washington D.C. called the Institute for Religion and Democracy. Its agenda is to combat the radical feminist theology that is penetrating the Protestant seminaries and encouraging women to, in the words of its former president, Diane Knippers, "re-imagine God in a new way."[44] Such a new way is against biblical orthodoxy and causes the decline in social mores and a rejection of God's will for humanity. Furthermore, the high price of social upheaval has not bought women any more happiness or peace but rather has made them restless and discontent and led to much suffering caused by the likelihood of divorce, bearing children out of wedlock, drug addiction, and poverty. A shift from the strict biblical message will only lead to unhappiness, failure, and social denigration. The answer to such problems, according to Rebecca Jones, a speaker for CBMW, is covenant relationships grounded in our covenant with God. In the Bible a woman finds God's will for the world and, by sacrificing her will to the will of God, she serves her family, thus making the world a better place.[45]

In the Roman Catholic world we see this same conservative viewpoint expressed by the group called Women for Faith and the Family. In its "Affirmation for Catholic Women" it claims that there exists a natural and essential distinction between the sexes. In her unique capability of childbearing, woman is endowed "with the spiritual capacity for nurture, instruction, compassion and selflessness, which qualities are necessary to the establishment of families, the basic and divinely ordained unit of society."[46] There is no mention here of the essential equality between man and woman, but there is a clear message that woman's place is in the home and that she is called to nurture her family by her selflessness. Since there is no mention of the man's role in the family, we understand that the roles of nurturer and instructor and the requirement of selflessness are especially placed on women, with men being the traditional supporters and heads of household.

Another similarity between the Catholic and Protestant women on this end of the continuum is their position against women's public ministry, which means preaching for Protestants and ordination for Catholics. "The Danvers Statement" of the CBMW claims that "some governing and teaching roles within the church are restricted to men (Gal 3:28; 1 Cor 11:2–16; 1 Tim 2:11–15)."[47] Similarly, the Catholic group Women for Faith and Family has written the following:

> We . . . reject as an aberrant innovation peculiar to our times and our society the notion that priesthood is the "right" of any human being, male or female. Furthermore, we recognize that the specific role of ordained priesthood is intrinsically connected with and representative of the begetting creativity of God in which only human males can participate. Human females, who by nature share in the creativity of God by their capacity to bring forth new life, and reflective of this essential distinction, have a different and distinct role within the church and in society from that accorded to men, can no more be priests than men can be mothers.[48]

Just as the evangelical women have understood the biblical verses in light of the teachings of the Southern Baptist Convention and the CBMW, so have these Catholic women understood Jesus' message in light of the pope's teaching. In his encyclical *Ordinatio Sacerdotalis,* Pope John Paul II noted that Christ called only men to be his apostles, not because he was conforming to prevailing customs, but freely and in a sovereign manner. "Therefore, in granting admission to the ministerial priesthood, the Church has always acknowledged as a perennial norm her Lord's way of acting in choosing the twelve men whom he made the foundation of his Church (Rv 21:14)."[49] These Catholic women, like their evangelical sisters, see no injustice in being excluded from the priesthood. In fact, the term *exclusion,* which is essentially a negative concept, is not within the framework of these women's thinking. They understand their role as women to be special and distinct and capable of providing them with a very rich spiritual life.

Another point held in common by both groups of women is their very serious objections to feminism and its effects on society. Just as the evangelical women's voices are a polemic against the women's movement, so are those of members of Women for Faith and Family. The very purpose of this Catholic group is to right the wrongs committed in the name of women's rights. These women are speaking out against elements in society that they believe are leading to moral confusion and the destruction of families. Unless the clear distinction between the roles of men and women is maintained, God's plan for humanity will be subverted and personal disintegration and the disintegration of society will follow.[50] These words carry the same message of the dangers of modernity as those of the conservative evangelical women.

Moving over slightly on our continuum of women's viewpoints, we encounter another conservative evangelical movement called Christians for Biblical Equality (CBE). While maintaining the authority and inerrancy of the Bible, the points of difference between this group and the ones previously discussed are significant within evangelical circles. First, the CBE believes that scripture is to be interpreted holistically and thematically and recognizes the need to distinguish between inspiration and interpretation. The first it defines as the divine impulse causing the whole canonical scripture to be the word of God, and the second as the human activity whereby we seek to understand the totality of scripture under the guidance of the Holy Spirit.[51] This being said however, one must make no mistake about the fact that biblical egalitarians base their view on the "full and objective truth and authority" of scripture and not on any secular movement. They loudly claim the label evangelical in their fidelity to the Bible, while still holding to a range of "theological, historical, hermeneutical, psychological and practical perspectives."[52]

The members of CBE and other evangelicals in the biblical equality movement, therefore, read the Bible as proclaiming the equality of men and women in all things including family roles and the church ministries of teaching and preaching. The editors of the recent collection of essays on the subject, Rebecca Groothuis and Ronald Pierce, use the word "complementarity" but have added the words "without hierarchy" because they understand the Bible to teach "mutually shared partnerships, without the trappings of male hierarchy that traditionally have accompanied such relationships, whether in marriage, in ministry or in cross-gender friendships."[53] According to the CBE's examination of scripture, it is a misinterpretation to say that the male is to be the head of the household and the woman his subordinate helper. Contrary to the CBMW's "Danvers Statement," which claims that Adam's headship was established by God before the Fall, the CBE understands the Bible to say that "the rulership of Adam over Eve resulted from the Fall and was therefore not a part of the original created order."[54] In her discussion of the Genesis account, Christiane Carlson-Thies claims that complementarians misinterpret Adam's aloneness before Eve's creation when they view God's creating Adam strong in and of himself and having authority over woman. The egalitarian interpretation is that Adam's aloneness was a deprivation, which God repaired by creating woman. The "let them rule" command of

Genesis 1:26 (repeated in Genesis 1:28) is collective and pertains to both the man and the woman. Those who would have another view would have to change the words to say "let *him* rule," and Carlson-Thies adds, "Is this not tampering with biblical truth?"[55]

Continuing her analysis, Carlson-Thies defines the Hebrew word for "helper," *ezer kenegdo,* and explains that when seen in context, it refers not to a competitor, nor to one who "stands by on the sidelines watching the man do all the heavy lifting of image-bearing." Rather, wife as helper is "clearly revealed as fundamentally, indispensably and *equally* called to the human task of imaging God and extending his rule throughout the creation."[56] Given this stance of complete gender equality, the CBE reads the Bible as teaching that the gifts of the Holy Spirit are given without gender preference (Acts 2:1–21; 1 Cor 12:7, 11; 14:31), that husband and wife are bound by mutual submission and responsibility (1 Cor 7:3–5; Eph 5:21; 1 Pt 5:2–3), and that "in case of decisional deadlock they should seek resolution through biblical methods of conflict resolution rather than by one spouse imposing a decision upon the other."[57]

Thus we see in that in comparison to the more conservative evangelicals, those who claim to be egalitarian hold a more progressive position on gender equality, some going so far as to call themselves evangelical feminists.[58] However, they base their position not on social movements that have advanced the place of women in society, but rather solely on the biblical texts, which reveal God's plan of total equality of men and women, not just in their persons and their call to holiness but in their familial and ministerial roles as well. These evangelicals are positioned on the conservative side of the continuum because they are upholding and supporting a traditional familial relationship, albeit with equal partners, not a head and a subordinate. Marriage between a man and a woman with children is still the personal goal and all other forms of nontraditional family arrangements are considered to be wrong in the eyes of God and contributing factors to social problems. While singleness in not condemned, it should be rare and viewed as a call to a celibate life emulating those virgins and widows in the early church.

Once again, we see in this evangelical position motivation to lead a spiritual life and to give glory to God. Instead of speaking in the language of rights of women, its proponents speak of accepting gifts of the Spirit. Instead of speaking of women in positions of authority and ruling a congregation, they speak of women in relationship with men together imaging God to the creation. In their systematic and faithful study of the scriptures and their attempts to discern the will of God, they are leading lives, not of selfish egoism, of which some in the more conservative position would accuse them, but of loyal submission to the Creator's original intent for the world and its creatures before they fell from Eden.

This stance on male-female equality as opposed to dominance and submission is to be found in a letter of Pope John Paul II and in a pastoral letter of the U.S. Conference of Catholic Bishops. The pope's letter *Familiaris Consortio,* written in 1981, states that both male and female bear the image of God. "Above all it is important to underline the equal dignity and responsibility of women with men. This equality is realized in a unique manner in that reciprocal self-giving by each one to the other and by both to the children."[59] The bishops of the United States affirmed this position in their pastoral letter of 1994: "Marriage is a vowed covenant with unique dimensions. In this partnership, mutual submission—not dominance by either partner—is the key to genuine joy."[60] The pope and bishops base their statements about equality on scripture, both the Genesis story and the sayings of Jesus, which reveal God's plan for creation. Furthermore, while the church does not permit women to be ordained, it is interesting to note that when the pope's and bishops' statements are read in full, they make provision for women taking part in church ministries, especially teaching, and also for their having professional lives, which are both necessary and rewarding. The bishops write that "when both spouses are employed, household duties need to be shared." When these letters are read as a guide to living a faithful Christian life rather than as a polemic against modern tendencies, they present a more progressive picture than that put forth by the more conservative Women for Faith and the Family. What we have here is proof that just as Protestant groups differ on their interpretation of the Bible, so Catholics differ on their interpretation of church documents. There are, then, conservative groups teaching the subordination of wives to husbands in both Protestant and Catholic worlds, and also conservative groups interpreting the authoritative sources as teaching the full equality of man and woman in both worlds.

At this point in the analysis of Christian positions, we draw attention to the one issue of gender that separates these conservative groups from all others. This issue, agreed upon by complementarians and egalitarians, by conservative Protestants and conservative Catholics, is the biblical condemnation of homosexuality. While it is true that there are other religions that believe homosexuality to be an abomination, it seems that the subject is particularly contentious in the Christian communities, because in their discourse homosexuality is inherently linked with the issue of women's roles and women's liberation. In her study of evangelical Christian women Julie Ingersoll explains that women's rights are identified with gay rights, and "there is a pervasive concern that equality for women (as defined by feminists) will result in an increased incidence of homosexuality and will leave no grounds from which to oppose homosexuality."[61] This concern makes sense when we understand the full implications of women's equality. If women wish to be equal to men in all things, then the distinction between the sexes will be blurred, and once this happens, God's design will be tampered with. Homosexuals, viewed as androgynes, represent such a tampering and therefore are aberrations and rejections of God's will for the sexes. Concerned that they will be misunderstood as approving of homosexuality, evangelicals for equality have written polemics to defend their position of biblical orthodoxy. One author, William J. Webb, writes, "Biblical egalitarians affirm, appreciate and seek to maintain a distinction between the sexes that honors God's creation design."[62] He then goes on to claim that while the sexes may be equal, they are still distinct, and that the biblical prohibitions against homosexuality emphasize the need to maintain male and female relationship boundaries as a way of honoring God, our Creator.

This concern that the movement toward women's equality leads to approval of homosexuality was also articulated by Joseph Cardinal Ratizinger, now Pope Benedict XVI, in his letter to the Catholic bishops in 2004: "The obscuring of the difference or duality of the sexes has enormous consequences. . . . [It] has in reality inspired ideologies which, for example, call into question the family, in its natural two-parent structure of mother and father, and make homosexuality and heterosexuality virtually equivalent, in a new model of polymorphous sexuality."[63]

Given the conservatives' position on homosexuality, it is obvious that they are also against homosexuals in the ministry. Even when the ministers are called to be celibate, as in the Catholic priesthood, the church warns against ordination of homosexual men. A 2005 document instructs bishops and seminary rectors to not ordain men with "'deep-seated' homosexual tendencies."[64] While the Catholic Church has always declared homosexual acts sinful, this document says also that homosexuality is, according to one priest explaining the document, not something neutral but rather an affective disorder that makes a man unfit for the priesthood.[65]

The debate regarding homosexuals in the ministry has been especially divisive within the more progressive churches, such as the Methodist and Episcopal churches. In March 2004 members of the Methodist Church engaged in a bitter internal debate about whether to defrock a self-avowed practicing lesbian minister, Karen Dammann. While the church court ruled in her favor, others in the church, including a president of a seminary, viewed Rev. Dammann as defiantly violating church law.[66] These dissenting voices were heard, and in December 2004 Rev. Elizabeth Irene Stroud lost her credentials after she disclosed she was a practicing lesbian. In 2003 the American Episcopal Church approved the ordination of Gene Robinson, an openly gay priest, as bishop of New Hampshire; as a result, two churches in Southern California dissociated themselves from the Episcopal Diocese of Los Angeles and became affiliated with a diocese in

Uganda.[67] In addition, as of November 2005 four Ohio congregations had split from the Episcopal Church USA and affiliated with a diocese in South America, and twelve Episcopal churches in Virginia have formed a network that separated from the Virginia diocese, accusing it of embracing a false gospel.

In spite of these arguments and objections, there are large numbers of people who both agree with their churches' ordination of gays and lesbians and still view themselves as being very faithful to the gospel and fully a part of mainstream biblical Christianity. These are the people who fall on the middle position of our continuum. They firmly believe that God's revelation in Christ as it appears in the Bible encompasses love, justice, and the full participation of men and women, gay and straight. Gender or gender orientation is not a barrier to holiness or to the reception of God's gifts for the community. The problem, they say, lies with the male power structures of the churches, Catholic or Protestant, which have misinterpreted and distorted the original revelation. Throughout history these male leaders have turned Christ's community into a patriarchal and hierarchal institution in which women can only be supporters not leaders, and homosexuals are abominations not normal persons.

CENTRIST POSITION

Most modern Christians, both Protestants and Catholics, fall in the middle section of the continuum. A few groups that illustrate this centrist position are the Evangelical and Ecumenical Women's Caucus (EEWC), the United Methodist Church, The United Church of Christ, and the Episcopal Church, which is considered Protestant because of its breach with the pope even though its sacramental system closely resembles that of the Catholic Church. The women in these religious institutions clearly proclaim their loyalty to the original revelation of Jesus in the Bible and the teachings of the church's founders. However, they are convinced that the history of this revelation has been tainted by patriarchy and that it is their calling to return to the original message, which, they claim, is one of inclusiveness and equality.

The EEWC has been criticized by other evangelicals as not accepting those aspects that define the movement: "the inerrancy of scripture, particular methods of biblical interpretation, and appropriate social conclusions that could be drawn."[68] In spite of these criticisms, however, its members strongly adhere to the term *evangelical* because they believe that the "the Bible is the Word of God, inspired by the Holy Spirit, and is a central guide and authority for Christian faith and life . . . [as well as] the good news for all persons."[69] Ann Eggebroten, a long-term member of the EEWC and a research scholar at UCLA, writes of the difficulty in organizing the 2004 conference. She wanted it to be recognized as evangelical but also ecumenical and definitely feminist. To meet these requirements, the conference had to be rooted in scripture, respect the authority of the Bible, but also offer an opportunity for its participants to get sound feminist exegesis, which she claims, is not offered in many churches. To this end she invited prominent women biblical scholars to be presenters. But it was not only the study of the Bible that made this conference evangelical but also the call to mission, "helping people to discover god's love and experience a personal relationship with God through Jesus of Nazareth."[70] What puts this group in the center of the continuum is its belief that the original inclusiveness of the biblical message was tainted by society's and the church's encouragement of male domination. These women are skeptical, therefore, about the social pronouncements of their churches that condemn homosexuals and keep women out of leadership. To them, being inclusive means welcoming members of various faith backgrounds, gender expressions, and sexual orientations. They consider themselves prophets in this regard and are willing to endure "getting stoned or burned for their efforts." Eggebroten writes, "Was Martin Luther widely approved by the church of his day? Not exactly."[71]

The EEWC's being both evangelical and inclusive has been healing for many women, who, while professing a strong biblical faith, have found themselves either uncomfortable in or excluded from their religious communities. One such woman is Peggy Michael-Rush, who writes a compelling account of her search for community and her discovery of the EEWC. Growing up, she experienced a dominating, patriarchal father; this made it difficult for her to image God as a loving father. Later, while attending a conservative seminary, she struggled against feminism because she had been indoctrinated with the idea that Christian feminism was an oxymoron. This thought, coupled with the harshness of the feminists she encountered, made her uncomfortable with the movement, yet, as a woman, she was also out of sync with her male colleagues, who, whether deliberately or inadvertently, caused her to feel inferior. When she discovered the EEWC website, her journey began. Through access to EEWC resources and attending EEWC conferences, she has found a place where she can feel safe, discover herself in the scriptures, and deepen her spirituality. What's more, she was empowered to enable other women to do the same.[72]

Another compelling story is told by Virginia Ramey Mollenkott, one of the founding members of the EEWC, a Milton scholar and professor emeritus of English at the William Paterson University of New Jersey. Born into a working-class Philadelphia family of extremely conservative evangelicals, she was taught that the deepest core of her being was evil and could only be saved by Jesus Christ's paying the price of God's anger. She writes, "Combine this with very early physical and sexual abuse and the early realization that I was a lesbian, and you can understand why I was well into my thirties before I was able to liberate myself from the fundamentalist belief system."[73] After careful study and "being challenged by feminist thinkers," Mollenkott began to use literary formats, historical context, imagery and symbol to read the biblical texts, and as a result, she was "radicalized by the Bible." She understands that its teachings support the sacred worth of all persons and, on the basis of this understanding, she helped establish the EEWC's policy of inclusiveness. She writes, "The Bible teaches the human dignity and equality of women along with men and all the in-betweens as well: intersexuals, transsexuals, homosexuals, bisexuals, nonconformist heterosexuals and gender transgressors of every type."[74] It is this belief that leads the EEWC to accept the validity of gays and lesbians in ministry and that caused other evangelicals such as the CBE to break and form their own organizations. Recognizing that evangelicals run the gamut of perspectives on sex and gender relationships, Mollenkott sees herself as more aligned with progressive Mainline Protestants, Catholics, Jews, and Muslims than with conservative evangelicals.

Two of the mainline Protestant churches that Mollenkott refers to are the United Methodist Church and the United Church of Christ, which also lie in the center of our continuum. The United Methodist Church's *Book of Discipline*, revised in 2004, states in its section on women and men: "We . . . reject the idea that God made individuals as incomplete fragments, made whole only in union with another. We call upon women and men to share power and control . . . to be complete and to respect the wholeness of others."[75] The Methodists have a clearly different interpretation of the Genesis story and of Jesus' message than that held by the more conservative Christian groups such as the CBMW. When discussing the status of women the Methodists make it clear that any inequality that may appear in scripture is a result of cultural attitudes and that Jesus "the Redeemer of human life, stood as a witness against such cultural patterns and prejudices. Consistently, he related to women as persons of intelligence and capabilities."[76] It follows from these statements that the United Methodist Church accepts women in the ministry today. However, full clergy rights were not granted to women until 1956, and the first woman bishop, Marjorie Matthews, was not ordained until 1980, indicating that a history of male domination had to be overcome before women became equal in leadership of the church. Jean Miller Schmidt, professor of Methodist studies at Illif School of Theology, notes that today's ordained women stand on the shoulders of laywomen who struggled to serve. "'We give thanks for all that has been accomplished,' she said. 'But the struggles still go on and go on.'"[77] The Methodists are also struggling with the extent of the church's inclusiveness. In 1984 the General Conference added a statement to the *Book of Discipline* claiming that the "practice of homosexuality is incompatible with Christian teaching." This was the key phrase that led to the trials of the two lesbian ministers in 2003 and 2004. However, the church does commit itself to supporting basic human rights and civil liberties for homosexual persons[78] and has constructed a task force to encourage further dialogue to struggle with the concerns in a civil manner that will benefit all. The church's willingness to grapple with the question of the roles of homosexuals rather than to make further dogmatic statements puts it in the position of listening to the Spirit in a changing world and making efforts to understand Christ's message in light of these changes.

The United Church of Christ (UCC) has a similar attitude toward the Bible, the roles of women, and the status of homosexuals. This church is grounded in a biblical faith: "The United Church of Christ acknowledges as its sole Head, Jesus Christ, son of God and Savior. . . . It looks to the Word of God in the Scriptures, and to the presence and power of the Holy Spirit. . . . It claims as its own the faith of the historic church expressed in the ancient creeds and reclaimed in the basic insights of the Protestant Reformers."[79] By affirming these beliefs, it is clear that the UCC accepts that the revelation as it appears in the Bible and as it was renewed by the reformers contains a message of justice and equality. However, it also understands that the social conditions within which that message grows is fraught with complicated problems. Therefore, the leaders of the church urge its members to engage in the daily challenge of discernment in order to separate "the wheat from the chaff, to discern essential truth from passing fancy."[80] It is in such discernment that the church attempts to apply its historic principles and practices to new situations. Over the years the General Synod of the UCC has taken positions on such issues as civil rights, equality for women, and respect and dignity for gay and lesbian people. In response to conservative criticism, it must be noted that these issues are not taken lightly nor are they studied solely in light of the secular sciences or popular culture. Rather, the church engages scripture scholars whose careful study of the text takes into account language, context, and other exegetical criteria to discern the meaning of the divine message regarding these contemporary questions.

The UCC also believes that the inclusion of homosexuals in the church and its ministry has biblical roots. On the justice section of the UCC website, Rev. Mike Schuenemeyer writes that contemporary biblical scholarship argues strongly against the condemnation of same-gender, loving people of God and finds a much more significant gospel message that supports the inclusion of gays and lesbians into the full life and mission of the church. While this scholarship is viewed as anathema by more conservative Christians, it is important to note that the UCC is devoted to God's message in the scriptures and is not merely bending that message to suit current trends. In illustration, Schuenemeyer gives an example of inclusion in biblical Christianity.

In the Bible, the book of Deuteronomy is very clear that the sexual minorities of that day—eunuchs—were not allowed to be members of the worshiping community; in fact, they were excluded altogether from Jewish life. However, in the book of Acts, we find the painful yet empowering story that poignantly demonstrates the life of grace we find in Jesus Christ—Philip's encounter with an Ethiopian eunuch. In short, this outcast wants to be baptized. Recognizing the boundless invitation of God's inclusive love in Christ, Philip receives the eunuch as a member of the church.[81]

"In 1972, the UCC ordained the first openly gay person into ministry, the Rev. William R. Johnson." Scheunemeyer continues: While the members of UCC are not all of one mind regarding this step, the movement for "full inclusion of LGBT persons continues to spread throughout all aspects of our denomination's life and witness."[82] In conclusion, it must be noted that these mainline Protestant denominations do not see that either the equality of men and women in all things or the blurring of gender distinctions in homosexuality is in any way contrary to God's plan. Rather, in their careful and scholarly study of scripture, they understand that the message of love, respect, and justice speaks so loudly from the pages of the Bible that its volume drowns out those passages embroiled in the cultural trappings of the day.

As stated earlier, each Protestant position on our continuum has its Catholic counterpart. Parallel to these mainstream Protestant positions are those held by Catholics who believe that the church's priesthood and sacramental system need to change in order to be faithful to the church's original message. They truly believe that the Bible reveals an early church that was centered on the sacraments, particularly baptism and the eucharist, and structured with deacons, presbyters, and bishops. The difference between then and now, however, is that in the beginning these positions were held by men and women and were in service to people of all ethnicities and social standings. This belief places these Catholics in the centrist position on our continuum because they blame the patriarchal church leaders throughout history for distorting this original message and, by working for change, they are being faithful to the will of God expressed in Jesus Christ and his original revelation in scripture.

The group that most represents this position is the Women's Ordination Conference (WCC), known globally as Women's Ordination Worldwide. This group's mission is to "reclaim the church's early tradition of a discipleship of equals," and its members are women and men who believe that "the church, in fidelity to the gospel, must be open to full and equal participation of women in all its ministries."[83] This group has worked diligently and patiently to remain within the Catholic Church in spite of objections and pronouncements from Rome, including excommunication. In its mission statement, Roman Catholic Womenpriests program, the training program for women candidates for ordination, claims that it "wants neither a schism nor a break from the Roman Catholic Church, but rather wants to work positively within the Church."[84] To this end, the members of the WOC have done extensive scholarship on biblical exegesis, church history, and church documents. They understand that the New Testament priesthood established by Jesus is one based on grace, not inheritance, and as such is shared by all the baptized. Also, they remind us of Paul's references to Phoebe, Evodia, and Syntyche as deacons in his letters to the Romans and the Philippians as well as his mention of the ordination of women deacons when he writes to Timothy. Also, in their study of early Christianity these women scholars learned that deaconesses existed into the fifth century, with their roles clearly spelled out at the Council of Trullo. There were also women priests (presbyters) as evidenced in a fifth-century letter of Pope Gelasius, who expressed annoyance that "divine affairs have come to such a low state that women are encouraged to officiate at the sacred altars."[85] It is obvious that such a letter would not be necessary were not some bishops indeed ordaining women. In addition, archeological inscriptions on tombs and other venues indicate that women were ordained in the early church; however, Rome is still insisting that these women belonged to heretical groups. One mosaic in the ancient church Santa Praxedis depicts four women, two saints, Mary, and a fourth with the inscription "Theodora Episcopa," that is, Bishop Theodora.[86]

Armed with this information, the members of the Women's Ordination Worldwide have countered Rome's argument based on tradition, and have moved forward with women's ordination in spite of being censured by the Vatican. In 2002 seven women were ordained in a secret ceremony on the Danube River. In 2003 two of those women received episcopal ordination, and they in turn ordained six women deacons in 2004 who were elevated to the priesthood on 25 July 2005 in a ceremony aboard a ship on the St. Lawrence Seaway. In order for these ordinations to be legitimate in the Roman Catholic Church, it is important that they be verified as following the line of apostolic succession. Dr. Judith Johnson, writing for the WOC, explained that the ordination of the two women bishops by male bishops in good standing was legally verified and documented by an Austrian notary, a procedure necessary to avoid the presiding bishops' excommunication by Rome. Bishops Mayr-Lumetzberger and Forster may have become the first Roman Catholic women in centuries to be ordained into the apostolic line of succession according to the rites and procedures defined by the bishops and the papacy. Their struggle to maintain this line of succession indicates these women's commitment and dedication to the Roman Catholic tradition. According to Dr. Johnson:

It is this respect for the essence of Catholic tradition, and for a sacramental theology wrapped in a divine mystery, that has inspired (and driven) the two new female bishops to follow in their ordinations the rites and procedures laid down by the Vatican. The RC Womenpriests have not spawned a new church. Rather, they have opened a door to a wave of women seeking Roman Catholic ordinations. And the movement of the Spirit—if the response of women around the world is any indication—is working to keep the potential ordinands coming.[87]

This need to remain Roman Catholic is often a puzzlement to many onlookers, especially non-Catholics. Why not simply become an Episcopalian? After all, the Episcopalian sacramental system is almost identical, and that church ordains women priests and bishops. Furthermore, other denominations have women in all types of leadership roles. I have heard secular feminist scholars accuse some Catholic feminists of suffering from battered-wife syndrome, and, if we consider them as being "married to the church," the accusation might apply. However, these women believe that the church is not the hierarchy of male leaders but rather the body of Christ, in whom there is "no longer Jew nor Greek, free nor slave, male nor female" (Gal 3:27–28). Given this strong conviction, lodged in the core of their being and forming their identity, these women who have been ordained in the Roman Catholic Church and have suffered censure from the male hierarchy are boldly committed to renewing the church by living out their prophetic vision of what it should be. As Dr. Johnson explains, they are proclaiming "by their act of receiving the sacrament of orders, the validity of women as equal participants with men in the priestly ministry of Christ, as handed down through the original apostles."[88] The Womenpriests' intention is to preserve the Roman Catholic heritage and traditions, not by leaving the church, but by renewing it and its priestly ministry.

PROGRESSIVE POSITION

Not all Catholic women who consider the church patriarchal and discriminatory want to see women priests. Many of them envision a renewed church in which the theology of priesthood takes on a different form, one free from any hierarchical overtones. These women fall on the progressive end of our continuum because, while they believe in the Christian message, they view the original revelation as necessarily distorted because of its parameters of time and location in history. It must be emphasized that the women we are speaking of are still believers in Christ and maintain their fidelity to his word. Most of them come out of the Roman Catholic tradition, a fact that makes sense, according to Episcopal priest

Paula Nesbitt, because "Catholic women's very exclusion from the ordination process has radicalized them to think creatively and innovatively, while those denominations ordaining women too often have co-opted them."[89] These women are not to be confused with those feminist theologians such as Mary Daly and Carol Christ who find the Christian revelation unredeemably patriarchal and have left the church to follow a goddess-centered faith. While these post-Christian feminists would be included in an interreligious dialogue, their rejection of the Christian tradition necessarily excludes them from an intra-religious project.

Two scholars coming out of the Roman Catholic tradition who fall into this progressive category are Elizabeth Schüssler Fiorenza and Rosemary Radford Ruether. Both of these women refer to their work as a reconstruction, that is, they are reconstructing the Christian message in order to view it in a liberating and egalitarian way, which, they believe, is the only faithful way to understand it. They are convinced that only in such a reconstruction can we truly understand Jesus' message of love and liberation from sin and all of its effects, including the patriarchal domination of the ancient world in which he lived. Schüssler Fiorenza's reconstructs biblical history, and Ruether reconstructs Christian theology. Schüssler Fiorenza recognizes what a powerful force the Bible is in women's lives, and she is committed to transforming it into a source of liberation rather than one of tyranny. Her biblical hermeneutics uncovers the women who participated in the teaching and preaching of the Christian message in the early church but were silenced by the patriarchal society in which they lived. Remembering them will reconstruct Christian beginnings and will be "a challenge to historical-religious patriarchy."[90]

Her reading of the New Testament understands that the world in which Jesus' words and deeds were recorded used the language and practices of domination. Therefore, we must utilize what Schüssler Fiorenza calls a hermeneutic of suspicion, that is, we must read the texts with an eye for traces of such domination. Rather than see all passages as divinely authoritative, they are investigated to determine how they functioned in the interest of the male power structure.[91] An example is the passage stating: "'Cretans are always liars, vicious brutes, lazy gluttons. That testimony is true" (Ti 1:12–13). Instead of seeing this passage as a direct message from God, we must read it asking why this passage was included in this literature and whom it was benefiting. She also calls for the reader of scripture to evaluate critically and to "reject those elements within *all* biblical traditions and texts that perpetuate, in the name of God, violence, alienation, and patriarchal subordination, and eradicate women from historical-theological consciousness."[92]

But Schüssler Fiorenza's hermeneutics do not only criticize, they also creatively imagine what would stand instead. To her, the reform of a male-dominated church is more radical than the ordination of women to the priesthood. In her keynote address to the Women's Ordination World-wide conference in July 2005, she speaks of a dream yet to be realized, not of women wearing the collar, being called Reverend, or saying Mass, but rather of a transformed ministry and church that is not a hierarchy but rather a discipleship of equals. She views women's ordination not as a struggle to move into male power but rather as a movement toward a new way of being church, one that does not rest on divisions between clergy and laity but rather on a radical democratic leadership that represents the poor and oppressed. It is in this context of new leadership that Schüssler Fiorenza places women's struggles for self-determination and bodily integrity.[93] Hers is indeed a progressive vision, which, while still identifying with Christianity, understands that fidelity to Jesus Christ requires a radical transformation of what is into what can be.

Many critics on the conservative end of our continuum accuse Schüssler Fiorenza and scholars like her of picking and choosing parts of the Bible that suit them and ignoring the more difficult commands and exhortations of Jesus. While space here does not permit a full explanation of Schüssler Fiorenza's work, suffice it to say that the extent of her scholarship and the intensity of her thought process speak of the seriousness with which she takes the Christian biblical tradition. Her work, which is anything but arbitrary, is extensive, deliberate, scholarly, and Christocentric. She has bravely and boldly seen Christian history in a new light and has thus reshaped a religious vision that works to transform the social, political, and religious communities of our time. Far from avoiding the difficult demands of Jesus, her transforming vision is perhaps more difficult than those of her predecessors.

Another Christian theologian on the progressive end of our continuum, whose work is also a reconstruction, is Rosemary Radford Ruether. She, like Schüssler Fiorenza, understands that the patriarchal bias of the early Hebrew and Greco-Roman worlds and of the medieval church have distorted the Christian revelation in such a way as to exclude women. She writes that "the imagery and understanding of God, Christ, human nature, sin, salvation, church, and ministry were all shaped by a male-centered, misogynist worldview that subordinated women and rendered them non-normative and invisible."[94] Because women were excluded from shaping Christian theology, such theology is distorted not only in its symbols but also in the very relation between God and humans and between men and women. Throughout the history of the Christian Church, claims Ruether, women have epitomized the evil human tendencies by causing sin to enter the world while men have been the norm of God's image. This distortion has resulted in a theology that has denied the full humanity of women. Ruether is able to critique this distorted theology by using the principle of "the promotion of the full humanity of women. Whatever denies, diminishes, or distorts the full humanity of women is, therefore, appraised as not redemptive. Theologically speaking, whatever diminishes or denies the full humanity of women must be presumed not to reflect the divine or an authentic relation to the divine."[95]

By using this principle, Ruether identifies the patriarchal influences in revelation, seeing them as part of the ancient culture and not divinely ordained. Her reconstruction of God's plan, therefore, is a liberating one and puts her on the opposite end of the continuum from those conservatives who believe that, from the beginning, God created man as the dominant creature and woman as his helper. Ruether believes not in the complementarity of the genders, one making up for what the other lacks, but rather in the full personhood of each. It is to be noted here that Ruether does not speak of the genders being identical or fused into one androgyne; rather, her view is that each possesses the potential to be a complete person and that each is to help the other to reach that potential, not to supply what the other is "missing."

In her theology of God, Ruether moves away from the symbol of father, which serves to reinforce patriarchal power, to that of creator and source of our being, which "fosters full personhood."[96] Her Christology understands that Jesus is not only the Logos or Word of God but also the Sophia, the Wisdom of God. By using both these terms, one masculine and one feminine, Ruether demonstrates that Christ transcends gender and, therefore, can be personified in both men and women. Her concept of church also is freed from its distorted image of a hierarchical institution to one of an inclusive and liberating community that is true to its roots as a countercultural prophetic movement.[97] Here Ruether distinguishes herself not only from the most conservative women but also from all others on our continuum. She does not agree that the ordination of women, or the inclusion of women in teaching or preaching ministries, is sufficient to eliminate the patriarchal influences in Christianity. Only when the church eliminates the hierarchical distinction between clergy and laity and embraces a form of relationship based on a discipleship of equals can it be true to its divine origins. The Catholic Church, in particular, which believes that the ordained episcopacy was established by Christ and that this apostolic succession is the source of clerical power, is evidence of the distortion of patriarchal influences. In Ruether's ecclesiology, this church, like all others that adhere to such clericalism, must be transformed into a liberating community not simply by admitting women and homosexuals to the clergy but by reaching out to all its members, including the poor, the oppressed, and the marginalized. Only when these others are embraced as equal members can the church truly witness to its founder, Jesus Christ.[98]

Catholic theologian Mary Hunt stands with Ruether and Schüssler Fiorenza on the furthermost end of our continuum. As director of the nonprofit organization Women's Alliance for Theology, Ethics, and Ritual (WATER), Hunt is in the forefront of educating about and working for justice and equality. In her presentation to the Women's Ordination World-wide conference, she warned against merely replacing male priests with women and urged those involved in change to "reconfigure the whole model of church," and to "live the vision of radical equality now, however imperfectly, rather than participate in what oppresses."[99] Her vision of feminist ministry is a justice-seeking activity that crosses religious boundaries. Ordination, for Hunt, is a distraction from the more important work of seeking justice within a collaborative framework. It is this vision that spurs its followers to develop intra-religious as well as interreligious connections so that women's issues of justice, which exist throughout the world in all socioeconomic classes and throughout all religions, can be attended to. Mary Hunt understands that, as important as women's and homosexuals' ordination are, the issues of poverty, abuse, HIV/AIDS, and sexual trafficking are also major concerns that demand our immediate attention.

Once again, looking at the wide range of views regarding gender issues in Christianity, the questions of dialogue become more pronounced and the possibility of mutual understanding undergoes intense skepticism. Yet, listening to the explanation of these views from these women allows us to more easily respect where they are coming from, even if we still find dialogue beyond our reach.

ISLAM

We now approach Islam, the third and perhaps most problematic—at least in the view of many feminists—of the three Abrahamic traditions. One difficulty, extrinsic to the essence of Islam but nevertheless problematic, is that after the events of 9/11 the world has been saturated with images and commentary that identify Islam with terrorism. Many Americans and Europeans appear not to realize that Islam has the same roots as Judaism and Christianity or that Muslims worship the same God, the God of Abraham, called Allah in Arabic. In spite of attempts to counteract this simplistic identification of Islam and terrorism, rhetoric within various Western nations, including the United States, has portrayed the whole of Islam as a violent faith that hates freedom and justice, particularly with regard to women. Images in the news show women in either full head-to-toe coverings *(burkas)*, or head scarves *(hijabs)*. Such pictures, accompanied by reports of women being unable to drive, being forbidden to leave home unaccompanied by a male relative, and not receiving an education leave Westerners with the distinct impression that the religion of Islam is not only violent but also misogynistic. Added to these news reports is an array of popular books and movies, both fiction and nonfiction, that depict Muslim women as victims of male oppression.

Not all of those portrayals are advanced by Americans and Europeans. For example, Iraqi American playwright Heather Raffo achieved success both in London and New York with her one-woman play *Nine Parts of Desire*, in which she depicts the lives of nine Iraqi women in the ten years from the Gulf War to the war in Iraq. The film *Osama*, the story of a destitute Afghani family living under Taliban rule that sends its girl-child out dressed as a boy to earn money, won several awards, including a 2005 Golden Globe for best-foreign film. The best selling novel *Reading Lolita in Tehran*, published in 2003, tells of a group of Iranian women who studied modern American novels in secret with the author Azar Nafisi, herself an American-educated Iranian. These art forms have brought Islam to the attention of the Western public. Unfortunately, while they may be truthful in their depictions of the time and place of their subjects, they fuel the impression that Islam as a religion oppresses women. To counter this image and to ward off hatred and discrimination after 9/11, college campuses and local communities throughout North America have held information events to educate the public about the truth of Islam. Even the popular television personality Oprah Winfrey devoted one of her programs in October 2001 to depicting women in *hijab* living their daily lives like any other Americans. Certainly the veiled Islamic woman who spoke to me of her freedom at our interfaith dialogue should cause us to think twice about generalizing or essentializing Islam, but whether Westerners will let go of the negative stereotypes is debatable. One thing is certain: Islam is now a topic of interest to all Westerners.

And well it should be, because Islam is one of the fastest-growing religions in the world today, claiming nearly 20 percent of the world's population or 1.6 billion people. It is the second-largest religion in the world, exceeded only by Christianity.[100] In order to understand its surge in popularity, it is necessary to examine the true Islam that lies beyond the current images. Only then can we learn what the women who practice this religion have to say about their situation and how their viewpoints fit on our continuum of women's voices.

Muslims consider themselves related to Judaism and Christianity in that they are People of the Book; that is, the Jews have the Hebrew Bible, Christians have the Old and New Testaments, and Muslims have the Qur'an. While it is true that the Qur'an is technically a book containing references to creation, Moses, Jesus, and other similar themes, it differs from the Hebrew and Christian Bibles in that it is believed to be the final revelation of the God of Abraham, whose previous self-revelations were misunderstood by the people. It also differs because Muslims believe that the Qur'an, "by its own testimony, consists of the words of God as recited in Arabic to the Prophet Muhammad through the Angel Gabriel (Qur'an 26:193)."[101] Muhammad did not compose these words in the same sense that the prophets or the evangelists wrote the Bible. He could not have done so because, Muslims believe, he was illiterate, which is proof that the melodic and poetic words could not have come from him but only from the voice of God. Muhammad recited them from memory to his followers, who later put them in writing. The revelation of God or the primal Qur'an[102] exists in heaven with God and descended to the heart of Muhammad through the Angel Gabriel, and, as such, "the Qur'an is inimitable, inviolate, inerrant, and incontrovertible."[103] It is the profound word of God, and both its meanings and its language are divine, infinite, and beyond human explanation.[104] Furthermore, for the Muslim, God is "unique and without associate and therefore . . . cannot be represented, except by His word, the Qur'an."[105] Thus, these words are more than a book; they are, in fact, the presence of God. The Qur'an, then, does not parallel the Bible in Christianity; rather, it signifies the presence of God for the Muslim as Jesus Christ, the Word of God, does for the Christian.

The Qur'an, therefore, is not just meant to be read or studied. Rather, it is first and foremost to be recited. God dictated the words to Muhammad, and he to his companions. Therefore, Muslims believe that "meaning is conveyed by the sound. . . . Only by recapturing the divine sound, as best one can, is one able to approach the presence of God, and apprehend His divine word."[106] The chanting of the Qur'an holds a special place in Islam and is, in itself, a religious experience that goes beyond human language and puts both the chanter and the listener into a communion with God. For this reason, all children, both boys and girls, are taught to memorize the Qur'an from their earliest years.

While the Qur'an is the primary source of divine revelation for all Muslims, it is not the only authority governing their lives. Islamic tradition also includes sunnah, hadith, and shari'a.[107] The sunnah refers to the Prophet Muhammad's words and practices, that is, how he lived out and taught the revelations he received from God. These accounts were transmitted orally by his followers and eventually written down in narrative form now known as hadith. As time went on and the life of the prophet grew more and more distant, these hadith were essential for the interpretation and adaptation of God's message. Even though "these records began to be compiled over a century after his death and were not completed until three hundred or more years later,"[108] they are often treated as though their authority is equal to that of the Qur'an. Riffat Hassan aptly describes the nature of the hadith as "the lens through which the words of the Qur'an have been seen and interpreted"[109] from the early days of Islam. However, the meaning and authority of particular hadith are sometimes disputed by scholars who, in recent years, include more and more women.

The other source of authority is the shari'a, the classical Islamic law derived from both the Qur'an and the hadith. However, there are diverse opinions about how much weight should be given to various revelations when constructing this law. As a result, the carrying out of shari'a reflects a wide diversity of opinion, which accounts for the differences we see in the customs and practices in various countries, all of which claim to be acting in the name of Islam. These various sources, the Qur'an, the hadith, and the shari'a are all to be considered when listening to women's voices. It is the particular weight of authority and the interpretations given to each that determine where these women's viewpoints lie on our continuum.

Before exploring the diverse women's voices in Islam, it is important to take note of a common thread woven throughout all of their discourse. Muslim women, both scholars and laywomen, conservative and progressive, make a very emphatic point of grounding their positions in Islamic traditions, thereby distancing themselves from two phenomena: (1) oppressive regimes in power in Islamic countries, and (2) Western concepts of women's liberation. They insist that the personal and ethical form of Islam rooted in its revelation is different from what Leila Ahmed calls the established version of Islam, the Islam of the politically powerful, which she says is authoritarian, androcentric, and hostile to women.[110] Hence, when regimes oppress women by denying them political rights, keeping them in seclusion, and oppressing them sexually, all in the name of Islam, the fault lies in the ruler's destructive use of power, not in Islamic tradition itself. Proof that these authoritarian regimes are "un-Islamic" is found in the Qur'an itself, which says in sura 2:256, "Let there be no compulsion in religion: Truth stands out from Error."[111] Further, these women blame colonialism and the anti-Islamic rhetoric of the West for the backlash of rigidity and oppression existing in the Islamic world today.[112] A very direct accusation is made by a political scientist from the University of Cairo, Heba Raouf Ezzat, who claims that the regimes that violate women's rights and human rights are "usually supported by Western allies."[113] She understands that secularism and materialism of the postcolonial era removed the religious-based shari'a and reduced Islam to a penal code, which was then used by totalitarian governments to violate human rights. Against this backdrop of an antireligious and anti-Islamic West, these women understand the Western feminist movement as a fight for the rights denied Western women in the secular world and see the Islamic women's movement as one that is grounded in Islam itself, not in secular philosophies. Their opinion is aptly expressed by Omaima Abou-Bakr, who declares that she will not "subscribe to any foreign/Western agenda or discourse on feminism and gender."[114] In other words, Muslim women's struggle to have their voices heard is portrayed as a result of the emerging education of women in the Islamic world and not due to any association with the Western feminist movement. On such a construction of the matter, parallels made here between the views of Muslim women and those of women in other religions are *mine* and do not imply any causal relationship between the two.

CONSERVATIVE POSITION

Having said this, we can now traverse the many Muslim women's viewpoints from conservative to progressive. On the conservative end of our continuum are those women who interpret all three sources, the Qur'an, the hadith, and the current shari'a as possessing God's unchanging message, which is that women are essentially different from men and that their primary roles are to be wives and mothers. By living under shari'a, which is divine, the state can return to the ideal days of the Prophet in which women's equality is restored.[115] Perhaps the most famous spokeswoman for this perspective is Egyptian Islamist activist Zaynab al-Ghazali, founder of the Muslim Women's Association, a spinoff of the Muslim Brotherhood. Her ideas were very much influenced by the founders of the Muslim Brotherhood, Hasan al-Banna and his successor, Sayyid Qutb, who encouraged women to join them as long as their activism did not detract from their domestic responsibilities. "Women have a natural capacity and skills for managing the household," wrote Qutb, "and it was their place to care while a man's skill was that of management."[116] Convinced that wives and mothers were the bearers of culture, Zaynab al-Ghazali set out to organize women's activities according to traditional Islamic norms. Like her mentor Qutb, she believed that, while a woman has the right to be active in public life, hold a job, own property, and do business, she can do so only if she has fulfilled her primary duty as wife and mother, which takes precedence over all else. She was also a staunch promoter of women's education, for she maintained that if women were educated in the precepts of the Qur'an and the Islamic tradition, they would learn that their God-given and most important roles are to be wife and mother, a fact that cannot be ignored. Al-Ghazali's activism and teachings essentialized women's roles in Islam and made the domestic sphere women's natural responsibility. Through this Islamist gender discourse the idea of equality was transformed into that of "complementarity, that is, women and men are equal, yet different, thus providing some grounds for a justification of some of the religious inequalities."[117] This concept of complementarity reminds us of the conservative Christian idea of the same name discussed earlier and espoused by those evangelicals who also lie on the conservative end of our continuum.

For her active opposition to the then-ruler of Egypt, Abd al-Nasir, al-Ghazali was imprisoned in 1965, tortured, tried in 1966, and sentenced to hard labor for life. In 1971 she was released by Anwar Sadat. She continued until her death in 2005 to be an active teacher of Islam. She taught that all Muslims should strive for the establishment of an Islamic state, one in which society would be divinely guided by the Qur'an and the sunnah of Muhammad. But as passionate as she was about her politics, in all her years as an activist she herself never neglected her husband or her family duties.[118]

Al-Ghazali's message is alive and well, and she continues to be a role model for modern Muslim women across the globe. College student Marya Bangee wrote in the online Muslim magazine *Alkalima* that al-Ghazali's courage and devotion to Islam made a powerful impact on her generation. When faced with adversity, young Muslims look to her as a model of steadfast faith and resilience.[119] This admiration for the Egyptian activist inspires young women to follow her lead and to be faithful to their religious calling, to be wives and mothers first and professionals and public activists when time and energy permit.

The belief in complementarity of genders is also held by a new generation of university-educated Islamist women who believe that it is the true message of Allah. One such scholar at Cairo University, Heba Raouf Ezzat, has as her motto, "Liberate women, and still keep the family."[120] Ezzat tackles some controversial hadith regarding women, such as "No success is destined for a folk whose ruler is a woman." In recounting its history, she concludes that, while the verse doesn't exclude all women from holding public office, "only few women can practically manage both the responsibilities of family and jurisdiction at [one] time."[121] Many women in Islam agree, and, although they actively participate in economics and politics, they are committed to guarding the culture by being wives and mothers.[122] To Ezzat and her Muslim sisters, unless women assume these roles as their first obligation, all Muslim society is in peril.

This perspective is not unique to women in the Middle East but is held also by Western Muslim women. In an interview for the British paper the *Guardian*, six young professional Muslim women, all university graduates, explained their dedication to Islam and their endorsement of gender stereotypes. They believe that women are more emotional and men are more rational, a situation due to natural differences in the genders rather than to socialization. In their minds Western science is catching up with the "Koranic insight into the profound differences and complementarity of the sexes." These women believe that that women really want to care for children and "a genuinely equal society would be the one that honours that role and provides them with the financial resources to concentrate on it."[123] Like al-Ghazali, they believe that women are free to work and be active in public life only after they have taken care of family responsibilities.

An American convert to Islam, Lois Lamya al-Faruqi, explains that the gender equality found in the Qur'an does not mean that the sexes are equivalent or identical. Rather, both sexes have different and special responsibilities in order to ensure the healthy functioning of society. "This division of labour imposes on men more economic responsibilities (2:233, 240–241; 4:34), while women are expected to play their role in childbearing and rearing (2:23; 7:189)"[124] She understands the passages in the Qur'an that grant men twice the portion of inheritance granted to women (4:19, 176) as alleviating the greater economic demands made upon them as heads of households. This idea of complementarity of gender, which al-Faruqi finds in the Qur'an, is for her the ideal for American women, an ideal that cannot be found in Western feminist movements.[125]

In spite of the appearance of oppression, many American women are experiencing Islam as liberating. Among them is a growing number of African American women converting to Sunni Islam (not to be confused with the Nation of Islam led by Louis Farakan) and espousing the idea of gender complementarity, which they understand as essential to the tradition. Why is this happening? To answer this question, Carolyn Moxley Rouse embarked on a study of Muslim women converts in South Central Los Angeles; she inquired about their motivations and their lived experiences. Rouse discovered that the reason for many conversions was that these women's lives were profoundly changed for the better because of their belief in Islam.[126] For them, Islam provided a way to create a moral and just world in the face of social chaos. "The Muslima (Muslim sisters) accept the religiously prescribed gender roles and codes of conduct, believing that liberation emerges out of these disciplinary practices."[127] One woman, Marwa, for example, believing that birth control was anti-Islamic, had given birth to eight children. In spite of the family's poverty and her inability to handle her oldest, who was learning disabled, she believed strongly that children are the source of women's respect and blessings.[128] Women like Marwa believe that the will of Allah comes before their material comforts, and they take literally the Qur'anic verse that says that Allah " 'creates what He wills. He bestows (children) male or female according to His Will' (42:49)." She and others also take to heart the conservative understanding of the Qur'an's teaching that Allah made the man responsible for woman because he is stronger and more able to deal with [business] affairs.[129]

By listening carefully to the voices of these Muslim women who espouse complementarity, we hear similarities to their Jewish and Christian counterparts. First, their espousal of traditional roles is religiously motivated and becomes the lived expression of their spirituality. Being a faithful wife and mother is a Muslim woman's way of relating to Allah and of achieving the Islamic ideal of oneness with the Divine. Rouse writes that the Muslim women she interviewed valued "religious asceticism over personal empowerment."[130] Second, by bearing and educating her children, the Muslim woman is assuring the purity, solidarity, and continuation of the *ummah* (Muslim community). These two motivations, spirituality and solidarity, are the foundations of the conservative Muslim woman's embracing a life that to outsiders appears to be repressive but to her is liberating and holy.

There is one aspect about this conservative position, however, that distinguishes it from the views of Jews or Christians, particularly those in the West. This is the issue of veiling. Because it is the most visible sign of Muslim identity, it is usually the first criticism made by Westerners who judge veiling according to modern American standards and see it as oppressive to women. However, there are many complex reasons why conservative Muslim women choose to wear the *hijab*. First, they believe it to be an act of religious devotion in obedience to Allah whose will is found in the Qur'an and the hadith. They cite as proof a verse that "instructs Muslims to speak to the Prophet's wives from behind a curtain, or screen: 'and when you ask his wives for anything you want, ask them from before a screen: that makes for greater purity for your hearts and theirs' (33:53)."[131] There are also particular hadith calling for women to veil, that, while controversial among scholars, are quoted by traditionalists as being authoritative. It is out of obedience and devotion to Allah that these women choose to wear the *hijab*. "The covering of the head is something that is commanded by God, not man," says Monowara Gani, a university student in Nottingham, England. "I can't explain why, it's something between me and God."[132] Zaynab al-Ghazali once told an interviewer: "I always encouraged women to wear the veil, because it is important for women to be religious. It is through them that men find Islam and this influences the family to be religious."[133]

This statement brings us to the second reason for Muslim women to wear the *hijab*, that is, to identify publicly with Islam and its values. Such identification is not only a sign of pride in one's tradition but also a rebellion against Western ideology and culture, which are viewed by these Muslim women as oppressive and promiscuous. In her discussion on veiling, Leila Ahmed explains that during colonial times Westerners saw veiling as a symbol of the backwardness and inferiority of Islamic societies, believing that women who were required to cover their heads were obviously oppressed.[134] In some Islamic countries, such as Iran and Egypt, women were prohibited from covering their heads by regimes under Western influence. Such degrees often provoked violent demonstrations among the general populations. Ahmed reports that "many women chose to stay at home rather than venture outdoors and risk having their veils pulled off by the police."[135] Thus the veil became the focal point of friction between those who sided with the Western powers and those who were faithful to Islam. Wearing it became an act of defiance and rebellion against Western imperialism and its values. It is interesting to note that after 9/11 the veil has once again been the focus of criticism and a symbol of Islamic oppression, and once again Muslim women have the need to assert their Islamic identity. These young women interviewed by the *Guardian* justified wearing the *hijab* as a statement of their political identity in a world where Islam perceives itself as under threat.[136] Journalist Geneive Abdo writes that even today, "from Tehran to Istanbul to Cairo, the *hijab* serves as the most potent homegrown symbol of the power of the Islamists."[137] As a result of this history and of the current political climate, wearing the veil for many Muslim women is as much a political statement as it is a religious one.

A third reason for wearing the *hijab* follows from this reaction against Western values. It is very important for Muslim women to avoid the dangers leading to what they see as the rampant sexual immorality of Western society. This can be done, according to traditional Muslims, by discouraging sexual attraction between men and women who are not husband and wife.[138] They believe that such attraction is dangerous and will cause chaos in society because of "women's power to engender uncontrolled lust among men."[139] Therefore, by covering their hair and wearing loose clothing, Muslim women can avoid the lustful and potentially dangerous glances of men. Many modern feminists look upon this idea as sexist because it stems from the notion that women are tempters of men and responsible for man's sexual desires getting out of control. Christian and Jewish women recognize such an idea from the ancient misogynistic interpretations of the Adam and Eve story. However, while to some this idea is ancient, Americans need only be reminded that until recently rape victims were often accused of being responsible for the crime because they "provoked" their attackers, and hence convictions of rapists were difficult to obtain. Many conservative women both in the West and East still hold to this stereotype; to them, wearing the veil protects them and gives them a freedom to move about without worrying about how they are affecting men's sexual drives. Leila Ahmed writes that the veil "protects them from male harassment. In responding to a questionnaire women stated that wearing Islamic dress resulted in a marked difference in the way they were treated in public places."[140] Similarly, the protection from male advances that the veil affords women means that they are able to be viewed for their worth as persons as opposed to being valued for their bodily features, which are considered superficial. Abdo recounts a conversation with an Egyptian woman who said, "When I put on the veil, I put on my brain as well."[141]

To sum up the veiling issue on the conservative end of our continuum, we see three motivations for covering one's head, which may exist either separately or simultaneously: (1) obedience and devotion to Allah, (2) repudiation of Western values, and (3) defense against sexual advances. It must be noted that none of these motivations includes obedience to a repressive regime. When the Taliban in Afganistan or the monarchy of Saudi Arabia imposes full coverings for women and executes penalties for noncompliance, it is not acting in accordance with Islam, for we are reminded that the Qur'an forbids compulsion in religion (2:256).

CENTRIST POSITION

The conservative position is disputed by many Muslim women whose views lay in the center of our continuum. These women understand the original revelation to be egalitarian and believe that the later texts, in which the revelation was preserved, incorporated many of the misogynistic and patriarchal ideas of the time. In recent decades many Muslim women who are studying the Qur'an and Islamic history are addressing some of the oppressive practices being sanctioned by governments in the name of Islam, one of which is the exclusion of women from education. Keeping women in ignorance assures their acceptance of male domination. Things are changing, however, as evidenced in a recent *New York Times* article. Several women were interviewed throughout Europe, and it was found that "young women are increasingly engaging in Islamic studies, a fast-growing field across Europe that offers a blend of theology, Koranic law, ethics and Arabic."[142] In the view of one woman, what we want is "direct access to religion, without depending on the rigid views of the clergy," because religious texts are more effective than secular arguments when fighting against the oppression of women in families and in the public arena. In addition to fighting for their rights under Islam, those who have been educated are taking up the cause of all Muslim women, especially those in rural areas of Islamic countries where the rate of literacy of women is among the lowest in the world.[143] Women scholars, such as Amina Wadud, Riffat Hassan, and Fatima Mernissi, are not only researching and writing, but they are also actively campaigning for literacy programs for Muslim women in order for them to experience their religion as liberating and not confining. They wish that all Muslim women could read and recite the texts for themselves and not have to hear them from the voices of men.

What these scholars have discovered is that the Qur'an itself, as it was spoken to Muhammad through the Angel Gabriel, carries a liberating message for women. However, problems of interpretation arose after the death of the Prophet. His words and deeds (sunnah) were passed on by word of mouth and eventually were written down in accounts known as the hadith. In this process the Prophet's teachings were subjected to various misogynistic and patriarchal attitudes of the times, and, as a result, disputes arose about the authenticity of both the oral and written accounts. Hence, these women scholars believe that many of the hadith, particularly those that are most harmful to women, have been misinterpreted and are not authentically attributed to the Prophet himself.

Throughout the history of Islam there has been so much concentration on the preservation of the hadith through the development of Islamic law (shari'a) and its application to politics, that attention was taken away from the study of the primary revelation, the Qur'an. According to Amina

Wadud-Muhsin, this shift in emphasis resulted in a separation from the intent of the original text. Further, these hadith and shariʻa, which have been interpreted through the world views of the various readers and teachers, have become more important and their authority more binding than the Qurʼan itself.[144] Therefore, many Muslims are living out, not necessarily the will of Allah, but its interpretations passed down by various male leaders. To discover the original message, Wadud-Muhsin, in her 1992 text *Qurʼan and Woman*, carefully analyzes the Qurʼan's original text, particularly those passages that refer to women, by putting verses into their context and by comparing them to similar verses and to overriding Qurʼanic principles. She also gives careful attention to the Arabic language and explains that, since this language contains no neuter terms, each word is designated as masculine or feminine. Therefore, references to male or female persons are not necessarily limited to that gender. The conclusion of her analysis is that the Qurʼan does not support the essential distinction between women and men that is held by conservative Muslims and that has been used to limit women's tasks and functions in society.[145]

This centrist position—that it is the hadith and not the Qurʼan that supports the inequality of women—is held also by Riffat Hassan:

> The cumulative (Jewish, Christian, Hellenistic, Bedouin and other) biases which existed in the Arab-Islamic culture of the early centuries of Islam infiltrated the Islamic tradition, largely through the hadith literature, and undermined the intent of the Qurʼan to liberate women from the status of chattels of inferior creatures and make them free and equal to men.[146]

Like Wadud-Mushin, Hassan carefully analyzes the Arabic language, which, she says, is incredibly rich, with multiple meanings to almost every word. By so doing she is able to reinterpret passages so that their meanings do not contradict the justice of God. She dispels the prevalent notions that women were created inferior to men, that women are responsible for the Fall, and that women were created to serve men, by doing a careful exegesis of the suras and verses of the creation story. She concludes that the Qurʼan makes it clear that men and women "stand absolutely equal in the sight of God" and that they are protectors of each other. "They are created as equal creatures of a universal, just and merciful God whose pleasure it is that they live in harmony and righteousness."[147] Her intense study reveals a Qurʼan that frees all human beings, women as well as men, from, in her passionate words, "the bondage of traditionalism, authoritarianism . . . tribalism, racism, sexism, slavery or anything else that prohibits or inhibits human beings from actualizing the Qurʼanic vision of human destiny embodied in the classical proclamation, 'Towards Allah is thy limit'"[148]

Fatima Mernissi, in her book *The Veil and the Male Elite*, carefully studies the disputes over the hadith that occur in historical sources. She explains how one of the most respected and wise companions of the Prophet, Umar Ibn al-Khattab, would not repeat hadith for fear of being inaccurate. He relied instead on his own judgment in moral and political affairs because he believed that memory of past events was "dangerously fallible" and that to assume to recall so many of the Prophet's words and deeds, as did Abu Hurayra, a prolific recorder of hadith, was irresponsible.[149] Mernissi explains that the only way scholars can determine the authenticity of hadith is "to check the identity of the Companion of the Prophet who uttered it, and in what circumstances and with what objective in mind, as well as the chain of people who passed it along –[and she concludes] there are more fraudulent traditions than authentic ones."[150]

With regard to the issue of veiling, Mernissi and Ahmed exemplify the centrist though still controversial position in Islam. They understand that the explicit notions of veiling are found in the hadith, while, as Ahmed points out, "it is nowhere explicitly prescribed in the Qur'an; the only verses dealing with women's clothing . . . instruct women to guard their private parts and throw a scarf over their bosoms (Sura 24:31–32)."[151] These passages and others that refer to the seclusion of Muhammad's wives can be interpreted in ways that don't require women to cover their heads. Veiling existed before Muhammad's time, and, according to Mernissi, it was a symbol of the pagan belief that the feminine was dangerously mysterious. Such an attitude was far from the message of Islam, which was to free its followers of such pagan attitudes and superstitions. Since veiling held such a place in the interpretations of the Qur'an, she questions the effectiveness of Islam's novel approach to women on the seventh-century Arabs. "Is it possible that the *hijab*, the attempt to veil women, that is claimed today to be basic to Muslim identity, is nothing but the expression of the persistence of the pre-Islamic mentality, the *jahiliyya* (preconversion disbelief) mentality that Islam was supposed to annihilate?"[152] It would be difficult and problematic for some Muslims to believe what Mernissi and Ahmed are saying, that is, that the veil was a practice of the paganism that Islam was meant to transform rather than an inherent part of the religion itself.

PROGRESSIVE POSITION

On the progressive end of our continuum are those women who believe that while religions' original revelations did introduce a new way of being and new life principles, these ideas came into a culture of misogyny and patriarchy and were presented within this framework. Therefore, in order to be faithful to the original message, one must sift through the texts to discover the revelatory message that lies within the cultural context. One woman performing this task within Islam is Asma Barlas, a Qur'anic scholar and political scientist who was forced to leave her native Pakistan in 1983 and is now teaching at Ithaca College in New York. Barlas understands that the Qur'an was addressing seventh-century Arabs and is spoken in a language and in a way that was relevant to those people's lives. It was revealed into an existing patriarchy, and this ideology influenced the way the divine word was interpreted. As a result, "Muslim women have a stake in challenging its patriarchal exegesis."[153]

Although Barlas accepts the authority of the Qur'an and holds, as do all Muslims, that it is the voice of God to the people, she realizes that in order to be faithful to God's message, we must recognize that there is a distinction between Divine Speech and its earthly realization. Further she questions the long held assumption that only men can interpret what God means and believes that it is this assumption that has caused so much of women's oppression in Muslim societies. She believes that God did not reveal a patriarchy; rather, it has been read into the text "in contextually problematic ways."[154]

In order to unleash this Divine Speech and its message, Barlas develops a hermeneutic that allows her to free the text from its patriarchal and misogynistic interpretations and to view it as liberating for women. This hermeneutic is based on the Muslim's understanding of God as learned from God's self-disclosure. What do we know of God and how does this knowledge influence how we read what God has said? "The failure to connect God to God's Speech (which has resulted in some extremely objectionable readings of the Qur'an) is inexplicable in view of the fact that the organizing principle of Islam, the doctrine of God's Unity *(Tawhid)*, stipulates that there is a perfect congruence between God . . . and God's Speech."[155] Barlas applies three aspects of God's Self-Disclosure to her reading of the Qur'an, Divine Unity, Justness, and Incomparability. In a clear and extensive analysis she applies these attributes to the verses of the text. Those that don't coincide with the nature of God must be reexamined and put into context. In the end, says Barlas,

> a reading of the Qur'an is just a reading of the Qur'an, no matter how good; it does not approximate the Qur'an itself, which may be why the Qur'an distinguishes between itself and its exegesis. Thus it condemns those "who write the Book with their own hands. And then say; 'This is from God.'"[156]

Barlas's hermeneutics gives the Qur'an a very different interpretation than those conservative women who side with the Islamists' view of gender. She does not endorse the belief that God assigned different roles to the genders based on biology, psychology, or any other factor. Rather, she believes that the Qur'an establishes and confirms the principle of equality of the sexes. In her book she demonstrates how these principles can be found in Islam through the study of the Qur'an and thus makes unnecessary and inferior any recourse to Western ideology for the establishment of women's liberation from patriarchy. In her recent work *Inside the Gender Jihad*, Amina Wadud similarly disconnects her feminism from Western thought by engaging in a reconstruction of human rights discourse that is appropriate to her Islamic origins. Like Barlas, she redefines what it means to be authentically Muslim and also a feminist.[157]

Finally, a study of progressive Islam would be incomplete without reference to a group of American Muslim women who are struggling to find their religious identities in a culture that is both secular and, since 9/11, increasingly focused on Islam. Like Asma Barlas, they believe Islam is fundamentally egalitarian and, while they distance themselves from American feminists, they do attribute their impetus to study and explore liberating interpretations of the Qur'an to the cultural freedom and diversity they experience in America. Saleemah Abdul-Ghafur, an American Muslim activist from Atlanta, brought together fifteen other American Muslims and edited their works in a volume called *Living Islam Out Loud*. While these women come from a diversity of backgrounds, they are all on spiritual journeys and "understand that following disempowering interpretations of sacred text"[158] is not for them. To them, Islam is in the midst of a global transformation, and it is their responsibility to let their voices be heard even at the risk of judgment from family, friends, and the Muslim community. Each one of these women has a deeply spiritual life and trusts that God, who is a God of mercy, speaks to her in the Qur'an. Saleemah writes: "The more self-aware I become, the more I feel that I am aligned with God's best plan for me. My faith grows stronger, no longer weakened by external forces. . . . What I now know is that for me, Islam is fundamentally a way of life emanating from God's mercy."[159] Yousra Y. Fazili, an attorney and scholar of Islamic law, discovered after intense study that Islam requires one to be faithful to one's self as well as to God. She writes: "I suppose my own understanding of Allah is of a God with infinite love and infinite kindness, a God who knows what is in our hearts. More than anything else, my God is a God of mercy and my God is a God of compassion."[160] The God that these women are committed to does not demand blind obedience to laws and practices that have come down through the interpretations of male authorities; rather, their God is one of kindness and love who asks nothing but the same in return.

This deep spirituality is reflected also in the story of Mohja Kahf, a writer and university professor. In her search for an Islam in which she could participate, she realized that something radical was needed. She did not wish to leave the tradition but rather to take the best strands of it and "create Islam afresh for a new generation." She exemplifies the progressive position when she writes:

If you think such a thing as "pure Islam" existed, even for five minutes in C.E. 623, think again. Islam is always manifested inside a
particular culture and in specific, earth-rooted human bodies, and
our job now is to birth a new Islam, a new Islamic culture. This
Islam-on-the-ground-as-a-lived-reality needs to step up and take
credit for the specific ways in which it oppresses women as well as
the ways in which it liberated women fourteen hundred years ago.[161]

Perhaps the most startling and most impressive piece in this collection
is one by a Muslim woman who is a lesbian. She writes under a pseud-
onym for protection, since being gay and being Muslim is "like sinning
automatically, for no reason, all the time."[162] She writes that in her culture homosexuality is a Western concept and choosing anything other
than family is considered the epitome of selfishness. She eventually found
a group of gay and lesbian Muslims to worship with, and to her surprise,
after doing so, she had the exuberant feeling of being cleansed. Her devotion to Allah has increased so much so that she now practices an Islam
that makes sense to her. She tells us:

> Progressive Islam operates under the belief that anything that sanc-
> tions discrimination against anyone is anti-Islamic. It is the belief
> that working toward social justice is an integral part of religion. . . .
> Patriarchy and sexism are not necessarily Islamic traits but are actu-
> ally cultural traits. Realizing this has allowed me to give religion
> another chance.[163]

How do these women view the veil? The answers to this question are
as varied as the women themselves. Precious Rasheeda Muhammad chose
to wear it because she wanted to stand out unmistakably as a Muslim. It
was a conscious choice that gave her "great feelings of serenity, security
and elation."[164] Yousra Fazili decided not to wear it at age nineteen because she decided to live according to the Qur'an and not a jurist's interpretation of what the Qur'an was saying. She understood that there is no
explicit reference to veiling in the Qur'an, only to modesty.

Perhaps the most distinguishing factor about the progressive stance on
the *hijab* is that there is no definitive stance. In fact, for the most part
progressive women believe that there is entirely too much made of the
dispute over the *hijab*. To Afra Jalabi, a member of the Muslim Women's
League, wearing the *hijab* depends on which country she happens to be
in. This is so because, she writes, "while I believe in modesty, I do not
define myself through the scarf, nor shy away from it. It is simply a way
of dressing that can be beautiful, empowering and protective but also, at
times, limiting, misleading and impractical."[165]

After looking at the various perspectives of Muslim women, we notice that they represent the conservative, centrist, and progressive positions on the continuum. The common thread among them is that they all claim that their views are authentically Islamic and not derived from any Western—or Jewish or Christian—ideas. While this fact is made clear by all these women, the way in which their viewpoints differ resembles the differences among the women in both Judaism and Christianity. The conservatives in all three of these traditions understand that their religion teaches that men and women are essentially different, with different roles in society, the male being dominant and the female subservient. The centrists believe that the original revelation was egalitarian and that the male elite who passed on the revelation were responsible for its misogyny. The progressives, on the other hand, believe that the society in which the original message was revealed was itself misogynistic, and only by their belief in the unity, justice, and love of God can they separate the original message from the social influences in the primary texts. The similarities in these women's perspectives will be a major point of discussion in the interreligious dialogue that will be the subject of later chapters.

4

Conflicting Viewpoints
in Hinduism and Buddhism

The religions of Hinduism and Buddhism, which had their beginnings in South Asia and East Asia, appear to be so different from the Abrahamic faiths discussed in Chapter 3 that one wonders what women's voices in these religions sound like. Is there the same amount of discord among women from these traditions as there is among women in the West? If there is, can these voices be placed on the same continuum as that used for Judaism, Christianity, and Islam? In my meetings with Hindu and Buddhist women, I found that opinions on topics of religion and its role in forming their female identity varied so much that I began to question the source of the discrepancy. Was it the area in India that a Hindu woman came from that made her ideas so different from her Hindu sisters? Was it the particular school of Buddhism that she belongs to that distinguished a Buddhist woman from Taiwan from the Buddhist women from Thailand? In my search for answers I found that women from these traditions are much like others in that they understand their origins and their sacred texts differently, yet in ways that resemble those of their Western sisters. In this chapter we examine the conservative, centrist, and progressive viewpoints of Hindu and Buddhist women living in various parts of the world.

HINDUISM

Hinduism, like Islam, has had, and is having, a very problematic relationship with the Western world. India's occupation by Britain for over two hundred years affected the country and the religion in ways that are seen by many Indians as negative. As a result, many wish to combat the move toward modern secularism by returning India to its Hindu roots. Nationalistic movements, known as Hindutva, claim that Hindus who share in these roots include those whose religions are indigenous to India, such as Jains, Buddhists, and Sikhs, as well as mainstream Hindus.

61

Supporters of this form of nationalism believe also that Hinduism, by its nature, is inclusive with regard to other religions as well as to various beliefs within Hinduism itself. Hence, if India becomes truly Hindu, it will not only be tolerant of but will embrace other faiths and avoid factions within its own. It was the British tactic of divide and conquer that many Indians believe has pitted Hindu against Muslim, Christian, and Sikh and caused the often violent political tensions in India today. Looking for India's roots, however, may not be that simple, for the search reveals that its origins and culture are engulfed in a very ancient and very complex belief system, which only comparatively recently has become known to the world as the religion of Hinduism.

While four out of five Hindus today live in India, Hinduism is represented on every continent. It has spread through migration and cultural contact rather than missionary activity, since Hindus are not concerned with acquiring converts.[1] It is important, however, for Hindu immigrants to let their religion and culture be known in their new countries, because Hinduism is one of the least understood of the world's traditions outside of India. Most Westerners are familiar with curried Indian food and the brightly colored women's saris, but deities with bodies of humans and heads of monkeys and elephants are far beyond their comprehension. Thus the underlying beliefs and practices remain a mystery to many.

As we start to become familiar with Hinduism, one thing that comes through very clearly is that the role of women is one of the most contentious issues for its followers living both in and outside of the subcontinent. There has been a tremendous increase in the number of women in the nationalist movement, but these women are not of one mind regarding the interpretation of their religious tradition. They fall, in fact, on all segments of our continuum. In India's new nationalism we find traditional women whose duty as mothers and wives is to support their men as they struggle for a Hindu *rashtra* or nation. At the same time, the movement is urging women in India to call for the state to grant equal rights to all its citizens, men and women alike.[2] Each of these positions, however contradictory, can be found in India's ancient religious traditions. That religion and its sacred texts are relevant to this issue may not be immediately apparent, but many Indians believe that at the core of the social structure are the ancient religious beliefs, particularly those regarding women. One such activist, Jyotsna Chatterji, associate director of the Joint Women's Program in India, writes: "Religion has provided the ideological and moral basis for the status and role of women in society. The people's notion about the proper role of women in the home and society and the social restrictions on women are all rooted in religious conceptions."[3]

It is impossible in this short space to describe adequately this religion that has so affected women. Actually, it is not one religion but rather consists of a variety of religious sects or traditions. Unlike the Abrahamic faiths, there is no single set of doctrines, no one founder, no particular text that is a basis for dogma.[4] There are, however, some underlying ideas that enable us to unite these diverse sects with some degree of accuracy. The first is that all the various schools of thought rest on the eternal laws of nature (Dharma), which bind the universe and its components together. These laws, found in the world's most ancient texts, called the Vedas, consist of three parts: hymns used in ritual sacrifices, instructions for the performance of the rituals, and philosophical treatises called Upanishads, which explain the religious significance of the rituals. Besides the Vedas, there are other texts widely revered as sacred throughout India and exerting tremendous influence on the lives and mores of its people. Some of the most important especially for the status of women, are the *Manusmriti (Laws of Manu)* as well as the two great epic stories of the gods and their cohorts, the *Mahabharata* and the *Ramayana*. The origin, authorship, meanings, and interpretations for women of these very ancient texts are very controversial. This literature is used by conservatives to support the idea that woman's role is to be homemaker, mother, and husband's helper. But, by the same token, it also is used by women in the center of our continuum to show that in ancient times women were equal to men and that the male power structure throughout history has distorted the original message. Progressive women also refer to these texts but are willing to rewrite them, not for the purpose of creating a new story, but rather to bring out the egalitarian principles that are inherent in what they consider to be true Hinduism.

The Vedas are considered by Hindus to be foundational scriptures. In the words of Sri Swami Sivananda, they are "direct intuitional revelations and are held to be . . . entirely superhuman, without any author in particular." Those who received the revelations were called *rishis* or seers. The thoughts were not their own; rather, they saw or heard the truths, which already existed. These truths are eternal, not created and not the composition of any human mind.[5] Historians have tried to pinpoint the date of the composition of the Vedas, some saying around 3500 B.C.E.[6] and others saying that they were revealed about 1500 B.C.E. but codified later, about 600 B.C.E.[7] But the evidence for such statements is indecisive. Regardless of the time of origin, the Vedas remain authoritative for Hindus, even though they are considered far too obscure for the average Hindu to read much less comprehend. Hindus themselves believe that they are symbolic, requiring special vision to understand and to use correctly. For this reason, a person has to be specially educated and trained in order to recite the hymns *(samhitas)* and perform the rituals. For many centuries, Vedic learning was restricted to Sanskrit-speaking Brahmins, scholars and priests who wrote down the sacred texts and explained them in commentaries (Upanishads).[8] It is in these treatises that are found the most basic concepts of Hinduism, including the idea of Brahman being the great oneness of all being, the essence of all things, and of karma being the moral cause and effect, that is, the result of our actions, which determines how we live in our reincarnated lives.

The Brahmin priests also codified laws and these "ancient sacred law codes of the Hindus are called *Dharma Shastras* or *Smrutis.* Law-givers . . . laid down rules to maintain certain manners and customs. Manu Smruti is the best known; it elaborates the four stages of life *(Ashramas)* and the division of labour through a class system *(Varna Vyavastha)*."⁹ These *Laws of Manu* contain rules for family life and for the correct relationship of the genders, some of which are contradictory and become, therefore, particularly important when women on all points of the spectrum examine their place in Hinduism.

While the Ultimate Reality in Hinduism known as Brahman "can be understood as an unmanifest, impersonal One," it is also understood to manifest itself in millions of divine forms, including gods and goddesses, many of whom are believed to have lived physically on earth. The stories of the most famous of these are found in the epic poems of the *Mahabharata,* specifically the section called the *Bhagavad Gita,* and the *Ramayana.* The *Bhagavad Gita* is perhaps the most popular spiritual book of Hinduism, and it is for a Hindu what the Bible is for a Christian. Hindus of all sects consider it the most important guide to self-realization. The *Bhagavad Gita* consists of a dialogue between the warrior Arjuna and the god Krishna, who appears in the form of a charioteer. It is in this exchange that Hindus learn about the three yogas or paths to salvation: the path of action *(karma)*, the path of knowledge *(jnana)* and, especially emphasized in this text, the path of devotion *(bhakti)*.

The other major epic, the *Ramayana,* tells the story of the god and goddess who are the ideal models for all Hindu men and women, Rama and Sita. Rama is the seventh avatar or manifestation of the Hindu god Vishnu and is considered to be the perfect human being. Sita, his wife, is a manifestation of Vishnu's consort, Lakshmi. When she reincarnated herself on earth as Sita, she endured great hardships in order to be a model of virtue for humankind. Sita is, for Hindus, the "prototype of noble womanhood."¹⁰ Rama and Sita provide Indian men, women, and children with ideal models of familial relationships. Every boy wants to be a perfect man, like Rama, and every girl is taught to strive to be the ideal wife and mother, like Sita. At the center of this long and detailed epic is the exiled King Rama, who is followed into the forest by his devoted wife, Sita. After she is kidnapped by the demon Ravana, Rama obtains her release with the aid of the monkey king, Hanuman. Athough Rama has missed Sita and is delighted to have her back, he asks her to prove that she has been faithful to him by walking through fire. She comes out unscathed because she is pure. In an episode that was appended to the story at a later date, Rama banishes the now pregnant Sita to a distant forest, where she lives simply and raises her twin sons. Due to a number of circumstances, Rama encounters the two sons and recognizes them. He calls for Sita, but, to appease his subjects, he asks her once again to defend her purity by walking through fire. But this time, instead of responding, Sita calls to the earth with the words, "O Mother! Please take me into your fold. My mission is over."[11] When she says these words, the ground quakes and Sita "disappears into the furrow from whence [*sic*] she came."[12]

It is in the interpretations of these basic texts, the Vedas, the *Laws of Manu*, and the epics, particularly the *Ramayana*, that we find the most controversy in the viewpoints of Hindu women. In her study of these textual traditions, Hindu scholar Mary McGee presents the various perspectives, not as a pure academic exercise but rather to show how the different interpretations of authoritative texts have implications for women's rights in modern Hinduism.[13]

CONSERVATIVE POSITION

Those on the conservative end of our spectrum understand the sacred texts of Hinduism to be proclaiming a gender complementarity, requiring women to be the dutiful servants of men, obedient, and in extreme interpretations, worshipful. The traditional Hindu believes that men and women have distinct gender roles, which make up their Dharma or path of virtue according to the eternal laws of the universe. One must live according to her or his Dharma in order to accumulate merit for the next life and eventually to achieve *moksha* (salvation). Men have been, and in some locales still are, the only educated ones, the heads of households, and the ones who eventually leave home to become ascetics. Women meanwhile learn how to keep a home, mother the children, and support their husband in all things. In traditional thought the woman would have to be reborn again as a man in order to become an ascetic, the final step before *moksha*.

Of the texts that support such a view, the earliest appear in the Rig Veda and are especially prominent in the wedding ceremony. One author, V. SadagOpan, in an introduction to a translation of the wedding hymns, writes that the Rig Veda, while describing the wife to always be the best friend of the husband, is also entrusted with maintaining family tradition and strengthening the family's spiritual affairs. He adds, "According to the Vedas . . . she does duty for duties sake. She sacrifices her individual pleasure and pain and serves the family."[14] This author is indicating that a woman's place is beside a man, her husband, and in the family. A translation of hymn X. 85.27, sung at wedding ceremonies, states:

In this new family of your husband, may you be happy and prosperous along with your off springs. Be watchful over your domestic duties in this house. May you unite your person with your lord, your husband; thus may you both, growing in age together, manage your household affairs according to gruhasthAsrama rules.[15]

Even though we do find women priests mentioned in the Vedas, conservatives note that women such as Gargi in the *Brihadaranyaka Upanishad* are exceptional cases and should not be considered when discussing the status of women in the Vedic period.[16] Instead, the same Upanishad in which the Gargi is mentioned contains strict instructions given to the male to exercise his control over the female in matters sexual and maternal.

Another text that must be considered when viewing the role of women in Hinduism is the *Manusmirti* or *Laws of Manu*. Many Indian women living in America have reported that they were not familiar with this text and only encountered it through American scholars. However, although the *Manusmirti* may not have been studied in and of itself, it has had a large influence on the Hindu concept of women because gurus or holy teachers have long considered it standard among the Hindu sacred texts and have taught it throughout the ages.[17] Its importance rests on the fact that it expresses what ancient India, under Brahmin influence around 500 B.C.E., understood to be the norms of domestic and religious life. Although it is well known that, at the time, only the elite were subject to such prescriptions and that the lower classes were more pragmatic, placing fewer constraints on women, these laws nevertheless still "have given posterity a celebrated portrait of the compleat [*sic*] Hindu woman (i.e., wife, for at the time of his writing, the two were synonymous)."[18] A current guide for teachers of Hinduism in England and America refers to these laws as the oldest and most authentic of revealed texts and to Manu as "the first lawgiver of mankind and . . . the patron saint of social thinkers."[19] Writers who extol this text admit, however, that there is much controversy today about the meaning of certain passages. Indeed, many devout Hindus do not consider them relevant to their lives. Be that as it may, the very fact that this text is still officially taught as authentic gives us reason to wonder about its role in modern Indian society. A further consideration is that the *Laws of Manu* was "imposed as the Hindu law code by the eighteenth-century colonial governor Warren Hastings, in consultation with Brahman [*sic*] priests,"[20] and as a result has left its mark on the subcontinent.

Conservatives wanting to show Hinduism's respect for women are fond of quoting verses 55 and 56 of Chapter 3, which state that "women must be honoured and adorned by their fathers, brothers, husbands, and brothers-in-law, who desire (their own) welfare. . . . Where women are honoured, there the gods are pleased."[21] When looking at the code as a whole, however, these positive verses seem to be outnumbered by those that present a different picture. For example, Chapter 9 contains the following admonitions:

> 2. Day and night woman must be kept in dependence by the males (of) their (families), and if they attach themselves to sensual enjoyments, they must be kept under one's control.
> 3. Her father protects (her) in childhood, her husband protects (her) in youth, and her sons protect (her) in old age; a woman is never fit for independence.
> 5. Women must particularly be guarded against evil inclinations, however trifling (they may appear); for, if they are not guarded, they will bring sorrow on two families.[22]

Furthermore, in this text we see the development of the principle of an eternal relationship between a man and his wife. "A man was like a god to his wife, for whom no other form of worship was necessary but attending to her husband with all devotion."[23] The eternal permanence of the relationship meant that in the event of his death she was never to remarry and must remain chaste for the remainder of her earthly life.

There is no doubt that these laws have influenced the relationship of women to men and have enforced the idea that the role of woman is synonymous with that of a wife for she is destined for the duties of maintaining the home and serving the man. However, this role both elevates and denigrates the nature of woman in the eyes of some conservative Hindus. On the one hand she is to be respected, but on the other, she is dangerous and in need of protection and control. The conservative woman recognizes these two positions and claims that the *Laws of Manu* instructs the husband to respect his wife while she must still obey and serve him. Vrushali Kene, a Hindu woman from Bombay now living in southern California, exemplified this view. She has a negative view of modern society because she sees in it less cooperation and more competition between husband and wife, whereas in a proper relationship they each revere the other in their respective roles. The wife should listen and obey the husband while he, in turn, must treat her with gracious respect. Vrushali herself gave up a fruitful architectural career to help her husband buy and run his own business and sees her choice as her duty. She supports her actions with a familiar saying from Swami Vivekananda, "Grease the duty with love." In other words, spouses must perform their respective roles willingly, without force or oppression. Abuses in the male role resulting in dominance and control are blamed by Vrushali on the British, who, during their two hundred years of control, coopted the Brahmins to think like them. She claims that they forced the Brahmins to change the scriptures making them much more male dominated, especially the *Manusmirti.*

In summary, whether it was changed or not, the *Manusmirti* still reinforces the notion that the ideal relationship between husband and wife is
one in which the male is the major decision-maker and head of the household and the wife is the submissive and self-sacrificing caregiver. This
ensures that the domestic domain is peaceful, which in turn upholds the
orthodox Hindu moral code, which in turn maintains a perfect world.[24]

Turning to the figure of Sita, wife of Rama in the *Ramayana,* we see a
similar variety of interpretations of her story affecting women's place in
society. Conservatives such as Vrushali understand that Rama is the perfect king and Sita is the ideal wife. Rama's questioning and testing of
Sita's fidelity are done only to adhere to Hindu scriptures and to demonstrate Sita's purity to his people, who are carefully observing his handling
of the situation. His duty as king, or *raja*, requires him to serve his people,
or *praja*, above all else, even above his own personal life. Rama must
respect his people and fulfill his requirements as leader. Thus he has to
have Sita prove her innocence to them, even though he knows she has
been innocent all along. In turn, Sita, according to this view, never crosses
Rama. She follows him into the forest when he is exiled, knowing that
"whatever the husband must go through, she goes with him."[25] Her words
to Rama convincing him to let her follow him are some of the most often
repeated in Hindu literature, both in homes and in temples:

> Oh, Rama! As per the command of the elders, I
>   also should go along with you. My life is to be
>   abandoned here, if I were separated from you.
> Oh, Rama! Verily such a thing was taught to me
>   by you, that a woman disunited from her
>   husband should not be able to survive.[26]

Sita also willingly undergoes the trial by fire to prove her purity because
she understands Rama's duties to his people.

The popular textbook version of the epic teaches that Sita is considered by all Hindu women to be the ideal of Indian womanhood. Her
obedience, fidelity, and willingness to suffer for her husband make her
not only the ideal wife but also elevates her to the status of virtuous woman.
Apart from her husband, Sita had no life. Hindu women whose lot has
been as hard or even harder than hers have seen her as a model to be
emulated by bearing their suffering ungrudgingly.[27] Even though there
have been other interpretations of the events in this epic, Sara Mitter
observes that "the Sita ideal is a part of a Hindu woman's psychic inheritance, and she inculcates it, both overtly and unwittingly, in her daughters."[28]

In an addendum to the original version of the *Ramayana* called the
Adhyatma Ramayana, Rama asks Sita to prove her fidelity and purity a

second time. However, rather than walk through fire again, she asks Mother Earth to help her. Just then there is a great earthquake, and Sita falls into the opening and dies. In one summary it is said that "Sita's mother (the earth mother) rose from a great chasm to reclaim her daughter."[29] Conservative and progressive women have interpreted this account of Sita's death differently. Vrushali's conservative view is that Sita was caught between duty to her king and her ego. She understands that it was Sita's own ego that caused her to hesitate in responding to Rama, and, in the process of asking Mother Earth for help, her life in this world was ended. So this version leads us to understand that it was not her deliberate choice to die. Her hesitation was merely her ego getting in the way of what she knew to be her duty. Thus, from the conservative viewpoint, this incident in no way contradicts Sita's status as the ideal woman or Rama's as the ideal king.

These interpretations of the Vedas, the *Laws of Manu,* and the *Ramayana* advocate the ideal of womanhood, which can be understood as becoming a perfect homemaker, a faithful wife, and a sacrificing mother. She who wishes to be such a woman will undertake these roles with religious zeal and ardent devotion.

Centrist Position

As India becomes industrialized, more and more Hindu women are becoming educated. As they do, they are studying and examining their roles both past and present, urban and rural. As a result, there are Hindu women of all social classes who share the centrist position on our continuum, that is, that the original message of the sacred texts was egalitarian and the males who dominated the later stages of history gave these later texts their misogynistic slant.

There appears to be an abundance of evidence indicating that women figured prominently in the Vedas. They functioned as priests, as seers, and as ascetics, and they also took part in the thread ceremony (initiation into the stage of student), which today is only administered to boys. In a lecture on women's roles, Swamini Niranjanananda explained that twenty-seven of the hymns of the Rig Veda were written by women, and, in spite of this fact, today women are not supposed to read the Vedas. She continues, "The *Rig-Veda* presents the picture of a woman as an equal of man in both secular and spiritual spheres."[30] When she learned of this history, Nanditha Krishna, an art historian, was quite startled and went on to discover that women students, *brahmavadinis,* went through the same rigorous studies as their male counterparts, the *brahmacharis,* and continued their study of Vedic texts even to the extent of *savitri vachana* (higher studies).[31] Women scholars have also found that all four Vedas have references to women ascetics reciting Vedic hymns and even creating mantras.[32] This egalitarian nature of the Vedas is no surprise to anthropologists and historians of religion who have studied the nature of society at the time of the Aryans. They found that for these semi-nomadic people women were partners in life and shared in its pleasures and hazards, its joys and sorrows. They also discovered that, while girls initially had participated in the thread ceremony, it was discontinued for them because the marriage ceremony replaced it.[33] In other words, girls' duties shifted over time from study to taking care of husband and home.

This shift indicates that, similar to this centrist viewpoint in other religions, women's position in Hinduism underwent a gradual decline, which is why the later texts such as the *Laws of Manu* and versions of the *Ramayana* portray a different picture from the liberating one in the Vedas. Centrist women attribute this shift to the changing situation of the times and not to any sacred revelation. They therefore put less religious importance on the misogynistic aspects of these later texts.

The decline of women's status begins during the period of the Upanishads, the philosophical explanations appearing at the end of the Vedas. The major ones, written down in the eighth and seventh centuries B.C.E., introduced into the Hindu tradition a shift from the importance of sacrifice to the need for asceticism, including celibacy. The general effect of such a shift was to see women as sexual temptresses possessing insatiable sexual appetites and therefore not only obstructing man's achieving *moksha*, or liberation, but being incapable of achieving it themselves. Thus, while women who lived their Dharma could be reborn into a better life, they would have to be reborn as a man in order to become an ascetic and reach *moksha*.[34] This is not to say that the role of mother and wife was denigrated but that now there appears a separation of family from asceticism, the latter being the holier stage in life. To be fair, scholars searching for evidence of women's presence in Indian history have discovered women *sannyasinis*, female ascetics, but their small numbers indicate that they were exceptions rather than the rule.

In the practical realm women became marginalized from Vedic knowledge and ritual for several reasons. For one, there was increasing concern over protecting a girl's virginity, which made lengthy studying in the home of a male teacher worrisome. Also, the priests desired more control over rituals, which they could have if they were the only ones educated in the Vedas and mantras. The resulting lack of education for women caused them eventually to be looked upon as equal to the *sudras*, the servants in society.[35]

In the first centuries of the common era the priests were concerned that the popular movements of Buddhism and Jainism were encroaching on orthodox Hinduism and hence they needed to unify and solidify Hindu society. The priests believed that this effort required the subordination of women. As a result, codes such as the *Laws of Manu* were developed, which reflect this attempt to control and marginalize women.[36] Since there are social and historical reasons for legitimizing such inequality of class and gender, modern women look upon such laws and recognize two things: first, they originated with male priests who were attempting to unify and control, and not by the ultimate law of the universe, or Brahman; and second, they applied mainly to the upper classes and, in fact, were generally ignored by other segments of society. "There is historical evidence that the lower classes, peasants and artisans, paid less attention to these prohibitions than did 'respectable' society. . . . Manual and agricultural work made them less fastidious and more pragmatic, perhaps, than the Brahman [*sic*] elite."[37] For these reasons, among more modern educated Hindu women those aspects of the laws that are so denigrating are not considered religiously binding. Lina Gupta presents this modern perspective well when she explains that these laws were not intended to be so forceful but became progressively so over time. She writes that the idea of men being guardians of women developed over time into the notion of their owning women, allowing men to suppress them as well as exploit them.[38] Such exploitation, in her opinion, is not the nature of Hinduism and leads us further away from the original egalitarian message of the Vedas. A further indication that these laws do not apply to many modern Hindu women is that those whom I've met in the United States who grew up in India never heard of them except from American scholars.

Many modern women today are also taking a new look at the figures of Sita and Rama in the *Ramayana*, so long held up as the ideal woman and the perfect husband and king. They are discovering versions of the epic that take a different view of the royal couple, one in which Rama is seen as treating Sita unjustly and Sita as rebelling against him. Furthermore, they are finding that these versions are not new. Women as well as some men in various times and social classes have long held this alternative view. The words describing Sita's death, "entered the earth," appearing at the end of the epic, have been seen by some Hindus as a euphemism for suicide.[39] If this is the case, the responsibility for her death lies not with Mother Earth but with Sita herself, and her request for help is really a conscious decision to die, which does not stem from her problematic ego but rather from her self-respect. One popular interpretation in the American Hindu community is that Sita had qualms about proving her fidelity again and because of her self-esteem would not do it, even though refusing meant going against her husband's wishes. So we see that Sita really is an ideal woman. Author Sara Mitter calls her suicide "an elegant, ultimate act of rebellion worthy of herself."[40] Hindu scholar Lina Gupta gives Sita's death a similar interpretation.

> She finally rebels. . . . The way I see her she has a sense of timing. In a sense she realized that there is a time and place to suffer, there is a

time and place to come and there is a time and place to leave. So the time came when simple pain and suffering and endurance would not work. It is time for her to act not necessarily to react. So she left.[41]

Rather than see her as an obedient wife, these women interpret Sita as rebelling against a dominating and controlling husband. Such a reinterpretation of Sita's actions is not really denying her image as model or ignoring her importance but merely seeing her from a different perspective. Rama, in turn, is still the perfect king, but in these women's eyes, that responsibility causes him to be less than loving as a husband. His duty to his people forces him to put unreasonable and unfitting demands on Sita, who responds by refusing to undergo the fire test again and commits suicide instead.

According to these centrist Hindu women, the misogynistic interpretations of Sita and Rama came about because of social conditions at the time the *Ramayana* was put down in writing. Just as the original messages of the Torah in Judaism, the Bible in Christianity, and the Qur'an in Islam were affected by the social mores throughout their history, so too was the *Ramayana* affected by the "general degeneration of the freedom of women."[42] The epic, therefore, like the *Laws of Manu*, needs to be revisited and given a reading that makes it more in keeping with the original Dharma or universal norms of equality.

Like their Jewish, Christian, and Muslim counterparts, Hindu women are recognizing that their sacred texts have been tainted by historical circumstances, and they are attempting to return to a more authentic egalitarian religious practice as seen in the Vedas and in the authentic Hindu stories, in which women have equal participation in public as well as private worship. It is true that the existence of the goddess in the Hindu pantheon gives a certain elevated position to women in parts of India. Durga, the female manifestation of the divine power *(shakti)* is believed to sustain the universe. She appears in many forms, two of which are the goddesses Kali and Mahishasura, who "manifest this feminine power to eradicate suffering caused by injustice."[43] The existence of this female power is cited by women in many parts of India as the source of their empowerment and proof that, far from being misogynistic, Hinduism embraces, respects, and encourages the strong and powerful woman. For women in the centrist segment of the continuum, this positive view of women is the real message and that which suppresses women is the tainted one.

This centrist position acknowledges that women have always performed rituals in devotional Hinduism but view these as very different from those in the more formal Brahmanic tradition. Women's rituals take place in the domestic sphere and pertain to familial situations. These *vratas* are domestic rites performed by Hindu women in order to receive bless-ings for their home and health and prosperity for their family.[44] They consist of stories and ritual actions that are taught to girls in rural India from the time they are very young. However, although in one sense these *vratas* indicate the importance of women as teachers and ritualists, they also represent the reinforcement of "the traditional values, in which women are submissive, self-sacrificing and obedient."[45]

With increasing knowledge of women's role in ancient India and the study of the ancient texts, many women are seeking a more public role in the practice of Hinduism today. Organizations and ashrams are springing up in several parts of the world to train and ordain women to perform priestly functions. In Pune, India, there are three popular centers that train women to chant Vedic mantras and perform the various rites that have traditionally been reserved for men.[46] In an open letter to "Respected Guardians of Our Ancient Faith," Hindu scholar Vasudha Narayanan requests that the Brahmanic roles be opened to women. She asks of the holy teachers:

> Can you, with your wisdom and compassion also encourage those women who have a propensity for learning our eternal Vedas to do so? Our literature speaks of women who have been learned in the Vedas in the past. Can we not make our women of today the inheri-tors of the treasures of our tradition and become well versed in sa-cred texts if they so choose to do so? . . . Can we not revive our own traditions of wisdom?[47]

Narayanan represents a growing number of women who are claiming the more public Vedic roles that have been denied them—teachers, seers, po-ets, mystics, and great yoginis—as duly theirs. Women themselves are creating and maintaining ashrams and centers for training.[48] One such center has ordained over seven thousand women from all castes since 1976. In Kerala, where only Brahmin men could have anything to do with Vedic rituals until as recently as 2000, thirty-seven non-Brahmin women have become priests. In the sacred city of Veranasi women are being trained as priests. "Not only are women being trained in priesthood in large numbers, the long-lost tradition of performing the sacred thread ceremony for girls to give them the right to perform all religious rituals in the family has also been evolved."[49] When many orthodox Hindus ar-gued against girls receiving their *upanayana* (thread ceremony) in Pune, India, women priests were able to produce ample literary references to women's thread ceremonies in the ancient Vedic culture.[50] Exemplifying this centrist position in the Hindu tradition is the historian Nanditha Krishna, who sees that, if we go back far enough, there is equality in Hinduism and cautions women that "next time we look for role models, let us look carefully and make sure the message they convey is correct. We have to go back 5000 years to find women who fit 21st century hopes and aspirations."[51]

PROGRESSIVE POSITION

On the progressive end of our continuum are the women who view all of the past as oppressive and the ancient culture of the Vedas as one of class and gender discrimination. Pandita Ramabai, an Indian feminist and Sanskrit scholar, argues that there never were any "glory days" of Indian Hindu womanhood, times when women were equal in status to men.[52] Therefore, while still remaining believers, these women are attempting to look beyond the given texts to a vision of a universe that has as its fundamental law the equality of men and women. Rights activists in this tradition are reexamining all the questions. They are taking nothing for granted in redefining themselves, their roles, and their images to fit the society in which they want to live.[53] These reformers, men as well as women, are viewing religious texts and traditions as culturally formed and in need of reworking so that their core values are maintained while the class and gender hierarchies that no longer apply to our modern society are eliminated. One group working for the spiritual equality of all Hindus is the Navya Shastra, a global Hindu organization of scholars, religious leaders, and social reformers. In support of their cause Dr. Arun Gandhi, grandson of Mahatma Gandhi, has written that "the new millennium now offers Hinduism an opportunity to change its ancient and orthodox ways to bring unity and harmony among its believers."[54] From these words we understand that he and those like him are willing to reform Hinduism and, in the process, radically revise those portions of the ancient texts that divide humanity by denigrating portions of society, including women. Vedic passages that view women as inferior creatures appear to contradict the basic tenets of Hindu philosophy. For example, we read in the Rig Veda that "Lord Indra himself has said that woman has very little intelligence. She cannot be taught" (8.33.17). And again, "With women there can be no lasting friendship: hearts of hyenas are the hearts of women" (10.95.15). Such statements, which reduce women to a status less than human, are understood by some feminists such as Soma Sablok to mean that all of Hinduism is oppressive to women and therefore should be abandoned and replaced by a secular state.[55] Progressive Hindu women believe, however, that there is a fundamental value in the Hindu religious tradition that contradicts such statements and supports equality. In the Upanishads we read that all things are essentially one. The ultimate source of everything, called Brahman, is the Ultimate Reality from which we all came and to which we will all return; it is the "unfathomable first principle, the Absolute Essence that preexists the gods."[56] The Hindu belief in this ultimate oneness, like the monotheistic religions' faith in God, requires that there be no dualities, including no distinction between male and female. This basic understanding of Brahman, therefore, will not tolerate the subjection or oppression of women or of lower classes. Such practices, according to the Navya Shastra, were cultural norms that have undergone change throughout different periods, whereas the message of the unity of all things proclaimed by the Hindu sages is timeless and eternal. What is needed at this time is a reworking of the early texts in order to bring the basic teachings to light. This distinction between the eternal truths and the social structure is emphasized by Nelia Scovill, who writes: "Despite Hinduism's endorsement of patriarchal social structure, the roots of Hinduism strongly argue for egalitarian and mutual relationships between the sexes. For if everything is Brahman, then ultimately there is no meaningful distinction between male and female. Such recovery of Hinduism's roots can provide fertile ground for improving women's lives."[57]

Unlike the dogmatic religions, such dynamic reworking of the text is nothing new to Hinduism. All through history Hindu texts have been selectively followed because local customs have interpreted them differently. Such flexibility in the understanding of texts has allowed for the legitimization of changes that are in keeping with progressive practices. It is possible, therefore, within such a flexible system, to allow the dictates of one's conscience to be a source of Dharma. Therefore, women, or anyone who feels marginalized, may appropriate or redefine rituals and traditions.[58] This unique characteristic of Hinduism explains why some women I have interviewed cannot see a problem with differing opinions about religion. There have always been such differences in Hinduism, a fact that they see as a positive rather than a negative characteristic.

If any part of the tradition can and should be reworked, the progressives agree that one of the first texts to undergo such a process should be the *Laws of Manu*. One holy teacher, Sri Swami Sivananda, even suggests that this text was intended for a former time and therefore must change with the changing conditions of time: "Our present society has considerably changed. A new *Smriti* [scripture] to suit the requirements of this age is very necessary. Another sage will place before the Hindus of our days a new suitable code of laws. Time is ripe for a new *Smirti*."[59]

Dr. Jaishree Gopal, a woman activist, commends the government of India for working to end discrimination, which, through the *Laws of Manu*, has been given a religious basis for continuing oppression of the lower caste. She applauds a new group of seers who represent the progressive mindset. These scholars are not explaining or reinterpreting the *Laws of Manu* but are doing away with them so that they may be replaced by a more suitable code, one that is more representative of Hinduism at its core, that is, of the unifying message of the one eternal principle of Brahman.[60]

This thought echos that of Swami Vivekananda, who claimed that the end of all religions is but one—reunion with God, or with the Divinity residing in all persons. Then, to reinforce the central message and as if calling out for reworking the texts, he says, "The ideal of all religions, all sects, is the same—the attaining of liberty, the cessation of misery."[61]

Among the progressives there are also radical retellings of the relationship between Sita and Rama in the *Ramayana*. Because changing the sacred stories is a natural exercise in Hinduism, progressive reworkings are not a new phenomenon. They have taken place throughout history and in many different geographical states of India. Vasudha Narayanan tells us that throughout the centuries from ancient civilization to the age of the Internet, Hindus have been able to meet the needs of the day and keep their tradition vibrant by interpreting sacred texts and assimilating and adapting practices. In this day, she adds, we need to make adaptations and adjustments to the great epics to allow for a "full range of possibilities and opportunities for men and women."[62] Such adaptations are not new ideas but have existed previously in Hindu history. For example, research has uncovered critical treatments of the *Ramayana* that were developed by women in low caste, folk, and dissenting literary cultures.[63] It is important, therefore, to rework the *Ramayana*, which has such an impact on Indian women.

When we examine the many retellings of the epic, past and present, we see that the feminist perspective presents two types of Sita. The first, coming mainly from educated women and some men also, tells of a rebellious, self-assertive Sita who defies Rama's demands. The other image, coming mostly from the oral tradition of lower-caste village women, emphasizes a struggling and suffering Sita who is unjustly treated by a tyrannical king obsessed with power.

In the first category of retellings we encounter an outspoken and rebellious Sita who was not robbed of her voice and personhood by patriarchal tradition. In 1919, a male poet, scholar, and social reformer from Southern India, Kumaran Aasan, published the *Chinthavishtayaya Sita*, or *The Brooding Sita*. In his version Sita criticizes Rama for his unjust treatment of her and refuses to go back to him, crying, "What? Does the emperor think that I should once more go into his . . . presence and once again prove myself? . . . Do you think I am a mere doll? . . . My mind and soul should revolt at the very thought."[64] One commentator on Asan's version writes: "The gentle, mournful, soft-spoken Sita of our schoolday's dreams vanishes, and in her place appears a critical, sharp-tongued, passionate woman speaking out for the legitimate rights of the women of all times."[65] Needless to say, at the time it was written, this depiction of a self-assertive Sita caused Asan's poem to be the center of great controversy.

Another example of this strong Sita is seen in a folk song from Uttar Pradesh published in the Indian women's journal *Manushi* in 1981. It tells of Sita's refusal to return to Ayodhya at Rama's request. When the messenger asks if she has taken leave of her senses, she replies:

> "Guru, that Rama who caused me such sorrow,
>   how can I see his face?
> The Rama who put me in the fire, who threw me
>   out of the house,
> Guru how shall I see his face? . . . I will never go
>   back to Ayodhya,
> and may fate never cause us to meet again."[66]

This image of Sita is hardly that of the obedient and subservient woman.

Some more modern versions of the epic have taken expression in plays and short stories. Snehalata Reddy's one-act play *Sita* (1973) contains the following exchange:

RAMA: Come to your senses! . . . My word is law! . . . I cannot take it back! . . . If you do not do your duty, I must reject you!
SITA: *(fiercely)* How dare you! It is I who reject you![67]

In an effort to announce such a Sita to the world, we find her mentioned in a documentary that tells us that Indian women "don't need many lessons from Western feminists. The examples and the message of true equality, of a genuine realization of self, are contained deep within India's own cultural traditions. . . . [They] ask Sita . . . to speak to tell her side of the story, a story that most women know instinctively but have suppressed for too long."[68] These portrayals of Sita are more extreme than the images presented by the centrists because Sita is not simply being self-assertive or rebelling against the necessary duty to her king, but rather, she is lashing out at Rama's injustice and conceit.

In those versions of the *Ramayana* coming mostly from lower-caste women Sita is not a rebellious wife but one who suffers great injustices, loneliness, and pain at the hands of her selfish and self-centered husband. The women who retell these versions severely criticize Rama as crazed and abusive. Interestingly, not all of these stories are products of the modern feminist mindset; some have been around since before the sixteenth century. Researcher Nabaneeta Dev Sen uncovered several versions of women's retellings of the epic. For example, a fifteenth century woman and *shudra* (servant caste) named Molla challenged the Brahmin court poets by writing a perfect classical *Ramayana* in her regional language. The Brahmins responded by forbidding her work to be read in the royal court. Another woman, Chandrabati, a sixteenth-century poet, based her version on an oral tradition in which Rama betrays Sita by banishing her when she is pregnant, refusing to carry out his parental responsibilities, and, worst of all, sending her into exile because he is jealous of the demon Ravana.[69] This version, originally rejected by literary historians as incomplete and weak, focused not on the the heroic life and achievements of Rama, but rather on the sufferings and sorrows of Sita.[70] These retellings of the *Ramayana* portray Rama as a cruel, uncaring, and weak-willed husband, which is hardly the picture of an ideal man. Down to this day, village women tell these versions of the story. They sing the work songs and ritual songs that tell of different moments in women's lives: attaining puberty, getting married, getting pregnant, and being abandoned to give birth. These women call the songs the *Ramayana*, but they are really singing about Sita. Nabaneeta Dev Sen calls these women "sisters in sorrow" because these exile songs touch the very core of Indian women's common experience of suffering. The following song speaks particularly of a pregnant woman in distress.

> Sita walks to her forest exile
> Girls, exile is written for Sita . . .
> In the third mile the pain arises.
> Now life wishes to be born, girls, call the
>   midwife, quick! . . .
> You take my golden bangle then,
> And cut the cord of the baby . . .
> Alas, if only Rama would understand![71]

For women in various parts of India, Sita is a symbol of womanhood, not because she is what a woman should be, as some would have us believe, but because she is a voice of the silenced suffering that is the stark reality of who women are.

Some of the more modern writings of the *Ramayana* give voice to these village women's versions and present Sita's plight in stories, plays, and even in Internet blogs. Sara Joseph has written four stories focusing on women in the *Ramayana*. Her translator, Vasanthi Sankaranarayanan, calls them commentaries that focus on the women characters, who have been marginalized in the original. In this way Joseph challenges the patriarchal version of the *Ramayana* and provides an alternative text.[72] One of these stories, "Asoka," focuses on a suffering Sita who willingly steps into the fire after having been tormented. In the opening words of this story, Joseph paints a vividly horrid picture of Sita.

Having spent a year in pain and suffering, Sita lowered her eyes and examined her body. The Body! Clay, battered and destroyed by continuous onslaughts of snow, rain, sunlight, lustful gazes, destructive stares, falling . . . scabs of severe brutalization, scabs of drying tears, wounds of humiliation. Trailing in mud and dust, hair so matted that the strands could not be separated. Nails grown long, distinct from fingers. Skin drying and peeling off.[73]

This story is told from the perspective of a suffering Sita, who sees Rama as powerless and impotent. "The earth that used to be wet and ready at his touch . . . was now dry and barren. Never again would his hands be able to rouse any feeling in the earth."[74]

In the play "Sanctuary," Hema Ramakrishna depicts Sita as endowed with gloom. "She loses speech, beauty, vitality and cowers in fear. . . . Rama, repelled by the changes, rejects her."[75] Here Rama is deglorified and loses his stature as the perfect man. In addition to these accounts, women's attitudes can also be found in many Internet blogs such as "Searching for 'Sita,'" which tells young women not to see Sita and Rama as ideals or to imitate Sita by allowing one's husband to behave unreasonably. The author sees Rama as "emotionally unreliable," a husband "who had been unjust in his dealings with Sita. . . . He behaved like a petty minded, stupidly mistrustful, jealous husband and showed himself to be a slave to social opinion."[76]

In conclusion, we note that there have been women in various ages who take what is considered here to be a progressive attitude; that is, they are willing to rework a sacred text to eliminate the misogynistic ideas. They do this not to say that the religion of Hinduism is not viable, but rather to rework it into a meaningful spiritual journey for both men and women, poor and privileged. It is their hope that the egalitarian practices that are in place in many parts of India today may become the norm throughout all of India. They believe that for this to be possible, equality must be the business not only of the state but of the religion.

BUDDHISM

The second major religion originating in Asia, and now with an increasing number of Western followers, is Buddhism. It began in northeastern India approximately twenty-five hundred years ago with the person of Siddhartha Gautama, a prince of the Sakya tribe. According to the sutras, Buddhism's sacred texts, he was raised in the confines of a royal palace, protected from the harsh realities of the outside world. When he came of age, he married and fathered a son. One day he ventured out of the grounds and encountered the three inevitable experiences of human life: sickness, old age, and death. In order to discover the meaning and cause of these human conditions, he left his family and his home, cut off his hair, and became an ascetic wanderer. After long periods of following various ascetic practices, he found that none of them gave him the answers he sought. Finally, he sat under a tree and entered into a state of deep concentration. While sitting there, a woman offered him some rice and barley, which he ate, causing his followers to leave because they assumed that he had failed at the life of an ascetic. His breaking the fast was a good thing, however, because it became the first step in what Buddhists call the Middle Way, which eventually became a major part of the Dharma, or doctrine of Buddhism. Here, after several stages of contemplation and some instances of temptation described in the texts of the Pali Canon, Siddhartha Gautama became awakened and henceforth was known as the Buddha, the Awakened One; the tree he sat under was the Bodhi tree.[77]

Shortly after this experience he began teaching those who came to him because they recognized his advanced spiritual state. These teachings were passed down orally and finally written down in the first century B.C.E. Because different lineages of monks preserved different versions of these oral accounts, the teachings themselves have undergone some scrutiny regarding their connection to the Buddha. In spite of the years of oral transmission, however, scholars have agreed that there is enough similarity in the accounts to justify attributing them to the Buddha. This authenticity is further assured by the fact that memorization was common when it came to important teachings, especially sacred teachings.

Among the many versions of these teachings, the only complete collection in existence is written in Pali, an ancient Indic language. This Pali Canon consists of three sections, referred to as the *Tripitaka,* or three baskets, so named because they were first written on palm leaves and kept in baskets. The first of these sections, the *Vinaya Pitaka,* contains the rules for the monks and nuns who made up the *sangha* (monastic community). It is in this section that we find the Buddha's reluctance to admit women to the *sangha,* which he eventually does after imposing eight extra rules on them. The second basket contains the *Sutra Pitaka,* accounts of the Buddha's life and teachings. It is here we find the famous teaching of his first sermon, that of the Four Noble Truths: "the truth of suffering, the truth of the origin of suffering, the truth of the cessation of suffering and the truth of the path that leads to cessation."[78] These basic teachings can be understood once we realize that all things in life are passing and that the more we desire them to continue, the more we suffer. Suffering is eliminated by ridding ourselves of these desires, which we do by practicing what Buddhists know as the Eightfold Path, "perfecting our training in the three areas of discipline, meditation, and wisdom."[79] The third basket is the *Abhidharma Pitaka,* comprising the Buddha's teachings in the form of lists, which serve as pedagogical tools enabling students to remember the Dharma and to interpret its more ambiguous passages.[80] In this last section parts of Buddhist teachings were defined and analyzed for perfect precision by the early monks.[81]

The Theravadin school, or the Way of the Elders, located in Sri Lanka, Thailand, Cambodia, Laos, and Burma, understands these texts to be directly attributed to the Buddha and hence authoritative. They believe that, according to these teachings, it is only through the strict discipline of monastic life that one can gain release from this cycle of life and death, *samsara,* and gain enlightenment. By supporting the monks the laity too can accumulate merit and, after many lifetimes, be reborn as a monk. The place of women in the monastic community of the Theravadin school has been a controversial issue throughout much of Buddhism's history. It is made even more so today due to scholars and practitioners reading and interpreting the Pali Canon with the tools of modern hermeneutics. Passages that are especially interesting for our purposes are those that appear to contradict current sensibilities regarding the nature of women and their potential for enlightenment. The differences in interpretations of these texts separate the views of women in this tradition.

About five hundred years after the death of the Buddha, when the monastic community had grown considerably, a counter movement began that resisted the belief that monastic life or total isolation from the world was the only way to achieve enlightenment. This movement, eventually called Mahayana, or the Greater Vehicle, gave more importance to laypeople by making the Buddha's teachings and the religious life more accessible to them. It taught that, rather than having to go it alone, help in achieving enlightenment was available to all from bodhisattvas, "beings who are dedicated not only to attaining enlightenment for themselves but, out of their immense compassion, to helping others to do likewise."[82] This form of Buddhism, begun in India, spread to China and eventually to Korea, Japan, and Vietnam, where it still exists today. As it traveled through these lands the religion was assimilated into the various cultures and took on many different forms, which grew into sects such as Pure Land, Cha'n (in China) or Zen (in Japan), and Nichiren. In spite of these diverse expressions, however, the main teachings of Mahayana Buddhism can be found in sutras that, along with the Pali Canon, are generally agreed upon as authoritative, that is, as originating with the Buddha himself. Perhaps the most important of these is the *Lotus Sutra,* an ancient text presumed by scholars to have been in existence since before 255 C.E. and to have been translated into Chinese several times, the most common version dating to 406.[83] Here we find the major teachings of the Mahayana school, which refute the Way of the Elders, or, as the Mahayanists call it, the Lesser Vehicle.

The concept found in the *Lotus Sutra,* as well as in other Mahayana texts, that is most significant for our study of women's place is that of Emptiness or *shunyata.* The traditional Theravadin meaning of the term was that all things are destined to change and pass away in time; hence they have no "inherent or permanent characteristics by which they can be described, changing as they do from instant to instant."[84] But the Mahayana school emphasizes more positive aspects of Emptiness, that of the oneness of all beings, a concept most related to the Western notion of nondualism:

> If all phenomena are characterized by the quality of Emptiness, then Emptiness must constitute the unchanging and abiding nature of existence, and therefore the absolute or unchanging world must be synonymous with the phenomenal one. Hence all mental and physical distinctions that we perceive or conceive of with our minds must be part of a single underlying unity.[85]

If this doctrine of Emptiness as put forth in the *Lotus Sutra* means that there are no distinctions and that everything is one, it is easy to see that Emptiness has a direct bearing on the issue of gender. For Mahayana women in both the lay and monastic communities there should be no gender distinctions. However, not all Mahayana women interpret this text in the same way, and like the *Vinaya* of the Pali Canon, the interpretations distinguish between conservative and progressive viewpoints.

Another Mahayana text that refutes Theravadin teachings and has particular significance for the topic of women's roles is the *Sutra of the Teaching of Vimalakirti*. In her book *Women in Buddhism*, Diana Paul recounts that this sutra "has been especially admired by the Chinese since the fifth century and by the Japanese since the time of Prince Shotoku."[86] Vimalakirti tells of an argument between a traditional monk, Sariputra, who speaks for all those who discriminate against women, and a goddess. After changing Sariputra into a female, the goddess tells him that "all things are neither male nor female when one views the world as Emptiness . . . [and] all phenomena are illusory."[87] She says to Sariputra, "Just as you are not really a woman but appear to be female in form, all women, also, only appear to be female in form but are not really women. Therefore, the Buddha said all are not really men or women."[88] What is to be made of these teachings? Are there really no differences between men and women who are striving for enlightenment, or are there real differences in this world that need to be accepted and dealt with before any further advancement on the path toward liberation can be made? The answers to these questions vary according to where the respondents fall on the continuum of viewpoints.

As a result of focusing on different texts, the schools of Buddhism are facing different controversial issues about women within their communities. The main concern for the Theravadins, who accept only the Pali Canon as authoritative, is women's ordination in the monastic *sangha*. The issue is important because equal opportunity for ordination reflects a belief that women are capable of achieving enlightenment and are willing and able to endure the hardships that are requirements for doing so. Another reason why ordination is so significant is the symbiotic relationship of the monastic community with the laity. Laypeople gain merit by supporting monks, and in turn, the monks teach the Dharma to the lay community. For this reason, immigrants from Buddhist countries often purchase land and build temples so that monks from their native county can live among them as Dharma teachers. In Theravadin communities, however, women renunciants are not ordained and donations to their *sangha* do not yield as much merit as do those given to monks. They are also not as educated and therefore are not considered official Dharma teachers. Obviously, this situation puts Theravadin nuns at an economic and political disadvantage. Hence, ordination has become a volatile issue in many Theravadin communities.

The Mahayana school does ordain women, but its issues focus on the subordination of the order of nuns, *bhiksunis,* to that of the monks, *bhiksus.* When the Buddha established the women's *sangha,* after being convinced to do so by his companion Ananda, he did so only if the women, led by Mahaprajapati, agreed to follow eight more rules, *gurudharmas* or vows of respect, "strictly subordinating them—institutionally but not spiritually—to the Order of Monks."[89] The interpretation of this apparently sexist text is one of the topics disputed between the conservative and progressive Buddhists.

Added to these interpretive concerns among the various sects is the issue of the spread of Buddhism to the West. An increasingly large number of European and American women have become practicing Buddhists. These women bring with them a self-understanding that is quite different from that of Asian women. As a result, the differences between conservative and progressive views of women in Buddhism, as well as all those views in between, can be understood as stemming as much from differences in culture and social context as from differences in schools.

CONSERVATIVE POSITION

In keeping with our continuum of perspectives regarding women and the sacred texts, the conservative Buddhist interprets the discourses in the Pali Canon as teaching that woman has a distinct nature complementing that of man. This nature inclines women to domestic responsibilities, including birthing and raising children and tending to the household. It is expected that women in traditional Asian Buddhist societies will fulfill these roles, and that the role of a monastic is more suitable for men. It follows therefore, that, since being a monk is a necessary step toward enlightenment, a woman has to be reborn as a man in order to achieve the ultimate goal of Buddhist practice. Another hindrance to entering monastic life, besides having to raise a family, is the fact that women are viewed as more worldly than men and more attached to things; therefore, leaving the world is much more difficult for them.[90] Even though Buddhist teaching is that all have equal potential for enlightenment, there are certain texts found in the Pali Canon that seem to tell a different story. In the *Anguttara Nikaya*, section II.82.3, for example, Ananda asks the Buddha:

> "Pray, lord, what is the reason, what is the cause why women nei-ther sit in a court of justice, nor embark on business, nor reach the heart of any matter?" To which Gotama replied, "Women are un-controlled, Ananda, Women are envious, Ananda. Women are greedy, Ananda, Women are weak in wisdom, Ananda. This is the reason why women do not sit in a court of justice, do not embark on busi-ness, do not reach the heart of the matter."[91]

It is passages such as these that give Theravadins cause to support the traditional roles of males and females. Karma Lekshe Tsomo, an Ameri-can Buddhist nun, says that in reality women are seen, and see them-selves, as less capable of actualizing their potential. "The assumption of women's spiritual inferiority and the neglect it engenders characterize most of Buddhist history."[92] Even today, women in traditional Buddhist cultures, including ordained nuns *(bhiksunis)*, assume that nuns must follow the eight *gurudharmas* that traditionally entail their subordination to monks.

In spite of this inferior status, there are many women in the Theravadin countries of Thailand, Burma, and Sri Lanka who have renounced the world and taken on the life of nuns. They are sometimes treated poorly, however, and lead much more difficult lives than their male counterparts. The nuns in Thailand, known as *mae chi*, have low status; their main responsibility is to prepare food for the monks and themselves. Conse-quently, they do not have opportunities to study or practice the Dhamma (Buddhist teachings).[93] This attitude toward women is widespread and of long standing, which means that the women themselves often have been socialized to accept it. For example, the *mae chi* as a group do not aspire to higher ordination but are content to be successful in the roles that are assigned them.[94] Karma Lekshe Tsomo writes:

> It is common to hear both nuns and laywomen state: "I don't care about equality. I only care about nirvana," or "What is the point of my getting an education? It is enough for me just to recite prayers." . . . It is common for Buddhist women to denigrate their own poten-tial and abdicate responsibility for their spiritual life to men, pray-ing for rebirth as a man in the next life.[95]

Even though their education and status are slowly improving in modern Thailand, nuns have yet to receive legal status and their position in rela-tion to the monks remains subordinate.

In Burma a similar situation exists, with nuns holding inferior positions in relation to monks. Even though there are nuns who are knowledgeable about the Dharma and are capable of teaching, and even though there are precedents for female teachers in ancient Buddhism, Burmese nuns are restricted to teaching in informal and private settings. This restriction has been internalized by the nuns themselves, and, as a result, they believe that it is not proper for them to hold public Dharma classes. Hiroko Kawanami reports that, while studying Buddhist women in Myanmar, most of the ones she spoke to "visibly shrank from the idea of preaching in public." She discovered that the reason for their reaction was that they were afraid their public image would be tainted and hence prospective donors would not sustain them. Some said, "Nuns should be modest and reserved. It is bad to do things that are too bold, such as preaching in public." Others said, "It is the role of monks to preach, not nuns."[96]

In Sri Lanka the issue of ordination of nuns is particularly poignant because this country is considered the home of Theravadin Buddhism and sees its practice as particularly authentic. In fact, it was the *bhiksuni* order from Sri Lanka that brought the women's *sangha* to China, although it died out sometime in the twelfth century. In the twenty-first century ordination is the subject of controversy. Those who object do so on the basis that the lineage has been broken. Others believe that the lineage could be restored through the orders in China and are struggling to reestablish ordination in Sri Lanka. There are, however, lay nuns who "accept the fact that, since the Theravada order of nuns died out there can never be the necessary quorum of nuns required by the *vinaya* rules to start the order again."[97] These same lay nuns deem their situation advantageous because, by not being ordained, they do not have to be subjected to the control of monks.[98] While this position appears to be liberating, in fact, it demonstrates the conservative interpretation of the sutras requiring nuns to follow the eight *gurudharmas*.

Another indication that lay nuns are not on a par with their male counterparts is the fact that they are to serve the monks. According to the monastic rules in the *Vinaya,* neither the *bhikus* nor the *bhikunis* are supposed to cook. In Sri Lanka and Thailand, however, lay nuns spend hours before sunrise until midday cooking for themselves and, in many cases, for the monks also. In Sri Lanka the following situation is an example of the inequalities between the nuns and monks.

> If the laity has gathered together both monks and nuns for an almsgiving, the lay nuns help the laity (usually women) distribute the alms to monks. In other words, the women serve and the men eat. . . . Only when the monks are fed, do the lay nuns receive *danaya* [alms] from the laity. . . . In short, the lay nuns themselves reinforce

male superiority. . . . Lay nuns argue that it is appropriate for them to support the *bhikkhu sangha*. They argue that such was the role of the ancient *bhikkhuni sangha*.[99]

A look at the Mahayana schools reveals a more progressive view of women. In February 1998 a milestone was reached. In Bodhgaya, India, site of the Buddha's enlightenment, 134 female practitioners from various Buddhist traditions participated in a full ordination ceremony.[100] Officiating at the ceremony were *bhiksus* and *bhiksunis* from diverse Buddhist traditions. Although this event was significant overall for women on various parts of the continuum, it must be noted here, in considering conservative views, that when the leading monks met to decide the future of the *bhiksuni* lineage in their countries, the nuns were remarkably reticent and were not encouraged to express their views. On the surface at least, they seemed to place their fate in the hands of monks. The authority of leading monks at the conference was never questioned; it was assumed that monks would decide the future of nuns.[101]

Finally, we can see that patriarchal interpretations of both Theravadin and Mahayana Buddhists texts exist in the practice of American Buddhists. Although it is true that the growth of Buddhism in America and the increasing number of American practitioners have contributed to the transformation of the tradition, there have been indications that it has not escaped its patriarchal roots. Sandy Boucher, an American Buddhist, believes that the the male Dharma teacher reinforces ingrained social patterns, which "reach deep into the conditioning of his female followers and elicit a subservience that may be obvious or subtle but is extremely hard to shake."[102]

Centrist Position

The centrist position on the continuum holds that the original insight of the tradition was egalitarian, but that male interpreters influenced by the cultures in which they lived were responsible for the sexist and misogynistic interpretations and trends. In other words, if one returned to the original texts and examined the writer's intent, one would find a religion that holds women in esteem and gives them an equal role, both spiritually and visibly.

Since the mid-twentieth century, more and more Buddhists, both women and men, have been scrutinizing the sutras using the historical and textual hermeneutics common in other traditions. This study has led many to the conclusion that the Buddha did teach equality of the genders, did recognize women's potential for enlightenment, and did give women an opportunity to attain it. In a classic study entitled *Women under Primitive Buddhism*, I. B. Horner tells us that the Buddha considered women to be approximately equal to men.[103] In fact, in condemning the existing hierarchical class structure and the ritual power of the Brahmins, the Buddha taught that liberation can be attained by one's own effort, regardless of class or gender. Given the attitudes of his day, the Buddha must have been "a man of considerable courage and a rebellious spirit to pronounce a way of life that placed woman on a level of near equality to man."[104] He spoke out against conventional religious views, and instead of dependency on Brahmanical rituals, he offered a spiritual path that was opened to all. In his study of the ancient practices, Alan Sponberg found that "the earliest Buddhists clearly held that one's sex, like one's caste or class *(varna)*, presents no barrier to attaining the Buddhist goal of liberation from suffering. Women can, we are told by the tradition, pursue the path. Moreover, they can (and did) become arhats, Buddhist saints who had broken completely the suffering of the cycle of death and rebirth *(samsara)*."[105] A famous passage in the Pali Canon's *Samyutta Nikaya* is often quoted to make this point. In it the metaphor of a chariot is used to carry the virtues of the Dharma, and then we read, "And be it woman, or be it man for whom such chariot doth wait, by that same car into nirvana's presence shall they come" (1.5.6).[106]

We know that, in fact, there were women who were in a *sangha* and attained enlightenment in early Buddhism. Historians tell us that after Buddha opened the doors for women's entrance into monastic life, "women flocked by the thousands to join the order of *bhikkshunis* . . . many . . . because the Budddha's teachings made sense to them, and aroused in them a desire for liberation."[107] In these *sanghas* at that time women had more freedom and independence than anywhere else in society. They were not anyone's slave or servant, and they had only to work toward enlightenment, which many of these women did achieve. Stories and poems attesting to their spiritual state are in a collection known as the *Therigatha;* these works were passed down orally for six centuries before being written in Sri Lanka in the first century B.C.E.[108] These poems are significant because they offer evidence that "women have the capacity to realize and understand the highest religious goals of their faith in the same roles and to the same degrees as men."[109] Only one who understands and experiences awakening could speak lines such as the following.

> Four or five times
> I have left my cell.
> I had no peace of mind,
> No control over my mind.
>
> I went to a nun
> I thought I could trust.
> She taught me the Dharma,

The elements of body and mind,
The nature of perception,
And earth, water, fire, and wind.

I heard what she said
And sat cross-legged
Seven days full
Of joy.

When, on the eighth
I stretched my feet out,
The great dark was torn apart.[110]

The women who wrote the *Therigatha* lived in the time of the Buddha, indicating that, from the beginning, women had access to enlightenment. Their existence provides evidence that in the beginnings of the new tradition women held a unique position that set them apart from their contemporaries.

Given this information, what can we make of the Buddha's hesitation to ordain women? Why did Ananda have to coax the Buddha no fewer than three times to set up the women's community, and why, after doing so, does the Buddha require eight more rules of them? One of these rules is that, even if they are 100 years old, they are to "rise, greet respectfully, and bow down before a *bhikkhu* ordained even that day."[111] Further, why would he tell Ananda that if women leave the household state and enter the monastery, the good law or Dharma will only last five hundred years?[112] To find the explanation for these passages that seemingly contradict the message of gender equality, scholars and practitioners in the center of our continuum look to the cultural norms in place both at the time that the Buddha was teaching and also at the time that these teachings were written down.

Many Buddhist scholars hold that the Buddha meant his teachings to be applied to women as well as men, with no discrimination, and that these seemingly sexist directives were for the purpose of assuring that the nun's *sangha* would not cause scandal to a local population, which held women in low esteem. It was necessary to put the nuns under the authority of the monks to avoid such scandal, for if the laypeople were scandalized, they would not support the order, thus causing its demise.[113] This thinking is quite similar to the passages in Paul's epistles in the Christian New Testament in which he instructs women not to speak in church and always to cover their heads. Scholars tell us that these verses were not meant to denigrate women, but, since only pagan and immoral women spoke out in public, and only prostitutes went out without their heads covered, Paul's intention was to spare Christianity from being associated with these evils. The Buddha's extra eight rules for Mahaprajapati, which were later applied to all nuns, was to protect the community from public outrage.

This interpretation seems all the more plausible when we read about the popularity of the *sangha* with women from all parts of society, including those that were not usually respected. Ayya Kema, the late Theravadin nun who helped revive the *bhikkhunis'* order in Sri Lanka, wrote that "women flocked from all classes of society to embrace the new life open to them."[114] Widows, bereaved mothers, childless women, and even maidens, slave girls, and courtesans came to experience the freedom of a life dedicated to study and meditation in the company of other women. We read in the *Therigatha:*

> Free I am free
> I am free from the three
> Crooked things
> Mortar, pestle and
> My crooked husband.
>
> I am free from birth
> And death and all
> That dragged me back.[115]

Knowing that disreputable women might be in the monastery would indeed cause laypeople to think twice before giving them food and sustenance, hence special caution had to be taken to ensure that women monastics would be above reproach.

Other scholars interpret these passages as additions to the Buddha's teaching made much later by the more conservative monks who put those teachings into writing.[116] No matter how egalitarian the ideals of Buddhism were, they were unable to stand up to or eliminate the deep-seated ideology of masculine superiority.[117] In a culture that understood karma as determining the nature of one's rebirth, to be born as a woman was interpreted as meaning that something had gone amiss in one's previous life. In such a male dominated social structure, the very idea of women being able to achieve a spiritual goal was too revolutionary.

The text of the Pali Canon also contains certain inconsistencies that point to the possibility of these sexist passages being later additions. Careful study indicates that women's subordination was not part of the original teaching but added after the *Bhiksuni Sangha* grew into an established monastic institution. At this time, writes Alan Sponberg, it became necessary to regulate the women's order to preserve and reinforce the conventions of male authority and female subordination. Sponberg sees the story of the eight rules not as a literal historical account, but as a symbolic means of solving tensions that arose in the monastic community centuries after the Buddha's death.[118]

Other answers to the problem of such androcentric passages come from a deeper reading of the texts in order to resolve apparent discrepancies. For example, Mahapajapati, the Buddha's stepmother, when seeking admission into the *sangha,* asks the Buddha, "Is it possible to respect *bhikkhus* and *bhikkhunis* according to seniority?" The Buddha answers that it is an offense for a *bhikkhu* to show respect to a laywoman, but nothing is said about *bhikkhunis,* which is what the question was. Kusuma claims that it is not likely that the Buddha would evade such an important question. This and other contradictions in the text lead her to conclude that "the *garudhammas* are not a *Vinaya* requirement, either as precept or as practice."[119] To her, they are later additions, not part of the Buddha's intention.

Whether the story accurately recounts the words of the Buddha or was a result of the influence of later cultural settings, the practitioners in the center of the continuum understand that the Buddha's original teachings hold no distinction between men and women either in practicing the Dharma or in achieving its goal of enlightenment. In the words of one Thai woman practitioner: "We must differentiate between the 'Buddhist teachings' as in the Tripitaka proper and the traditional Thai customs. In his supreme selflessness the Sammasambuddha never makes mistakes in his timeless teachings whereas ordinary human customs can integrate certain ancestral or foreign influences."[120]

Many Mahayana Buddhists also fall into the centrist position on the continuum. An example is a sect of the Pure Land school called Fo Guang Shan, which has its headquarters in Taiwan. One of its many temples is the Hsi Lai Temple in Hacienda Heights, California, which is supported by a congregation consisting of Asians, Asian Americans, and Americans of all ethnicities. The resident nuns here teach the Dharma and officiate at the temple's many ceremonies. When asked about the place of women in Buddhism, Mae Chu, a member of the temple, responded that any differentiation according to gender in Buddhist practice would lead us off the track and into the trap of bias. She explained that according to the teachings of Fo Guang Shan, the Buddha taught many precepts that are not suitable for modern society, and that, in order for his message of compassion and light to be brought to all peoples, the order must be flexible. For example, because the nuns at this large temple work hard serving many people, the nuns should eat three meals a day and not be restricted to eating only before noon, as was the Buddha's custom.[121]

Regardless of the lay orientation of American Buddhism, many monks and nuns strive to live in accordance with the Vinaya rules:

Indeed, every move or gesture [the monastics] make reflects the "Three thousand splendid rules, eighty thousand minute details."

These bhiksus and bhiksunis are not only well versed in the multiple chores and skills of a conventional monastery but are also equipped with the knowledge and capacities needed for writing and theorizing, monasterial management and accounting, social work and teaching, and dealing with computers and the day-to-day technical and mechanical needs. Combining the Dharma as the essence and world knowledge as the tool, is the way to liberate all sentient beings.[122]

To this end the sect runs orphanages, mobile medical-care units, and various Buddhist colleges throughout the world, including the University of the West in southern California. It is interesting to note that in this very structured organization, according to 1994 statistics, there were only 225 men *(bhiksus)*, but 937 women *(bhiksunis)*. At Hsi Lai Temple the *bhiksunis* are the teachers and officiants even though there are usually some *bhiksus* living near the property. One reason for the large number of women monastics is that Fo Guang Shan provides opportunities for education and career advancement that few, if any, other Buddhist organizations can match.[123] In a patriarchal society such as Taiwan these opportunities are especially appreciated. In addition, laywomen also view Buddhism as a spiritual refuge and enthusiastically devote their services to its advancement.[124] A similar situation exists in the traditional Korean society, where one writer, Choi Hee An, tells us that women are the main supporters and propagators, financially and spiritually, of both Buddhism and Shamanism. Korean nuns and laywomen actively participate in Buddhist practices and exhibit a devoted faith and strong spirituality.[125] Considering these cultural differences, American women might not be quick to join such a structured organization, but they can appreciate the opportunities it gives women of other cultures.

Even though Mahayana Buddhism allows women to be ordained and puts more emphasis on the ability of the laity to be enlightened, there are other problems posed by the misogynistic influences that crept into the Buddha's teaching. One is the issue of gender transformation recounted in several Mahayana texts. The Mahayana ideal, like that of the Theravadins, is to reach Buddhahood, but, unlike the Theravadins, the newer sect teaches that the average practitioner can take a bodhisattva vow, which commits one to attaining enlightenment eventually through having compassion for all sentient beings. A bodhisattva postpones Nirvana to help others reach this spiritual goal. Some sutras, including the *Pure Land Sutra*, require a woman to be reborn as a man before she can become a bodhisattva. Others acknowledge woman's virtues and merits and indicate that she may become a bodhisattva in this life, but not until she is transformed into a man. Diana Paul notes that in the *Lotus Sutra*, the *Sutra of the Perfection of Wisdom in Eight Thousand Verses* and the *Collection of Jewels*, the lower-stage female bodhisattva sexually transforms into a male prior to achieving Buddhahood. In her study of Mahayana sutras, Paul explains that "when one's religious practice was perfected, the desired sexual change from female to male would necessarily result."[126] There are a very few sutras, however, representing the view that women need not be transformed but are able to achieve Buddhahood as women. These are the *Diamond Sutra* and the *Vimalakirtri Sutra,* which explain the Mahayana teaching of Emptiness and interpret it as saying that all phenomena are impermanent and insubstantial, and, as a result, "there are not self-existent entities with inalienable and unchanging characteristics such as 'maleness' or 'femaleness.' There is no male or female."[127] To acknowledge such distinctions is to have an unenlightened mind.

But what are we to make of the stories that require a sex change? Are they not claiming that a male body is superior and the pinnacle of spiritual attainment? Interestingly, these stories pose no problem for the Buddhist woman who understands her tradition as being one of equality. One Korean woman writes that her study of sexual-transformation stories in the sutras leads her to conclude that they do not represent sexism but rather "an iconoclastic position intended to correct prejudicial views toward women. The idea of sexual transformation for enlightenment appears to be a strategy that eventually led to a theory of enlightenment in a female body."[128] In other words, the androcentric climate of the times was such that the idea of women's enlightenment came about gradually and had to be promulgated strategically. Rita Gross gives the same rationale by explaining that the main point in these stories is not that the woman eventually changes her sex,

> but that *she already had become a Bodhisattva and had already made the resolution to attain* Buddhahood, which she could demonstrate both by her understanding of *dharma* and by her magical power. . . . The point of doctrinal interest is that the woman standing here *now* could well be an advanced Bodhisattva and certainly is capable of rousing *Bodhicitta* [the thought of Enlightenment], contrary to conservative Buddhist opponents' opinions about her.[129]

In Mahayana texts, there are also celestial bodhisattvas, who have supernormal powers and act out of consideration for others. They are mythical figures who often assume the position of deities and are most often male. The figure of Avalokitesvara, common in India from the fifth century, appears as a male in the Sanskrit texts of the *Lotus Sutra.* In China, however, this bodhisattva of compassion is depicted as a female known as Kuan Yin. Another female bodhisattva is Prajnaparamita, who is the personification of transcendent wisdom. The existence of these female figures in early Buddhism is noted by Buddhist women as significant for the evolution of ideas about women's spiritual capacities. Rita Gross suggests that early Buddhists, as uncomfortable as they were with female spirituality, "did realize that a religion of compassion cannot condemn half its members to perpetual inferiority."[130] She notes that the problem of gender was solved in the *Sutra of Sagara, the Naga King* because here the Naga King's daughter displays her ability to transform her gender at will. Diana Paul's translation states, "The one who perceives through enlightenment has the Dharma, which is neither male nor female."[131] These scholars indicate that early Buddhism was egalitarian, in theory at least. They claim that whatever parts of the texts tell a different story are there because of the Buddha's respect for the sensitivities of his culture or because later, more conservative monks added to the teachings either inadvertently or deliberately in order to ensure the religion's acceptance by and support from local populations.

PROGRESSIVE POSITION

At the far left of the continuum lie those women who hold that the misogynistic culture that provided the soil for the growth of the Dharma not only shaped the community of Buddhist monastics and laypeople, but also influenced much of the teaching itself. In her introduction to *Meetings with Remarkable Women,* Lenore Friedman speculates that in spite of accepting women into the *sangha,* the Buddha "was not immune to the ingrained prejudices of his time and place."[132] Rita Gross echoes this idea when she says that the Buddha's insight does not include accurate scientific or historical statement or eternally valid institutional forms and rules. Rather, we must "distinguish the essential insights from non-essential cultural trappings."[133] So, the task for the modern woman who is Buddhist, either by birth or by conversion, is to decipher the meaning of the Dharma as it applies to her today, so that she can live the Buddha's message authentically.

Buddhist nun Karma Lekshe Tsomo understands that this deciphering means not only studying sexist texts for authenticity, as those in the center position do, but also engaging in a total reevaluation of the tradition's historical, philosophical, and sociological meanings. Today, progressive Buddhists are examining basic beliefs such as enlightenment, change, and Emptiness in order to discern their meaning and application in today's world.

Belief in the goal of spiritual enlightenment must be viewed "not simply as an abstraction, but as a concrete possibility available to all human beings, women included."[134] In Theravadin Buddhism ordination is essential for spiritual cultivation, monastic administration, and financial support.[135] It is also necessary that women be educated in order to receive the full benefit of the teaching. Therefore, if the goal of enlightenment is to be truly universal, women must have equal opportunities for ordination and education. Traditional ideas such as the preservation of lineage and subordination of nuns to monks can and must be rethought in order to preserve the essence of the Dharma, which is the oneness of all.

Buddhist teaching also includes the belief that change is intrinsic to human experience and essential for the world's and our own transformation. For Buddhist women to follow this teaching means that they should be agents for change. Tsomo encourages Buddhist women, monastic and lay, to acknowledge and work to fulfill their own spiritual potential and to support women's spiritual practice. She writes, "Women's increasingly active engagement in social and spiritual renewal may yield quite a revolutionary outcome."[136] To document the engagement, Tsomo has collected stories of women—monastic and lay, Asian, European, and American—who already are working to change Buddhism, women who are "breaking the mold in applying Buddhist ideals to issues of race, communications, sexual ethics, human rights, violence, and peace."[137] There are nuns in Theravadan Buddhist country of Nepal, for example, who have traveled to Taiwan to receive ordination from the Mahayana sect of the Fo Guang Shan. Even though they are not recognized by most Nepalese monks and have even been "severely castigated" by some, they continue to construct their own religious identity outside of traditional teachings.[138] Women who are thinking progressively believe that ordination, necessary for women's spiritual advancement, should not be denied them, and they have undertaken to change the satus quo.

These nuns, along with other women on the progressive end of the continuum, are confident that they are abiding by the spirit of the Buddha's teaching, which, if it is to last, must question and reevaluate the letter of that teaching. The letter may contain gender discrimination, but these women are certain that the message of enlightenment does not. From her study of early Buddhism, Ellison Banks Findly concludes that it is the spirit not the letter of the law that should motivate women to change existing practices. She writes, "If the letter of the law does not necessarily demonstrate parity between the nuns' and the monks' ordination process, it is possible that the spirit is more persuasive."[139] Such spirit should also dictate parity in the qualifications to teach the Dharma and to lead the monastic community.[140] Discerning the spirit of the Buddha's teachings is absolutely essential for its preservation, say the progressives.

The Mahayanist concept of Emptiness must also undergo progressive reinterpretation if it is to be an effective tool of social change. In some traditional perspectives, the idea of Emptiness is used to say that all distinctions are false, that differences between men and women are only relative and not really significant. If this is the case, asks Rita Gross, then why are the gender roles "insisted upon so absolutely and so rigidly, and why are they so carefully socialized into people?"[141] Even among Buddhist women there exists this idea that inequalities don't matter because all things are ultimately empty, hence there is no obligation to get involved in change. Gross says, however, that this attitude poisons the true idea of Emptiness by making it seem like an "allegiance to nothingness." She adds, "Because things are not absolute but only relative does not make them irrelevant or non-existent."[142] In other words, the lack of distinctions resulting from the idea of Emptiness should be an argument for the equality of genders, not for the irrelevance of present inequities.

Tsomo is thinking along these same lines when she tells us that the most liberating ideas in Buddhism are in its psychology. The enlightened mind, being totally pure and perfected, is not limited by gender or anything else. Since this goal of Buddhist practice has nothing to do with gender, as the teaching of Emptiness tells us, then "why should access to teachings and practice be limited by gender?" She proceeds to make the connection between psychological liberation and social liberation, saying one is dependent on the other, and concludes her book by saying that "women need only embrace the liberating opportunities that are intrinsically theirs."[143]

As the religion of Buddhism gains more and more women practitioners, many of whom were raised in Western cultures and with feminist ideologies, the face of Buddhism is gradually changing. Western women are making innovative contributions to the practice, the study, and the social consciousness of Buddhism. As a result, both Asian and Western women are being found on the progressive end of our continuum. They are reexamining the concepts of Emptiness and no-self, meditation, and ordination to extract what is essential and liberating from the teaching and to identify those parts that can be let go. One group attempting to unite the effort of all women who have embarked on this endeavor is Sakyadhita (Daughters of the Buddha). Buddhist nun Karma Lekshe Tsomo founded this organization, otherwise known as The International Association of Buddhist Women, in 1987. The members come from all traditions and work together to improve both the spiritual endeavors and the social situations of women practitioners throughout the world. By bringing together women of all sects, and by fostering education among them so they can become teachers, the association has done much to bring harmony to the religion as well as to make a contribution to world peace by reaching out to other religions. In its inclusiveness and its willingness to deal with difficult issues, this organization can provide a model for both intra-religious and interreligious dialogue that is needed in all traditions.

PART II

Proposing Some Solutions

5

Bringing Women Together

Bringing people of very diverse religious and political viewpoints to-gether appears to be an idealistic endeavor. While it is evident that the rifts between the conservative, moderate, and progressive contingencies are devastating to the cause of peace, mending such rifts seems to be im-possible. Why would one willfully enter into a conversation with the op-position? Why would one expose oneself to the frustration and anxiety of argumentation? Certainly no one wants to be converted to the other's view, and trying to change the other would only lead to more anger and deeper frustration. It is for this reason that the current interfaith dia-logues consist mostly of like-minded people, that is, people on the pro-gressive end of the continuum who subscribe to a more pluralistic view of religions. But, as stated in our first chapter, herein lies the problem. To be productive in the cause of peace, dialogues must be truly inclusive, that is, all positions must be represented. The following section presents some suggestions for methods and topics that might make such an inclusive dialogue possible.

WHY MEET WITH THE OTHER SIDE?

As one Hindu woman said to me recently, women speak on a very practical level. Ideological issues become secondary when women join forces to work out solutions to practical problems. In first-world coun-tries, on the local level, women of all religions and religious perspectives come together to improve the quality of their children's education and the safety of their neighborhoods. In third-world and war-torn countries, women are making valiant attempts to stop the killing of their children, to bring murderers and drug dealers to justice, and to begin cottage in-dustries so that they may provide for their families. In its 2005–6 annual report Religions for Peace indicated that groups of women are already working in war-torn communities to provide care and to advance devel-opment. As individual neighborhoods in all parts of the world become more integrated with peoples of all religious and ethnic backgrounds, such collaborations of women become profiles of diversity. This religious diversity enables women's groups to work for peace and sustainable development in such varying situations.[1]

On a broader, more global scale, women are working together to address problems that fall on all sides of economic or geographical boundaries: domestic violence, sexual exploitation of women and children, lack of clean air and water, and religious and ethnic intolerance. These issues are motivating women from all parts of the world to join together to effect change. Women who are members of these groups are forming bonds that transcend religious or political differences. But it is important that, in working together for practical causes, such differences are not shoved under the rug, but rather become the subject of dialogue so that misconceptions can be clarified, stereotypes eliminated, and true change can be accomplished. Because religion permeates so many of the world's problems, while at the same time representing the best of human values, it becomes a crucial meeting point. Whether an interreligious dialogue occurs as a result of or as a prelude to working on an issue, it is an essential part of cooperation among participants. Without mutual respect and understanding, no goal can be accomplished.

A recent study for the *Los Angeles Times* revealed one California neighborhood where differences in religious beliefs permeated all personal and moral issues, and, as a result, friendships were destroyed and children were made to feel excluded from school and neighborhood activities. But by the same token, when one resident was diagnosed with breast cancer, the entire neighborhood "rallied around with cards and casseroles and offers to drive her to doctor's appointments."[2] What can we make of this dichotomy between the personal and the ideological, one uniting persons and the other dividing them? One interpretation of the phenomenon is that individual needs can transcend ideological differences; another is that, in order for the bonds to be stronger than those caused by an emergency, an understanding that goes beneath the surface is needed. For such understanding to happen, dialogue is essential.

One example of the immediate necessity rippling out to broader understanding is a group of women in central New York State who have named themselves Women Transcending Boundaries. After the attacks of 9/11, some Islamic women in Syracuse experienced fear in the face of prejudice against Muslims. In an effort to reach out to them, one Christian woman, Betsy Wiggins, called the local mosque to offer some help. She was put in touch with Danya Wellmon, an American who had converted to Islam ten years before. Betsy writes of Danya's experiences: "One day, when she was wearing a traditional head scarf and a long coat, a man approached her in a mall and said, 'Why don't you go back where you came from?' She answered, 'I'm an American. My husband fought in Vietnam. Where would you like me to go?'"[3] The meeting of Betsy and Danya led to the gathering of a number of women of different faiths who wanted to eliminate prejudice and promote understanding. It has since burgeoned into an organization dedicated to dialogue and service. These women meet regularly to learn about one another's beliefs, to share experiences, and also to do service, which consists of donating time and money to projects aimed at alleviating social problems in Syracuse and in Muslim countries. The rapid growth of this one group formed to address one problem and sustained by mutual education and understanding indicates a willingness and a need on the part of women to work together.

While there are several women's interfaith organizations throughout the world that are working together for peace, there are few that welcome the kind of dialogue that is proposed here, that is, within traditions as well as among them. The Buddhist organization Sakyadhita is the rare example of one that is attempting to promote harmony and understanding among women from the various points on the continuum and to overcome the divisions that separate the Theravada from Mahayana traditions. This type of intra-religious dialogue is essential for other faiths as well. The World Council of Churches recognized this need when, at the very end of its consultation statement on interreligious dialogue, it states, "While actively engaging in interfaith dialogue and action, people in living faiths must also continue to maintain intra-faith dialogue, as well."[4] I wonder if the writers of the statement understood the profound implications of their words or how immensely difficult it would be to carry them out. Perhaps they did and therefore choose to end the statement there and not speculate any further.

OBSTACLES TO DIALOGUE

Mutual understanding and cooperation among conservative, centrists, and progressives are difficult to achieve because of the many obstacles preventing these groups from coming together. In order to develop a method of successful dialogue that will overcome these obstacles, they must be first be understood and addressed. Three specific obstacles considered here are stereotyping, receiving only selective information and fearing a loss of identity.

STEREOTYPING

Webster's dictionary defines *stereotype* as "a standardized mental picture . . . that represents an oversimplified opinion or uncritical judgment." Critical-thinking classes call this an overgeneralization, that is, a fallacious judgment in which a characteristic of some members of a group is applied to every member. It is true that we all make generalizations, which sometimes can serve a very good purpose. If the last three cars that I owned were Chryslers and I liked them, chances are that if I buy another Chrysler, I will like that one also. Marketers use generalizations all the time to target audiences for their products. The truck commercials that take place during the Super Bowl football game are targeted to young men whom the advertisers assume are watching the game and like to drive trucks—generalizations about young men. There are exceptions, of course, but it is good business to generalize. However, negative stereotypes or generalizations that are unjustly applied to all members of a group are far different. Unlike marketers' generalizations, which are based on surveys and trends, most negative stereotypes are based on anecdotal experience and little hard data. For example, some welfare recipients in the United States have abused the system and used taxpayers' money to gain wealth without working for it. As these cases are made known through the media and political speeches, many members of the American middle class become outraged and, as a result, stereotype all welfare recipients as lazy and irresponsible. Likewise, after 9/11, anyone with an Arabic name was suspected of being a terrorist. Paranoia was rampant, and many U.S. citizens of Middle Eastern descent, whether Muslim, Sikh, or Christian, were stereotyped as terrorists and became targets of discrimination. In each of these cases stereotyping was the result of the strong emotions of anger and fear.

Stereotyping also results from assuming that we understand what our opponents are thinking. We judge their position, label it, and then fit all people who are connected with our opponents into that category. Such was the case in that California neighborhood discussed earlier; both sides of the political divide were certain that they already knew what to think of the other. When asked what words came to mind when hearing "Republican," the Democrats said things like "uptight," "staid," and "anti pro-choice." The Republicans described Democrats as "hippie-types," "stubborn," and "anti-business." Each side labeled the other "intrusive."[5] Each side secured its position by attaching labels to the other. In an article about stereotyping in the work place, Sondra Thiederman warns that "even the most enlightened among us resist giving up the stereotypes that make us feel more secure and in control."[6] When we have labeled a group as having some characteristic to which we are opposed, it is much easier to avoid all members of the group than to have to make distinctions or to put our opinions at risk. But it is this very state of isolation from the other that reinforces stereotypes, isolates us from whole groups of people, and promulgates the ignorance that divides and antagonizes.

In Chapter 3 we met Jewish Orthodox women and rabbis and Roman Catholic women and priests who labeled women seeking ordination as selfish and self-centered. We also met conservative evangelicals who considered progressive Christians as worldly and turning their backs on God because of their positions on biblical interpretation and the role of women in the family. Likewise, the Muslim women on the conservative end of the continuum viewed the progressive Muslim women as irreligious and straying from the message of Islam.

Chapter 4 indicates that conservative Hindu women see those who follow a path independent of or contrary to their husband's wishes as violating the ideal of womanhood as seen in the goddess Sita. In Buddhism, those women who are attempting to be ordained as *bhikksunis* in the nuns' community are viewed by some Theravadin nuns as striving for power and not true to the Dharma.

The various religious conservatives tend to blame the progressives for the decline in religion and morality in the modern world. By the same token, however, progressives have stereotyped conservatives as narrow-minded, insecure, and out of touch with the real world and its global problems. The liberals accuse the conservatives of maintaining antiquated views of women that contribute to their oppression and foster their inequality. Those in the center of the continuum, of course, see those at each end as extremists who add little more than a great deal of animosity to the cause of their religion. It is because of the extremists, say those in the middle, that synagogues, churches, and mosques have declining memberships and that the Hindu and Buddhist communities are losing the dedication of their young people. The animosity among factions is largely due to these labels.

SELECTIVE INFORMATION

I remember being at a dinner party where one conservative Christian was expressing dislike for feminists by labeling them relativists. One feminist in the group, expressing her disagreement with relativism, responded "Rape is wrong no matter where it occurs or to whom." This retort did give the accuser some pause to rethink his assumption. But how often would people with such opposing views meet one another? And how often would there be the freedom to have such an exchange?

For the most part, people on the various points of the continuum live and communicate with like-minded people. In a world that is becoming more and more polarized, people increasingly gravitate to those who share their views. Also, in these modern times there is always a local organization, a radio program, a TV network, and several Internet sites that will cater to specific viewpoints and provide us with the most offensive representatives of the opposite side. In other words, we can surround ourselves with selected information that gives us only those facts and opinions that support our position, leaving little incentive for us to move outside our ideological comfort zone. As a result of this isolation and of listening to only our way of thinking, we remain ignorant or form wrong notions of other ideas. Such ignorance or wrong information only serves to entrench us more deeply in our prejudices and widen the divide between positions. I have encountered numerous people in my community who no longer subscribe to one or the other of the two local newspapers because it presents an opposing view to their own, suggesting that they will only read what they agree with. My husband and I subscribe to both publications and, when we compare notes, find that each one gives a distinctive slant to world and local events in the attempt to support one position or another. Which slant is true or more accurate? That is the dilemma. Perhaps both hold truth and the difference only lies in our perception of things. Samuel Johnson once said, "Inconsistencies cannot both be right, but . . . they may both be true." It is the human perception of the facts that spins them in different and sometimes opposing directions. Both the beauty and the struggle of dialogue is to arrive at points of understanding that reveal how ideas and opinions resemble each other and yet are different at the same time.

FEAR OF LOSS OF IDENTITY

The third obstacle to an honest and productive intra-religious dialogue is the fear of losing or changing one's identity. We all look for meaning and purpose in our lives. If one looks to religion to provide this meaning and purpose, then religious belief will become a large part of one's sense of self. We are also by nature social beings whose membership in a community establishes our personal identity. Belonging to a religious community, then, also contributes to making religion a part of our identity. When religion makes up such a large part of a who we are and what we do, we rely on our faith to support us in adversity, answer complex moral questions, and comfort us when we face our own or our loved ones' mortality. Is it any wonder that we become anxious in the face of those who question our beliefs? Such anxiety can cause defensiveness, which then leads to anger and argumentation. Such personal investment in one's religion naturally leads to avoidance of, separation from, and eventually conflict with those who hold opposing religious beliefs, especially within our own tradition.

The stereotyping of the other, the selection of information, and fear of identity loss are obstacles to any discussion with those who think differently. I propose, though, that they become exaggerated when we encounter people of our own faith who are on opposing parts of the continuum. We think that they should share our beliefs because we claim the same tradition. This expectation serves to highlight differences even more, and each tends to put blame on the other for veering off the straight path.

So, how can there be a dialogue? Very carefully. If we are convinced that the opposing viewpoints must be met and addressed, and we are willing to exert effort to do this, we can begin to sort out the steps necessary to engage in a fruitful interaction. Two of these steps, deciding on a methodology and on the topics to be discussed, are discussed in Chapters 6 and 7.

6

Methods of Women's Dialogue

An effective dialogue reduces stereotyping and increases mutual understanding. Through dialogue, people who seem intractably opposed often change the way they view and relate to each other—even as they maintain the commitments that underlie their views. They often discover shared values and concerns which may lead to collaborative actions that were previously unthinkable.[1]

This observation made by the Public Conversations Project clearly expresses the main objective of dialogue. This nonprofit organization has been facilitating dialogues on divisive issues since 1989, and, while its mission is to deal with social conflicts in general, some past dialogues have been directly concerned with religious topics including abortion, homosexuality in communities of faith, and prejudice in Muslim and non-Muslim communities. Specific guidelines that grew out of these experiences have been published in the project's workbook *Fostering Dialogue across Divides*. Among the many practical steps explained in this text, three stand out as especially important. First, the purpose of coming together must be made very clear. Second, personal stories must be used to introduce the participants. And third, participants must be taught how to engage in active listening.

CLARIFYING THE PURPOSE OF COMING TOGETHER

I once met a woman who was a leader of a conservative Christian activist group. During our conversation she explained her group's interest in a Muslim/Christian dialogue and its attempts to work out guidelines for such an encounter. When I expressed interest in her work, she said that her group's dialogues differed from the liberal ones in that, while liberals were willing to give up their principles, her group saw no problem with attempting to convince the Muslims of the truth. When I returned home and researched her group's guidelines for such a dialogue, I saw no mention of conversion or persuasion in them. I was uncomfortable with both our conversation and with my findings in the guidelines, and, upon reflection, was able to articulate my problems. First, what she was referring to sounded more like debate than dialogue. Debate is the arguing of two sides of an issue to decide which side is correct or true, or in other words, which side wins. It is quite acceptable in a debate to prove that your side's point of view is the correct one and to expect the other, after considering your persuasive arguments, to agree and move to your side. In a dialogue, however, participants seek to develop mutual understanding, and, in order to do so, put aside arguments and adversities. Doing so does not mean that they put aside their claims to the truth, but there is a recognition that no one person has, at any one moment, total knowledge of all the truth. Such understanding of their limitations leaves participants open to hearing what others have to say and to listening closely to who is speaking and what that person believes. It is essential however, to understand that in the process of listening, participants are in no way asked to abandon what they believe.

The urge to try to convince the other of your point of view is especially tempting in an intra-religious dialogue. In interreligious dialogue it is clearly understood that the other is truly "other" in that they subscribed to a completely different belief system. In intra-religious dialogue, however, there is the presumption of similarities in basic principles. The question becomes one of where the similarities in belief end and the differences begin. Although conservative, moderate, and progressive Christians believe that Jesus Christ is both God and man, they may disagree about his human qualities. I have heard conservative and progressive Christians get into quite heated arguments over whether or not Jesus knew he was God. The conservatives cannot fathom a God that is not omniscient; the progressives believe that Jesus grew in age and wisdom like other humans and that the full realization that he was God did not occur until after the resurrection. Each side of the argument firmly believes that the other side is wrong and therefore either quits talking or tries very hard to change its views. Likewise, I have witnessed Muslims in the United States get into quite heated discussions about veiling. Even though both conservative and progressive Muslims believe that the Qur'an is the direct word of God and that Muhammad is God's messenger, the directive that women must cover their heads in public has been given many different interpretations. Muslims are more likely to engage in debate—not dialogue—with other Muslims over this issue than with non-Muslims. It is far more difficult to refrain from proselytizing people of one's own tradition than people of other traditions. Therefore, when people of the same tradition engage in dialogue, there is even more need to lay out clearly the nature and purpose of the meeting than there is for an interreligious dialogue.

My second problem with my companion's comments is her claim that liberals are willing to relinquish their principles. In my several years of engaging in interreligious dialogue, I have not witnessed an abandonment of belief by any of the participants. In all that has been written about the effects of interreligious dialogue, there is never a mention of compromising one's faith. Instead, faith in one's own tradition often becomes deeper and more meaningful when placed in the larger perspective of the world's religions, because seeing the world and ourselves through the eyes of the "other" brings new dimensions to our own convictions. A good example of this experience is explained by Diana Eck in her book *Encountering God: A Spiritual Journey from Bozeman to Banaras*. After spending a year in Banaras, the spiritual center of India, Eck discovered that the pantheon of Hindu gods and goddesses manifesting one spiritual truth actually shed light on and gave strength to her own faith in the Christian Trinity.[2] Not only did she not give up the basic principles of Christianity, but she became more appreciative of them. This growth in the appreciation of one's own faith also is an essential point of two of the pioneers of interreligious dialogue, Leonard Swidler and Ashok Gangadean. Stage four of their seven stages of deep dialogue explains that participants in deep dialogue can enter into and understand the world view of the other but then return to their own world, bringing with them new knowledge of how to think and act. They see this experience as dramatically deepening one's sense of self, one's identity, and one's religion.[3] Engagement in interreligious dialogue, therefore, does not ask a Christian to abandon belief in Christ as a personal savior, or a Muslim to denounce Muhammad as God's messenger, or a Jew to forget the Torah. What it does demand, however, is to open ourselves to understand how another could believe what we ourselves could not. We are asked to understand that they believe, not to believe what they believe.

The subject of concern of Eck, Swidler, and Gangadean is interreligious dialogue; however, their principles can be applied to intra-religious dialogue as well. It is one of the erroneous presumptions of religious peoples that they understand the world view of those who claim the same tradition but stand in different positions on the continuum. The stereotyping described in the previous chapter is one of the results of such a presumption. Would participants have to give up their convictions about a married priesthood, a woman rabbinate, the veiling of women in public, or Sita as the ideal wife, if they dialogued with more conservative or more progressive members of their own faith? I would hope the answer would be no. If dialogue is truly for the purpose of mutual understanding and not persuasion, then there should be no fear of losing one's perspective. If anything, explaining our perspective to others will make our convictions clearer and our faith stronger. At least this goal, not conversion, should be the one for which we aim.

The third problem I had with my encounter was that, when I read the guidelines for dialogue published by her organization, there was no mention of attempting to convince the Muslims of Christianity. In order for there to be a sincere exchange of ideas and experiences, trust is essential, and the biggest obstacle to trust is a hidden agenda. I feared that the agenda of conversion, which she expressed in our conversation, was indeed hidden and that therefore the motivations for dialogue were not clear, thus leading to mistrust and a breakdown in the process. Without a clear articulation of the goals of mutual understanding and cooperation prior to an encounter, it is doomed to failure. To avoid such failure and to foster a respectful environment, the Public Conversations Project has participants put forth communications agreements before dialoguing. One of the points states: "We will not criticize the views of others or attempt to persuade them."[4] By having all participants agree to such statements, there will be no hidden agenda of proselytizing. The articulation of this statement will raise the consciousness of all participants and any attempt to convince the others to change their beliefs will be recognized as a failure to dialogue. I recall one incident of a hidden agenda early in my interreligious work. I was responsible for the Thanksgiving interfaith prayer service at a small college in New York. This was long before there were any Muslims, Hindus, or Buddhists in our neighborhood, so the representatives were a rabbi, a Catholic priest, and a Protestant minister. Each selected a reading for the day. The Protestant chose the story from the New Testament in which a Pharisee approaches the altar and thanks God for giving him virtue, while a tax collector stands in the back of the temple and asks for forgiveness for his sins. In this story Jesus condemns the Pharisee but praises the sinner. Whether or not the minister understood that Jews of today are descendants of the Pharisees was not clear, but there was definitely discomfort in the room at the not-so-subtle insult to the rabbi. While such a situation would probably not happen in a modern dialogue, it is not far-fetched to imagine such an agenda being part of an intra-religious dialogue.

People have chosen their position on the continuum and have rejected other places. It is very difficult and requires much patience to listen carefully to why others have chosen different positions, to not interrupt or to not assume to know what is coming next. It takes trust to listen to opposing views without feeling that the other is trying to persuade or without wanting to convert the other. That this type of trust is difficult is all the more reason why a clear articulation of the purpose of dialogue is essential.

PERSONAL STORIES

In my previous work, *Women Speaking, Women Listening*, I explain why it is important for women's interreligious dialogue to begin with the telling of personal stories. While this procedure sounds rather simple and ordinary, it is often overlooked in dialogue circles in which the main concern is similarities and differences in teachings and beliefs. However, when we focus first on structure and begin by telling personal stories, there is an impact that is far more powerful than one would expect. Each one of us has a particular perspective on reality; no one, not even the empirical scientist, can see the truth as it exists in itself.[5] Furthermore, our particular perspective has been shaped by what we have learned and experienced in our lives, and no two persons have received learning or experiences in the exact same way. Psychologists tell us that even siblings growing up in the same family have had different experiences and different perceptions depending on a variety of factors such as their place in the family, their gender, and their extended relationships. When we tell our stories—where we came from, our family background, our formative experiences—we are really explaining how we acquired our particular way of believing and why we perceive things the way we do. It is difficult to be angry or exasperated when one listens carefully to another's story. It is also difficult to maintain stereotypes when we hear each person's unique situation.

When I first moved to California from New York City, little did I know how isolated I had been. Being born and raised in a big city made me think that I was quite cosmopolitan. However, in California I met people who had migrated to that state from all over the country. Eventually I became good friends with a woman from a very small town in the Midwest. It wasn't until years later, when I joined her for a visit to her home town that I could envision and better understand the experiences she often spoke about. It was sharing these totally different stories of our growing up in different geographies and different social settings that made us appreciate each other's perspective. I told her stories of how my father, the only Catholic in his elementary class in a small Connecticut town, was bullied by the Baptists on his way home from school everyday, causing him to dislike Baptists into his adulthood. She, in turn, told me of her Baptist grandmother's belief that Catholics performed some kind of magic ritual when they ate the body and blood of Christ. Telling these stories made us appreciate the limitations of our backgrounds and made our discussions about our religious differences all the more valuable.

Another value to telling personal stories is that they reveal how a woman sees herself as opposed to how others see her. If no two people experience or perceive life in the exact same way, then one person, even in the same culture, cannot speak for another. Considering this fact, it would be difficult if not impossible for an American woman to speak for a third-world woman, or for a white woman to describe the experiences of a black woman. For this reason, over the years, the women's movement has produced scholars from all over the globe who are examining their particular culture's take on feminism. Katie Cannon and Delores Williams have used

Alice Walker's term *Womanism* for their work on the black woman's experience in America to distinguish it from that of white American women. Women of the Third World are writing and speaking aloud in their own voice in order to be heard over the voluminous works of first-world women.[6] Gender widens the perspective gap even further, making men's descriptions of women's place in religion practically unrecognizable to the women they are describing.

If these misperceptions of the other occur in interreligious dialogue, they are more likely to occur in a dialogue with those of our own tradition, because in these encounters assumptions are more easily made about what others think. Growing up as a Catholic in an Italian neighborhood, I had little occasion to meet with Protestant Christians, who were rare in my section of the city. The first time I experienced an interreligious dialogue with Jews and Protestants, I found that the Protestants' experiences of Jesus were quite different from mine, and I wondered how to explain these differences to the Jewish participants, whose view of Jesus was yet different. At the beginning of the twenty-first century, as dialogue becomes more common and engages more participants, more sects and divisions of the religions are represented. For this reason intra-religious dialogue has become an important prerequisite or component of interreligious dialogue. I recall a meeting of Jews, Christians, and Muslims at which the Orthodox Jews and the Reform Jews spent the evening contradicting each other in their explanation of an issue to the non-Jews of the group. While this meeting was an interesting encounter for all to observe, it demonstrated the need to incorporate intra-religious dialogue into the interreligious experience.

I am convinced that the only way the different factions of the religions will be able to join in the dialogue is if there is trust among them, and the way to establish this trust is with the telling of personal stories. After listening to the various views in the first part of this book, we hear women on all points of the continuum express a sincere desire to be religious. It is very difficult to appreciate or trust that our sisters who profess the same faith, but differ on so many expressions of it, really have a religious life. We can only know this by hearing their personal stories.

ACTIVE LISTENING

In order for the telling of these stories to be effective, however, the participants must also engage in active listening. In my college classroom I have often watched students looking through books or flipping through notes during the lecture. When asked if they would please give me their attention, they reply, "But I am listening." These students are mistaking *hearing* for *listening*. Active listening is doing something, not the absence of doing something, such as not talking. Many believe that if they are not speaking in a conversation, they are listening. However, while they may be being silent, is their mind silent as well? Very often, in discussions, especially lively ones, we are already formulating our next comment while the other is speaking. We are so invested in getting our points across that we really do not grasp the significance of what the other is saying. We also make assumptions about the other that cause us to believe that we already know what he or she will say. Such assumptions cause us to stop listening to the one speaking and begin listening to our thoughts about what is being said. To listen actively, on the other hand, is to clear our minds of our own ideas so that we have room to entertain those of the other. It also means that we suspend judgment on the content and form of the other's speech so that we can learn about the other in his or her own words and not in our interpretation of them. We do not have to agree with the other or believe in the same way in order to listen. Only this type of listening, that is, actively and deliberately clearing our minds and suspending our judgments, can give us a true understanding of another person and that person's experience, which is the goal of dialogue.

Active listening is not easy, however. For most of us it does not come naturally but must be learned and is mastered only after much practice. Teaching the art of listening, especially in interreligious dialogue, is the goal of Kay Lindahl, director of The Listening Center in Los Angeles. She believes that "learning how to listen to and speak with each other are essential skills for creating relationships that lead to mutual respect, dialogue, understanding , and peace. . . . Listening encompasses much more than words. Listening is a way of being in the world."[7] Two of the many requirements for attentive listening that Lindahl stresses in her workshops are preparing ourselves to listen and asking for points of clarification. In our world of high-speed Internet, jet travel, and fast food, there is seldom time to pause, to be still, and to reflect. When I bring my students to the Zen monastery and they taste five minutes of meditation, the usual response is that the time seemed more like hours than minutes, so unused to silence are they. However, it is only in silence and peace that real listening can take place. So, if we are not used to being calm in other activities, then we won't be still and able to listen when we are in dialogue with people who hold opposing views. Lindahl says, "Listening for true wisdom to reveal itself is a slowing down, waiting, practicing patience."[8] She believes that just as a speaker must prepare to give a presentation, so those in dialogue must prepare to listen. We do so by making it a practice to be quiet at some point during the day, by occasionally turning off the radio in the car or the television in the evening, or by practicing some form of meditation.

Besides slowing down, we also must practice letting go of the desire to be right. Lindahl also warns that "it takes practice to loosen our attachments to our own agendas."[9] In intra-religious dialogue there is a special temptation to "correct" others of our faith about their "erroneous" ways. As soon as we hear them say the words that represent what they believe and that we have heard so often, we have a spontaneous urge to correct them. In Christian circles the mere mention of a progressive theologian can turn a conservative off to anything another says. By the same token, a progressive Christian hears nothing after the conservative says "to be saved, one must. . . . " But have we really listened to what the speaker has to say? Have we suspended our judgment or, as Lindahl suggests, "loosened our attachment to our agenda?" Doing so takes practice indeed.

In order to facilitate our listening and to aid our understanding of the other in dialogue, it is important to ask questions for clarification. These are not questions to trip up the speaker or to put the person on the spot, but rather questions such as "What do you mean by . . . ?" Or "Could you please elaborate on that point?" Not only are we helped by these questions, but our dialogue partners are encouraged to speak because they realize that we are really hearing and are interested in what they are saying.

Active listening to personal stories affects not only the listener but also the speaker, the teller of the story. In the mid 1980s feminist Nelle Morton wrote a powerful sentence in her autobiography that has often been used by advocates of dialogue: "Word heard into speech creates and announces new personhood—new consciousness awakened in the human being."[10] The more we are listened to, the more we speak, because we feel heard and understood; and the more we speak, the more we can clarify our own ideas. Instead of these ideas, especially the ones about our deeper issues, revolving in circles in our minds, they are freed of the repetition and take a linear path to further clarification. This liberation happens because someone has invited the ideas out into the open by listening them into speech. Nelle Morton points out that this active listening can actually cause others to explore verbally their identity, to begin to see themselves as they truly are instead of how others see them. If we explain to others where we came from and why we think the way we do, and if those others are truly interested and listening to our story, then we will be encouraged to explore new ideas about ourselves and our positions. This new perspective on our identity can only occur, however, in an atmosphere of trust, and such an atmosphere can only be fostered when participants are engaged in active listening.

7

Topics and Issues
for Women's Dialogue

Although it is unnatural to separate *what* is being said from *how* it is being said, we must face the question of what would be talked about at a meeting of women coming from opposing viewpoints. When working on pressing social issues, there must be a level of discussion that addresses the deeper, more controversial concerns in order for a group's work to be effective. After listening to the voices of women from the conservative to the progressive points on the continuum, four important topics stand out as being the most contentious. Although the problems they present will not necessarily be solved, a clarification of the topics and an appreciation of their complexities will go a long way in improving both intra-religious and interreligious dialogue. The four topics to be considered are women's spirituality, sexuality and gender roles, the relationship of the past to the present, and the nature of religious authority.

WOMEN'S SPIRITUALITY

One of the most important realizations that comes from listening to a woman's personal story is that she has been on a journey of discovery, finding out about herself, her world, and her tradition. In other words, she has a spirituality that gives her life its meaning. I have found that one of the most prevalent misconceptions that fuels the fire of contention among women on opposite poles of our continuum is that the "other" is not sincerely religious or following a spiritual path. To the progressive, the conservative is motivated by fear and insecurity, causing her to cling to past traditions and to allow men to dominate and define her. To the conservative, the progressive is motivated by her ego, her need for power, and her love of the world, causing her to pick and choose the parts of the tradition's teachings that suit her. In other words, she fashions the religion to her own convenience. Neither side takes into account the spirituality of the other. Neither the progressive nor the conservative gives the other credit for striving for, or for having had, an authentic religious experience.

Listening to the voices of women in Chapters 3 and 4, we are struck by how often they proclaim a commitment to the spiritual journey. When Orthodox Jews such as Wendy Wolfe Fine talk about women being especially suited for intimacy with God and being the keepers of the holy temple, it is clear that these women who adhere to strict Jewish law are not afraid or insecure but rather very fulfilled in their inner spiritual life. Likewise, when conservative Jewish women listen to Adena Berkowitz talk about watching the faces of women who finally see the inside of a Torah scroll and read from it for the first time, they can appreciate why progress is important. By the same token, when progressives hear the same story, they appreciate the need to maintain the traditional framework.

Listening to conservative Christian women, we hear that they submit to their husbands not out of weakness but out of spiritual conviction. They view their family role as glorifying God and living in fellowship with him through Jesus Christ. This position was articulated in the voices of Dorothy Patterson and Kim Pennington, which, far from sounding soft and cowering, were loud and strong when explaining their relationship with God. We also heard the voices of conservative Muslim women in America who accept the gender roles and codes of conduct prescribed by their view of Islam. They feel liberated from the demanding and largely immoral social norms because they are following the will of Allah. They have found in the Qur'an a safe haven for living and communicating with an all-loving God. It is very difficult to listen to these stories and not be moved by the transforming power of these women's experiences. The more progressive women need to encounter these conservative women with a new mindset, one that destroys the old stereotypes.

In Hinduism the conservative woman who is a devotee of Sita sees her as the ideal wife and the model of patience and forbearance in the face of difficulty. By striving to be the ideal wife and mother, therefore, the Hindu woman is expressing her devotion to the goddess. The perspective of the conservative Buddhist nuns is also based on their spirituality and not on weakness. This spirituality is clear when they tell us that their goal in this life is not to be equal to the monks but to be successful in their assigned roles. They believe that getting an education or achieving independent status from the male monks does not help them to achieve enlightenment and therefore is irrelevant to their pursuit. These Hindu and Buddhist women are reminding us that their spiritual lives and experiences are valid and to be respected by all in the community.

The conservative women face a similar challenge when listening to the spirituality of the other, more progressive women in the dialogue. The

Orthodox Jewish woman who sees the woman rabbi as violating not only Jewish law but the standards of humility fails to understand the rabbi's spirituality. The more progressive Jewish women have told us that in their prayer and reflective study they have experienced God as a God of justice and a God of relationship. As such, justice becomes the underlying principle of God's law, the Halacha, which makes equal roles for men and women in the synagogue not only possible but imperative. Also, if God is a God of relationship, and if women are called to be in this divine relationship, the Jewish woman must see herself not as better than other religious persons, which the word *chosen* might imply, but as possessing a uniqueness that contributes to the whole. In striving to become close to God and to emulate God's justice, the progressive woman has much to share with her Orthodox sister.

When considering the more progressive women in Christianity, it would be very difficult not to be moved by the personal journeys of Peggy Michael-Rush and Virginia Ramey Mollenkott, whose strong biblical faith brought them from feelings of being inferior and inherently evil to the safety of the love of God. Mollenkott's description of her intimate relationship with a loving God who accepts her for who she is, a lesbian Christian feminist, gives the conservative some understanding of how one can see the Bible as teaching the human dignity of all persons regardless of gender and sexual orientation. Once again, if the purpose of this dialogue is understanding, not conversion, and if the conservative creatively listens to these stories containing such controversial topics, then the goal of the meeting will have been realized.

Like the progressive Jewish women, Christian and Muslim women on this end of the continuum also have an experience of a just God. In their eyes, justice refers to the equal treatment of all human persons whom God created. They strongly believe that God does not show preference in loving one over another and therefore we are to be open to the dignity and holiness of all. The Christian progressives Rosemary Ruether and Mary Hunt have a deep-seated faith in Jesus Christ and the community that must witness to him by embracing all as equal members.

The voices of progressive Muslim women have also been raised, telling of their relationship with Allah, a relationship that was cultivated in spite of some strong opposition from their families and colleagues who see them as unbelievers. In Chapter 3 we heard from a group of American Muslim women who have found a deep spirituality in Islam and believe that it reveals a God of mercy, love, and justice. When we hear Yousra Fazili speak about her God being a God of compassion, and Asma Barlas speak about God's self-disclosure in the Qur'an as divine unity and justice, it becomes clear that these women are speaking from their spiritual experience and not from what they have heard from the imam at the local mosque. To listen actively to these progressive Jewish, Christian, and

Muslim women is to respect them as sincerely seeking a relationship with God and to afford them some degree of understanding, even if one is journeying on a very different path.

In Chapter 4 we read similar perspectives from Hindu and Buddhist women about their roles in their traditions. Those Hindus who are re-evaluating the epic stories such as the *Ramayana* and those Buddhists who are reevaluating the concepts of lineage and traditional ordination are doing so not because they want to mold the traditions according to their needs, but because they genuinely seek to make the lessons of these teachings alive in the world of the twenty-first century. In a world where women's suffering and oppression are obvious evils, devotion to Sita means emulating her strength and justice as much as her obedience to Rama. In a world where woman's spiritual potential and ability to teach the Dharma are being recognized by more and more women and men, ordination is important for both women's growth and the growth of the entire Buddhist community. These realizations can come only if we are actively listening to the stories of these progressive women.

SEXUALITY AND GENDER ROLES

Perhaps the most glaring difference between conservative and progressive viewpoints is their approach to sexuality and gender roles in family and religious institutions. Much of this controversy was sparked by the Western feminist movement that began in the 1960s and became associated with bra burning and male bashing. These associations created a backlash by critics who blamed the movement for many of society's ills, including the breakup of families, unwed motherhood, and even the glorification of lesbianism. These attitudes persist to this day. Conservatives use the label feminist to refer to a selfish, egotistical woman who abandons her natural tendencies to nurture in order to pursue a man's role in society. They think that feminists want power and liberation from the bondage of housework and from the oppressive role of wife and mother. Very often many of my women students agree with equal pay and equal opportunities for women in the work place while insisting that they are not feminists. When asked why not, they tell me that they love their families and that they believe mothers should take care of their own children. That they view these values as incompatible with feminism reveals the negative stereotypes that have been attached to the movement.

When we listen to the conservative voices in Judaism, Christianity, and Islam, we hear them stereotyping not only the word *feminist*, but the whole women's movement as well. Blu Greenberg admits that she had a difficult time convincing Orthodox Jewish women to stop seeing the word "feminist" as meaning that men are enemies and the family is the locus of oppression. Conservative Christian groups—such as the Council for Biblical Manhood and Womanhood, and Women for Faith and the Family—denounce modern feminists because they see them as putting ego before God and contributing to the breakdown of society with their arrogance and self-centeredness. We heard the voice of Carolyn McCulley, who urges women to be "liberated from feminism," claiming that its marginalization of men has caused such problems as pornography, child abuse, fatherless children, and sexually transmitted diseases. We also hear Muslim women justify wearing the veil because they want to separate themselves from the American women's movement, which they believe encourages women to reject modesty and chastity.

Even though Hindu and Buddhist women have not used the word *feminism* in their discourse, they do maintain the attitude that marriage and motherhood define womanhood. Not to be married, usually to a spouse chosen by one's family, is seen as an aberration to the conservative Hindu and a distortion of the natural order of things. Even as more Hindu women become educated and enter professions, their family responsibilities are their foremost consideration. This fact indicates that women's gender roles are deeply ingrained in their world view.

In some conservative Buddhist circles we saw that women and men believe that a woman must be born again as a man to reach enlightenment, because being born as a woman is an indication of something amiss in the previous life. A woman, they believe, is suited by nature to bear children, and that is her function in society. This emphasis on her sexuality makes her too physical, too attached to the material world and to her own beauty to achieve Emptiness or the concept of no-self. Her sexuality is a powerful force that, as in Hinduism, can wreak havoc if not controlled; if it *is* controlled, the effort is so strained that life in a monastery would be quite difficult.

Progressive women in the five traditions, as we would expect, have a very different perception of the women's movement and women's sexuality. They see a conservative woman as accepting the male view of her tradition as the way things should be. To the progressive, these conservative women have allowed the current norms, which have been created by the male power structure, to define their lives, what they want, and who they envision themselves to be. Even though the conservative woman believes that she is free and happy, the progressive distrusts the fact that the conservative really speaks for herself because, says the progressive, the words sound like the male view being spoken in the female's voice. For example, the progressives in the traditions believe that women who see themselves as having to obey their husbands as heads of household are adhering to the standards set up not by the religion but by the male-dominated structures within which the religion grew. For example, those centrist Christian women who seek ordination or traditional leadership roles in the institutional church are viewed by progressives as having been coopted by males to continue the power roles. The progressive woman's plea in all religions is for women to find their own voices, determine their own gifts, and choose their own fulfillment independent of what males think they should be. In summary, what we have is two points of view that appear to be in a deadlock. The conservative calls the progressive selfish, and the progressive calls the conservative unaware. What to do?

Once again, we must listen carefully and actively to the stories of those in each group, and we must trust in the sincerity of what they are saying. We listen to the stories of women's fulfillment in their traditional roles of wife and mother, of their love for and devotion to their families, and of their involvement in their religious communities, and we are struck by their ability to rejoice in the gifts their traditions have laid out for them. I have heard conservative women talk about how fulfilled they are because of their feelings of importance and the respect they receive from their family. We heard the voice of Naomi, who joined an Orthodox Jewish women's community because it was there that a Jewish woman can be herself. Often, when these women observe their more liberal neighbors and friends, they see children disobeying, husbands taking their wives for granted, and general discontent in the household. These observations tell the conservative that she has chosen the better way. If the progressive woman hears these positive perspectives from the more traditional wife and mother, and understands that she sees her role as liberating rather than restrictive, perhaps the progressive woman's need to raise her consciousness and make her more aware would be put to rest and understanding and acceptance would replace it.

On the other hand, if the conservative listens actively to the stories of progressive women with openness and trusts their sincerity, perhaps she will hear something much different from ego and selfishness. She will hear the spiritual journey of self-discovery and the awakening and acceptance of spiritual gifts. She will then hear the deep frustration at not being able to exercise these gifts because the male establishment has forbidden women to do so. The Orthodox Jew will hear Susannah Heschel's feelings of sorrow and hurt at being turned away from a synagogue when she wanted and needed to recite the *kaddish* (mourner's prayer) after her father's death. Heschel explains that the men making up the minyan told her that they were not able to pray with a woman present.[1] Conservative Catholics, if truly listening to the stories of the women who were ordained on the St. Lawrence Seaway, will realize that they are not simply defying the pope in order to obtain power, but that, after much prayer and discernment, they experienced a call to minister to the people of God, a call that would not be recognized by the male hierarchy solely on the basis of the women's gender. Also, although it may be extremely hard to hear, conservative Muslims will listen to the stories of American Muslims in the collection *Living Islam Out Loud*, not with judgment, but with compassion and understanding. They will hear why these women are following Islam and what moral obligations it imposes on them, and on society, even if the conservative women see these obligations as different from their own. To respect the progressive woman as being sincere in her obedience to and love of Allah is the point of the dialogue, not to try to convince her to obey in the more traditional way.

I am especially convinced that those who oppose homosexuality so vehemently have not really listened to the stories of those who grew up becoming slowly and painfully aware of their sexual orientation. The very word *homosexual*, like the words *abortion* or *feminist*, brings with it baggage that triggers an automatic response that prevents not only rational thought but the important ability to listen. The Judith Plaskows of Judaism, the Virginia Ramey Mollenkotts of Christianity, and the Khalida Saeds of Islam have very compelling stories to tell, stories that are crying out to be listened to. Besides being contrary to the purpose of dialogue, it would be offensive and much too simplistic to tell these women that they can or ought to change. It is in the telling of these stories that the conservative is most challenged to listen actively to the "other" and perhaps, just perhaps, to develop an understanding of her, for it is only through understanding that judgment can be suspended and bridges can be built.

RELATIONSHIP OF THE PAST TO THE PRESENT

Another major difference underlying the rifts between the conservative and progressive positions is their attitude toward their history. To the conservatives the ideas and doctrines that were formulated in the past are immutable, whereas to the progressives they are malleable and adaptable to modern circumstances. One's position on this issue depends on one's view of history and its relevance to the present day. The religions that we are dealing with are based on a sacred revelation that took place back in time, and each religion has grown considerably since then. But how have they grown? Some might think that they have grown only in numbers, with each new generation producing population growth and, in some cases, conversions as well. As a result, these religious traditions have had to accommodate larger numbers and diverse cultural expressions. According to the conservatives on the continuum, it is necessary that, wherever the religion is practiced and however many people are practicing it, the sacred doctrines remain intact (that is, as they were revealed) in order to represent the divine will or the founder's insight. For these people, history is a phenomenon of time rather than a process of change.

For those at other points along the continuum, history is an explanation of the present. It is not something to return to, but rather to build on.

For these people, tradition is a developmental process; all historic events, including the divine encounter, need to be understood within their contexts of time and place. Religious dogmas, then, can and must be developed in order for their message to be understood and practiced by new generations of people in various cultures.

Part of this disagreement about the development of doctrine has to do with the differing views about the moral worth of historical change. The conservatives view modern developments as bad; the progressives view them as good. The conservatives believe that modernity has brought with it some terrible attitudes and behaviors, to the great detriment to humankind. They attribute social ills to a growing secularism in which more trust is placed in an individual's talents and ego than in God's mercy or in spiritual discipline. Further, psychology has emphasized the importance of personal freedom and self-esteem to such an extent that there are no longer any firm moral guidelines by which to determine family structure or sexual norms. People tend to believe that what feels good is right, and one person's standards are not necessarily anyone else's. These modern-day attitudes have, according to the conservative, resulted in a disregard not only for objective moral codes, but also for religion, divine revelations, and sacred traditions. They view today's society as a chaotic world in which gender definitions are blurred and sexual mores generally ignored. When Lynn Davidman listened to modern Jewish women tell why they espoused strict Orthodoxy, she heard them say that they "were troubled by the confusion over gender in the wider society and by the lack of comfortable, established patterns for forming nuclear families."[2] In the same vein, evangelical Christians tell us in "The Danvers Statement" that modern culture is full of "uncertainty and confusion" and that changes in the Christian church are merely accommodations to the "spirit of the age at the expense of wisdom."[3] Perhaps the clearest condemnation of modernity comes from the conservative Muslim women. Many of them consider the modern world, exemplified in Western society, filled with rampant sexual immorality. Conservative Muslim women both in the United States and abroad respond to the modern social trends, especially the women's movement, by wearing the veil and maintaining the separation of the sexes in all but formal social situations until after marriage.

The progressives, on the other hand, see the good in modernity. While they do not deny that evils exist, they believe that progress in the scientific, social, and theological realms has, for the most part, resulted in greater respect and value being placed on the human person; this, in the progressive's eyes, reflects the divine will. Scientists are finding more and more cures for diseases; slavery, while still existing in some parts of the world, is now viewed as immoral; and racism and sexism are more in the spotlight of concern. The very fact that these issues are so glaringly in need of attention means that we have grown as a global society to recognize them, for it was not so long ago that slavery, infanticide, child labor, and gender and race discrimination were, for all but a few reformers, accepted practices. As a result, a seeming paradox occurs. The more we become conscious of social evils, the more we notice them; the more we take notice, the more there seem to be. However, taking notice means that we have become sensitized to the problems. So, if the world seems more evil now, perhaps it is because our moral conscience is developing. To put it another way, the worse society seems to be, the better we are becoming. What is more, the progressive believes that there is a direct link between the social world and faith in God. The most dramatic expression of this idea comes in the Christian Social Gospel and in liberation theology. The women who subscribe to these movements, such as Rosemary Ruether and Mary Hunt, believe that Christ liberated us not only on a spiritual level but on a worldly level as well. God is a God of justice and freedom; therefore, God's followers must work to bring about this justice and freedom in our world. Change, particularly social and theological change, say the progressives, is not always bad, because without it God's continuing work of redemption cannot be accomplished.

But how do these opposite points of view meet in dialogue? Although it is true that each sees modernity differently, it is also true that both views hold truth. No one can deny the increase in divorce rates, single-parent families, and sexual promiscuity. But at the same time, we also have to admit that there are some positive points to progress. There is an increased sense of justice and responsibility to work for it in the political, economic, and religious spheres throughout the world. Our global awareness has put us in touch with such grave issues as starvation, poverty, and the AIDS epidemic, so that we can no longer shut our eyes to these problems as we were able to do in the past. The world is truly a global village. Even the most conservative religious groups are recognizing this fact and using modern technology to communicate their message. Hence, all will admit modernity has its advantages. If we listen to the stories, we will be able to tell how each person has been affected by the changes in society and perhaps understand why some can embrace them and others must retreat from them. In either case we will know that there are two perspectives and appreciate that of the other.

NATURE OF RELIGIOUS AUTHORITY

The one factor that underlies the other three issues can be determined by asking some key questions. How do we know what to do or how to behave? How do we know what to believe? Whom can we trust to tell us the truth? The answers to these inquiries point to what each of us takes to be the authority in our religious life: What has to power to tell us what to do and what to believe as true? The final major difference between conservative and progressive believers is the nature of this religious authority. For the conservative religious woman, the authority that dictates what is good and true lies outside of her and is found either in the sacred texts or in the officials or teachers who have the power to interpret these texts. For the woman in the centrist position, the authority also lies in the texts or the official interpreters but is tempered by the belief that the text must be read in its historical and linguistic context. For the progressive religious woman the major authority that answers these questions lies within her after she has absorbed the underlying messages found in the texts and their sources. If anything in the texts or in the officials' interpretations does not match what she understands is the nature of God or the nature of the original insight, then that part cannot be authoritative. For example, if the God of monotheism has been revealed as a God of love and compassion, then any part of the text or institution that does not exhibit love and compassion must not be authoritative. If the original message of the Buddha was impermanence and the emptiness of all concepts, then to consider gender a reason for inequality must not be authoritative.

Misunderstandings abound among women on this issue. Progressives label conservatives narrow-minded when the latter continue to quote the text as proof of moral and doctrinal positions. Conservatives believe that progressives are denying the sacred authenticity of the texts and accuse them of ignoring specific passages and conveniently interpreting others to support their positions. Both sides claim that the other already has an agenda and is merely using the scriptures or the official teachings to support that agenda. However, what would happen if, after listening to the women's stories, each side trusted that the other's beliefs were truly formed out of its understanding of the text? What would happen if we understood that the other is as dedicated to the texts as we are? My suggestion is that, if we truly listened, we might not only gain an understanding of the other's position but also discover that the text itself can be understood in various ways.

When women speak of specific texts making a difference in their lives and in their relationship to their tradition, we are forced to listen to how they have interpreted these texts. What meaning are they deriving from these same words that others have read time and time again but never seen in quite the same way? For example, Conservative Jew Diana Villa gives an interesting interpretation of Deuteronomy 17:8–12. This passage, dealing with a court of priests and judges making decisions about criminal matters, is read by Villa as meaning that the "wise of each generation can reinterpret the law in accordance with its necessity, so that commandments may truly be upheld."[4] On the other hand, this text, which brought Villa to the point of accepting that some modern practices can be incorporated into the Jewish law, might be read by other Conservative

Jews to mean that the rabbi's decree must be obeyed. By the same token, conservative Christians read Saint Paul's words in Ephesians 5:21–23, which say that a husband is the head of his wife, to mean that wives should submit to the authority of their husbands. Progressives, however, believe that Paul was teaching about Christ's headship of the church by using an analogy from the old Greco-Roman household codes.[5] Muslim women have the same differences in interpreting the Qur'an's injunction to modesty; some view it as Allah's directive to wear a veil, and others think that modesty implies not a head covering but simply a woman's overall demeanor. Not only does the Qur'an contain such problematic passages, but Islam has the added problem of the disputed authority of the hadith and the shari'ah. There are hundreds of such disputed passages, and to discuss them would result in an unending and volatile debate. There is much that can be learned from discussion of the treatises on hermeneutics and scriptural criticism, but such learning is not the goal of the intra-religious dialogue that we are concerned with. The problem for us here is what to do with the differences in opinion about the authoritative sources of belief when engaged in an intra-religious dialogue.

If we remember that the purpose of our dialogue is mutual understanding and not conversion, then we must return to the telling of personal stories; it is in these stories that we come to appreciate the reasons why certain passages with certain interpretations take on so much authority in a woman's life. The conservative woman recognizes a need to be grounded in a conviction that serves the community as a whole. Such unity can be realized only when there is one authoritative source that guides and protects the community from error. She understands the problem of human limitation and recognizes that each of us, if left to our own devices to determine religious truths, would be isolated, for we are each unique. There must be some central unifying factor, and somehow people must agree on interpretations; someone must make certain educated decisions about how a text should be viewed. The stories that we have listened to from these conservative women reveal that they have looked to their authority, whether the text, the church, or the surrounding religious community, for such guidance, especially in a modern world fraught with moral ambiguity.

From the progressive's point of view such external authority itself is fraught with problems. Texts have the problem of language and historical context; the church has the problem of being a male power structure; and the surrounding religious community is often split on current issues. The progressive woman then must turn inward to search for the values that she has herself found—in her prayer and in her study of the texts—to find the anchor to which she can attach her religious beliefs and moral actions. Each side must admit that without both the external and internal guides, no authority can be adhered to absolutely. The progressive could not judge the conservative for looking to the text itself or to the officials for authoritative guidance. The conservative, on the other hand, after listening to personal stories, will understand that the progressive woman is not just randomly giving a text the meaning that best suits her situation but is using definite criteria by which the message can be discerned. Finally, each will see that the other has used the sacred text as a guide to her actions, even though the specifics within the pages are understood very differently. So in the end, although neither side will have converted the other, at least there will be a greater awareness of the diversity within the text and within the community's interpretation of it.

More than likely there are many more topics that would be on an agenda of a dialogue of women within the various religious traditions. Although this is not meant to be an exhaustive list, these four topics can provide matter for a fruitful discussion that, it is hoped, will break down barriers, dissolve animosities, and build bridges to a future of understanding and peace.

8

Hope for the Future

In the 1970s, during the huge tidal wave of change that swept over the Catholic Church, I taught theology and scripture in parishes made up of adults who were extremely upset that their church had been taken from them. The Gregorian chant, the Latin prayers, and the quiet privacy of Sunday Mass, which gave them a sense of the holy and lifted their minds and hearts to God, were no longer. Now the congregation members had to sing mediocre folk music and to greet the stranger sitting next to them instead of spending time in quiet prayer. All of this was quite upsetting. As I would listen to the complaints and try to explain the reasons for the change, I realized that the problem was not an intellectual one at all. The feeling of the sacred had been destroyed and replaced by a poor attempt to create community among strangers. What had happened, it seemed to me, was that the transformation of the ritual in most parishes was overwhelming. By this I mean that, in trying to bring the Catholic Church out of the Middle Ages and into the present, no vestige of the recognizable past remained. It seemed as if the old saying held true: The baby had been thrown out with the bath water.

On reflection, this situation said a lot about the process of change, particularly changes in sacred traditions, which is the concern of those on all points of the continuum. How do we change while remaining faithful? To do so, two things are essential: the administrative structure, or the guardians of the message; and the prophetic process, or that which enables adaptation. Without both, the religious tradition would never withstand the test of time. It is true that we have discussed in these pages many sects and divisions of the five religious traditions under consideration. However, the amazing fact is that, in spite of all their internal differences, each of these traditions maintains an essential identity. The different versions of each tradition all stem from one beginning in one era of time. It is true that influences varied, so the teachings took on different forms and, in some cases, were added to; nevertheless, they remained discernable and different from the teachings of other world religions. This consistency could not have happened had there not been some unifying factor that pulled in the strays and kept the underlying, basic message intact.

On the other hand, these traditions would not be around today if they had not been able to adapt to changing times. Only by such adaptation were they able to keep followers and attract new ones. Those traditions, such as the Shakers, that did not adapt did not survive. Innovations to the traditions did not come about easily or quickly; in fact, those that were not accepted by a community often caused one group to split from another. However, even in the splitting there was the element of returning to the intention of the founder while adapting the message for a new time. The Protestant Reformation returned to Jesus' message while making use of the printing press so individuals could read the Bible for themselves. The Reformed Jewish movement kept the Torah but adapted to the new status of citizens of the state. The Episcopal Church and various Protestant sects have maintained Christian rituals while incorporating the modern view of gender by ordaining women as priests and ministers. The point here is that the conservatives' purpose of maintaining the original message is essential for the continuance of the tradition, but so also is the progressives' message of the need for adaptation in order to carry the message from the past to the present.

On the theoretical level, the need for both perspectives may seem obvious. But our preconceptions and our stereotypes can cause us not to see the issues clearly. The truth is that both the conservative and the progressive perspectives are needed for a religion to stay alive. Conservatives need to conserve the essentials, and the progressives need to make sure that these essentials can be lived in the present.

Now, at the beginning of the twenty-first century, the world's scientific, technological, and intellectual progress is proceeding at such a rapid rate that education, politics, and businesses are finding it hard to keep up. This situation seems to be causing religious conservatives to work harder at protecting the message and progressives to work harder at trying to bring religion into the fray. As a result, the two extremes of our continuum, like two ends of a tug-of-war, are pulling harder and stronger, moving away from each other. It seems that the range of our continuum is getting larger and larger as the distance between the two ends expands. This situation is causing factions and animosities that militate against the peace toward which religions claim to be working. As long as interreligious dialogue ignores the conservative perspective and as long as conservatives believe that to conserve means to isolate, there will not be the mutual understanding so essential to laying the groundwork for peace.

Because it will take much caring and patience to hear each other into speech, and because I believe—although I realize not everyone will agree with me—women have been better at doing this, particularly in interreligious dialogue, I believe that the difficult task of bringing women on the two opposing ends of the continuum together can be accomplished by a women's dialogue. The evidence of such work exists in groups like the Women's Interfaith Institute in Seneca Falls, New York; Women Transcending Boundaries in Syracuse, New York; and the international Buddhist nuns' group, Sakyadhita. These groups are models for others that can help the cause of peace and mutual understanding.

Along with others in the interfaith movement, I look forward to the day when conservatives and progressives—and all those between—can join together to work for justice and to reach out to one another in mutual understanding and respect, bringing about a more peaceful and humane world.

Only then will the prophecy of Isaiah 65:25 have a chance to be fulfilled.

> The wolf and the lamb shall feed together,
>   the lion shall eat straw like the ox;
>   but the serpent—its food shall be dust!
> They shall not hurt or destroy on all my holy
>   mountain,
>   says the LORD.

Notes

PART I: UNDERSTANDING THE PROBLEM

1. CHALLENGES FOR A FRUITFUL DIALOGUE

1. Ingrid Schafer, ed., "The Power and Promise of Deep-Dialogue," Global Dialogue Institute (7 March 1998) (on WWW, 27 February 2007, astro.temple.edu/~dialogue/case.htm).

2. Institute for Interreligious Dialogue, 2001-3, "Introduction" (on WWW, 27 August 2007, iid.org.ir/IIDE/AboutUs.asp?Menu=2).

3. Hans Kung, "Replacing Clashes with Dialogue among Religions and Nations," in *War or Words*, ed. Donald W. Musser and D. Dixon Sutherland (Cleveland: The Pilgrim Press, 2005), 19.

4. Benjamin Hubbard, "Let's Talk: Some Christians Ignore Interfaith Dialogue," *Los Angeles Times,* January 11, 2004, B16.

5. Peter Huff, "The Challenge of Fundamentalism for Interreligious Dialogue," *Cross Currents 50*, no. 1-2 (Spring-Summer 2000) (on WWW, 27 February 2007, crosscurrents.org/Huff.htm).

6. Joan Chittister, "Calling the Power of Women," *Spirituality and Health* (October 2005), 36.

7. Majella Franzmann, *Women and Religion* (New York: Oxford University Press, 2000), 3.

8. Anne Davison, "Learning to Live in a Europe of Many Religions: A Curriculum for Interfaith Learning for Women." World Council of Churches (2000) (on WWW, 3 September 2005, wcc-coe.org/wcc/what/interreligious/cd35-18.html).

2. THE PROBLEM OF DEFINITIONS

1. Carol Schick, JoAnn Jaffe, and Ailsa M.Watkinson, "Considering Fundamentalism," in *Contesting Fundamentalisms*, ed. Carol Schick, JoAnn Jaffe, and Ailsa M. Watkinson (Halifax: Fernwood Publishing, 2004), 2-3.

2. Ibid., 7.

3. Janette Hassey, "Evangelical Women in Ministry a Century Ago," in *Discovering Biblical Equality: Complementarity without Hierarchy*, ed. Ronald W. Pierce and Rebecca Merrill Groothuis (Downers Grove, IL: InterVarsity Press, 2004), 55.

4. Ronald W. Pierce, "Contemporary Evangelicals for Gender Equality," in Pierce and Groothuis, 59.

5. F. Volker Greifenhagan, "Islamic Fundamentalism(s): More than a Pejorative Epithet?" in Schick, Jaffe, and Watkinson, *Contesting Fundamentalisms*, 63-75.

6. Ibid.

7. Arij A. Roest Crollius, SJ, "Interreligious Dialogue: Can It Be Sincere?" *SEDOS Bulletin on Net* (20 July 2000) (on WWW, 19 July 2005, sedos.org/english/Crollius.html).

8. Linda E. Thomas, "Womanist Theology, Epistemology, and a New Anthropological Paradigm," *Cross Currents* (Summer 1998) (on WWW, crosscurrents.org/thomas.htm).

9. Ibid.

10. Susannah Heschel, "Judaism," in *Her Voice, Her Faith: Women Speak on World Religions*, ed. Arvind Sharma and Katherine K. Young (Boulder, CO: Westview Press, 2003), 151.

3. CONFLICTING VIEWPOINTS IN JUDAISM, CHRISTIANITY, AND ISLAM

1. Leila Gal Berner, "Hearing Hannah's Voice," in *Daughters of Abraham*, ed. Yvonne Yazbeck Haddad and John L. Esposito (Gainesville: University Press of Florida, 2001), 35.

2. Pnina Nave Levinson, "Women and Sexuality: Traditions and Progress," in *Women, Religion, and Sexuality*, ed. Jeanne Becher (Philadelphia: Trinity Press International, 1990), 47.

3. Wendy Wolfe Fine, "Modern Orthodox Judaism as an Option for Professional Women," *Journal of Jewish Communal Service* (Winter/Spring 1995): 154.

4. Shoshana Nannas, "Feminism within Ultra-Orthodoxy," *The Jewish Observer* (October 1998), 44.

5. *Judaism 101: A Glossary of Basic Jewish Terms and Concepts*, a project of the Union of Orthodox Jewish Congregations of America (on WWW, 12 October 2005, ou.org/about/judaism/m.htm).

6. Lynn Davidman, *Tradition in a Rootless World: Women Turn to Orthodox Judaism* (Berkeley and Los Angeles: University of California Press, 1991), 49.

7. Ibid., 109.

8. Quoted in Davidman, *Tradition in a Rootless World*, 130.

9. "Who We Are," JOFA: Jewish Orthodox Feminist Alliance (on WWW, 13 October 2005, jofa.org/about.php/about).

10. Blu Greenberg, "Orthodox, Feminist, and Proud of It," Beliefnet, Inc. (2004) (on WWW, 8 October 2005, beliefnet.com/story/47/story_4714.html).

11. Ibid.

12. Fine, "Modern Orthodox Judaism," 162.

13. Rochelle Furstenberg, "The Flourishing of Higher Jewish Learning for Women," *Jerusalem Letter* (26 Nissan 5760/1 May 2000) (on WWW, 8 October 2005, jcpa.org/jl/jl429.htm).

14. Ibid.

15. Adena Berkowitz, "An Orthodox Feminist Speaks—In Response to Our Critics." *JOFA Journal* (Winter 1999-Shevat 5759) (on WWW, 8 October 2005, jofa.org/pdf/JofaWinter1999.pdf).

16. Malka Bina, quoted in Furstenberg, "Flourishing," 13.

17. Wendy Amsellem, "Living within My Era," Drisha Institute for Jewish Education (on WWW, 9 October 2005, drish.org/viewpoints/wendyamsellem).

18. Melissa Nunes-Harwitt, "Masekhet Sukkah," Drisha Institute for Jewish Education (on WWW, 9 October 2005, drisha.org/viewpoints_archive/melissa_nunesharwitt.htm).

19. Furstenberg, "Flourishing," 10.

20. Greenberg, "Orthodox, Feminist, and Proud of It."

21. Susannah Heschel, "Judaism," in *Her Voice, Her Faith*, ed. Arvind Sharma and Katherine K. Young (Boulder, CO: Westview Press, 2003), 148.

22. Ibid.

23. Lisa Katz, "All about Judaism Branches of Judaism," on the About Religion and Spirituality website (on WWW, 11 October 2005, judaism.about.com/od/conservativejudaism/Conservative_Judaism.htm).

24. See "Studies and Responsa," JTS: The Rabbinical School (on WWW, jtsa.edu/rabbinical/women/excerpts.shtml).

25. Dr. Anne Lapidus Lerner, "On the Rabbinic Ordination of Women," JTS: The Rabbinical School (on WWW, 15 October 2005, shamash.org/lists/scj-faq/HTML/faq/08-02.html).

26. Judith Hauptman, "The Challenge Facing the Conservative Movement," *The Jewish Week* (7 August 2005) (also available on WWW, 22 May 2007, shefanetwork.org/shefajournal5766.pdf).

27. Diana Villa, "The Status of Women in the Halacha," *Hagshama* 11 (January 2001) (on WWW, 11 October 2005, wzo.org.il/en/resources/view.asp?id+152).

28. Helene Aylon, "Jewish Women and the Feminist Revolution," Jewish Women's Archive (on WWW, 14 October 2005, jwa.org/feminism/_html/JWA002.htm).

29. Judith Plaskow, "Transforming the Nature of Community: Toward a Feminist People of Israel," in *After Patriarchy: Feminist Transformations of the Word Religions*, ed. Paula M. Cooey, William R. Eakin, and Jay F. McDaniel (Maryknoll, NY: Orbis Books, 1991), 98.

30. Plaskow, "Transforming," 102.

31. Drorah Setel, in Maura O'Neill, *Women Speaking, Women Listening* (Maryknoll, NY: Orbis Books, 1990), 72.

32. E. M. Broner, "Jewish Women and the Feminist Revolution," Jewish Women's Archive (on WWW, 14 October 2005, jwa.org/feminism/_html/JWA006.htm).

33. Savina Teubal, "Jewish Women and the Feminist Revolution," Jewish Women's Archives (on WWW, 14 October 2005, jwa.org/feminism/_html/JWA006.htm).

34. Heschel, "Judaism," 167.

35. Maria-Teresa Porcile-Santiso, "Roman Catholic Teachings on Female Sexuality," in Becher, *Women, Religion, and Sexuality*, 199.

36. Kim Pennington, "Resources for Women," The Council on Biblical Manhood and Womanhood (on WWW, 7 November 2005, cbmw.org/resources/women-intro.php).

37. "The Danvers Statement," The Council on Biblical Manhood and Womanhood (2005) (on WWW, 8 November 2005, cbmw.org/about/danvers.php).

38. Rebecca Jones, "Does Christianity Squash Women?" speech, Bryn Mawr, April 2000, (on WWW, 8 November 2005, www.cbmw.org/resources/articles/christianityandwomen.pdf).

39. Thomas Aquinas, cited in Rosemary Radford Ruether, "Catholicism, Women, Body and Sexuality: A Response," in Becher, *Women, Religion, and Sexuality,* 221.

40. Ibid., 222.

41. David Wegener, "Southern Baptists Lead the Way: CBMW Interview with SBC Committee Member Dr. Dorothy Patterson," *Journal for Biblical Manhood and Womanhood* (Summer 1998): 3.

42. Dorothy Patterson, "The High Calling of Wife and Mother in Biblical Perspective," in *Recovering Biblical Manhood and Womanhood: A Response to Evangelical Feminism,* ed. John Piper and Wayne Grudem (Wheaton, IL: Crossway Books, 1991), 372.

43. Carolyn McCulley, "Liberated from Feminism: The Personal Testimony of Carolyn McCulley," The Council on Biblical Manhood and Womanhood (2005) (on WWW, 8 November 2005, cbmw.org/resources/articles/mcculley.php).

44. Diane Knippers, quoted in Laurie Goldstein and David D. Kirkpatrick, "Conservative Group Amplifies Voice of Protestant Orthodoxy," *New York Times,* 22 May 2004 (on WWW, 10 October 2005, theocracywatch.org/split_churches _times_may22_04.htm).

45. Jones, "Does Christianity Squash Women?"

46. Women for Faith and Family, "Affirmation for Catholic Women" (2005) (on WWW, 15 November 2005, wf-f.org/EngAff.html).

47. "The Danvers Statement."

48. Women for Faith and Family, "Affirmation for Catholic Women."

49. John Paul II, *Ordinatio Sacerdotalis* (May 1994), on Women for Faith and Family website (on WWW, 15 November 2005, wf-f.org/OrdSac.html).

50. Women for Faith and Family, "Affirmation for Catholic Women."

51. Christians for Biblical Equality, "Men, Women, and Biblical Equality" (1989-2005) (on WWW, 7 November 2005, cbeinternational.org/new/about/ biblical_equality.shtml).

52. Rebecca Merrill Groothuis and Ronald W. Pierce, "Introduction," in *Discovering Biblical Equality: Complementarity without Hierarchy,* ed. Ronald W. Pierce and Rebecca Merrill Groothuis (Downers Grove, IL: InterVarsity Press, 2004), 14.

53. Ibid., 17.

54. Christians for Biblical Equality, "Men, Women, and Biblical Equality," creation, no. 5.

55. Christiane Carlson-Thies, "Man and Woman at Creation: A Critique of Complementarian Interpretations," *Priscilla Papers* (Fall 2004) (WWW, 7 November 2005, cbeinternational.org/new/free_articles/ManandWomanatCreation.pdf).

56. Ibid.

57. Christians for Biblical Equality, "Men, Women, and Biblical Equality," family, no. 3.

58. Groothuis and Pierce, "Introduction," 16.

59. John Paul II, *Familiaris Consortio* (Rome: Libreria Editrice Vaticana, 1981) (on WWW, 10 November 2005, vatican.va/holy_father/john_paul_ii/apost _exhortations/documents/hf_jp-ii_exh_1911122_familiaris-consortio_en.html).

60. United States Conference of Catholic Bishops, *Follow the Way of Love: A Pastoral Message to Families* (1994) (on WWW, 10 November 2005, usccb.org/ laity/follow.shtml).

61. Julie Ingersoll, *Evangelical Christian Women: War Stories in the Gender Battles* (New York: New York University Press, 2003), 42-43.

62. William J. Webb, "Gender Equality and Homosexuality," in Pierce and Groothuis, *Discovering Biblical Equality*, 401.

63. Joseph Cardinal Ratzinger, "Letter to Bishops of the Catholic Church on the Collaboration of Men and Women in the Church and in the World" (31 July 2004) (on WWW, 7 April 2007, www.vatican.va/roman_curia/congregations/cfaith/documents/rc_con_cfaith_doc_20040731_collaboration_en.html).

64. John Allen, *Talk of the Nation*, National Public Radio, 29 November 2005.

65. Fr. Joseph Fessio, *News Hour with Jim Lehrer*, Online News Hour, 29 November 2005 (on WWW, 1 December 2005, pbs.org/newshour/newshour_index.html).

66. Ted Olsen, "Weblog: Methodist Court Acquits Homosexual Minister," *Christianity Today* (22 March 2004) (on WWW, 1 December 2005, christianitytoday.com/ct/2004/112/11.0.html).

67. Jan Nunley, "Two Southern California Parishes Vote Alignment with Uganda Diocese," *Episcopal News Service* (17 August 2004) (on WWW, 27 November 2005, episcopalchurch.org/3577_48614_ENG_HTM.htm).

68. Pamela D. H. Cochran, *Evangelical Feminism* (New York: New York University Press, 2005), 178.

69. "About EEWC," Evangelical and Ecumenical Women's Caucus (on WWW, 22 June 2005, eewc.com/About.htm).

70. Ann Eggebroten, "On Being Evangelical and Ecumenical," *EEWC Update: Newsletter of the Evangelical and Ecumenical Women's Caucus* (Summer 2003) (on WWW, 6 November 2005, eewc.com/Update/Summer2003OnBeing.htm).

71. Ibid.

72. Peggy Michael-Rush, "A Reluctant Feminist," *EEWC Update: Newsletter of the Evangelical and Ecumenical Women's Caucus* (Spring 2004) (on WWW, 6 November 2005, eewc.com/Update/Spring2004Reluctant.htm).

73. Virginia Ramey Mollenkott, "Feminism and Evangelicalism," *EEWC Update: Newsletter of the Evangelical and Ecumenical Women's Caucus* (Spring 2005) (on WWW, 6 November 2005, eewc.com/Update/Spring2005Feminism.htm).

74. Ibid.

75. United Methodist Church, "Women and Men," in *The Book of Discipline of the United Methodist Church, 2004* (Nashville, TN: United Methodist Publishing House, 2004).

76. United Methodist Church, "The Status of Women," *The Book of Resolutions of the United Methodist Church, 2004* (Nashville, TN: The United Methodist Publishing House, 2004).

77. "Historian: Women's Place in Methodism Inconsistent," United Methodist News Service (20 August 2003).

78. United Methodist Church, "Equal Rights Regardless of Sexual Orientation," in *The Book of Discipline, 2004*.

79. "The United Church of Christ: A Family of Faith for a Global Community" (on WWW, 8 November 2005, ucc.org/aboutus/family.htm).

80. Ibid.

81. Rev. Mike Schuenemeyer, "About Our Lesbian, Gay, Bisexual and Transgender [LGBT] Ministries," United Church of Christ (on WWW, 8 November 2005, ucc.org/lgbt/about.htm).

82. Ibid.

83. WOC, "Introduction" (on WWW, 3 December 2005, womensordination .org/intro.html).

84. Roman Catholic Womenpriests, "Mission" (2005) (on WWW, 5 December 2005, romancatholicwomenpriests.org/index.htm).

85. WOC, "Why Ordination" (on WWW, 5 December 2005, womensordination .org/why.html).

86. Ibid.

87. Dr. Judith Johnson, "Ordination on the St. Lawrence," *New Women, New Church* (Winter 2004-5) (on WWW, 5 December 2005, womensordination .org/pages/art_pages/art_2005Ord.htm).

88. Ibid.

89. Rev. Paula D. Nesbitt, Ph.D., "Women's Ordination: Problems and Possibilities," WOC 2000 Plenary Talks, Women's Ordination Conference (on WWW, 3 December 2005, womensordination.org/pages/art_pages/Nesbitt.htm).

90. Elisabeth Schüssler Fiorenza, *In Memory of Her* (New York: Crossroads, 1983), xix-xx.

91. Elisabeth Schüssler Fiorenza, *Wisdom Ways* (Maryknoll, NY: Orbis Books, 2005), 175.

92. Schüssler Fiorenza, *In Memory of Her*, 32.

93. Elisabeth Schüssler Fiorenza, "We Are Church—A Kingdom of Priests," Catholic Network of Women's Equality (22 July 2005) (on WWW, 7 December 2005, cnwe.org/WOW-AKindom-ElisabethSFtalk.doc).

94. Rosemary Radford Ruether, "Christian Feminist Theology," in *Daughters of Abraham: Feminist Thought in Judaism, Christianity, and Islam*, ed. Yvonne Yazbeck Haddad and John L. Esposito (Gainesville: University Press of Florida, 2001), 66-67.

95. Rosemary Radford Ruether, *Sexism and God-Talk: Toward a Feminist Theology* (Boston: Beacon Press, 1983), 18.

96. Ibid., 70.

97. Ruether, "Christian Feminist Theology," 70.

98. Rosemary Radford Ruether, "The Church as Liberation Community from Patriarchy: The Praxis of Ministry as Discipleship of Equals," Catholic Network for Women's Equality (5 August 2005) (on WWW, 4 December 2005, cnwe.org/ wowtalk.doc).

99. Mary Hunt, "Different Voices Different Choices: Feminist Perspectives on Ministry—A Contribution from the United States," talk presentd at WOW conference, 23 July 2005 (on WWW, 4 December 2005, cnwe.org/ DifferentVoicesMaryHuntWOWtal.doc).

100. Hibba Abugideiri, "My Faith, My Sustaining Guide," in *Geography of Religion: Where God Lives, Where Pilgrims Walk,* ed. Susan Tyler Hitchcock with John L. Esposito (Washington, DC: National Geographic Society, 2004), 386.

101. Muhammad Hashim Kamali, "Law and Society," in *The Oxford History of Islam,* ed. John L. Esposito (New York: Oxford University Press, 1999), 118.

102. Michael M. J. Fischer and Mehdi Abedi, *Debating Muslims: Cultural Dialogues in Postmodernity and Tradition* (Madison: University of Wisconsin Press, 1990), 103.

103. Asma Barlas, *Believing Women in Islam* (Austin: University of Texas Press, 2002), 33.

104. Fisher and Abedi, *Debating Muslims,* 97.

105. Sheila S. Blair and Jonathan M. Bloom, "Art and Architecture: Themes and Variations," in Esposito, *The Oxford History of Islam,* 230.

106. Fisher and Abedi, *Debating Muslims,* 102.

107. Riffat Hassan, "An Islamic Perspective," in Becher, *Women, Religion, and Sexuality,* 93.

108. Barlas, *Believing Women in Islam,* 42.

109. Hassan, "An Islamic Perspective," 94.

110. Leila Ahmed, *Women and Gender in Islam* (New Haven, CT: Yale University Press, 1992), 225.

111. *The Holy Qur'an: English Translation of the Meanings and Commentary* (Madinah, Saudi Arabia: King Fahd Holy Qur'an Printing Complex, n.d.).

112. Ahmed, *Women and Gender in Islam,* chap. 8.

113. Emran Qureshi and Heba Raouf Ezzat, "Are Sharia Laws and Human Rights Compatible?" Qantara.de: Dialogue with the Islamic World (11 December 2004) (on WWW, 28 December 2005, qantara.de/webcom/show_article.php/_c-373/nr-6/i.html 2.

114. Omaima Abou-Bakr, "A Muslim Woman's Reflections on Gender" (on WWW, 13 March 2007, crescentlife.com/thisthat/feminist%20muslims/muslim_womans_reflection_on_gender.htm).

115. Amina Wadud, "A'ishah's Legacy," *New Internationalist* 345 (May 2002) (on WWW, 27 December 2005, newint.org/issue 345/legacy.htm).

116. Sayyid Qutb, as quoted in Roxanne D. Marcotte, "Egyptian Islamists and the Status of Muslim Women Question," *Journal for the Study of Religions and Ideologies* (Summer 2005) (on WWW, 13 March 2007, jsri.ro/old/html%20version/index/no_11/roxannedmarcotte-articol.htm).

117. Marcotte, "Egyptian Islamists."

118. Sahba Mohammad, "Zainab Al-Ghazali Dies at 88," *Al-Abrar* (3 August 2005) (on WWW, 22 December 2005, abrar.org.uk/English/modules.php?name=News&file=article&sid=2120).

119. Marya Bangee, "The Flight of Our Rights: Zaynab al-Ghazali," *Alkalima* (October 2005) (on WWW, 22 December 2005, alkalima.com/?page=Archives&vol=8&issue=1&id=90).

120. Heba Raouf Ezzat, quoted in Marcotte, "Egyptian Islamists."

121. Heba Raouf Ezzat, "Women and the Interpretation of Islamic Sources," Islam21—International Forum for Islamic Dialogue (October 1999) (on WWW, 4 January 2006, crescentlife.com/thisthat/feminist%20muslims/women_and_interpretation_of_islamic_sources.htm).

122. Heba Raouf Ezzat, "Rethinking Secularism . . . Rethinking Feminism" (7 January 2002 (on WWW, 4 January 2006, islamonline.net/English/contemporary/2002/07/Article01.shtml).

123. Madeleine Bunting, "Can Islam Liberate Women?" *Guardian Unlimited,* 8 December 2001 (on WWW, 26 December 2005, guardian.co.uk/Archive/Article/0,4273,4314573,00.html).

124. Dr. Lois Lamya al-Faruqi, "Women in Qur'anic Society" (20 October 2004) (on WWW, 28 December 2005, crescentlife.com/thisthat/feminist%20muslims/women_in_quranic_society.htm).

125. Dr. Lois Lamya al-Faruqi, "Islamic Traditions and the Feminist Movement: Confrontation or Co-operation" (20 October 2004) (on WWW, 28 December

2005, crescentlife.com/thisthat/feminist%20muslims/islam_and_feminist
_movement.htm).

126. Carolyn Moxley Rouse, *Engaged Surrender* (Berkeley and Los Angeles: University of California Press, 2004), 17.

127. Ibid., xiv.

128. Ibid., 29.

129. Ibid., 39.

130. Ibid., 28.

131. Geneive Abdo, *No God But God: Egypt and the Triumph of Islam* (Oxford: Oxford University Press, 2000), 142.

132. Zaynab Al-Ghazali, quoted in Paula Dear, "Women Vow to Protect Muslim Hijab," *Al-Abrar* (15 June 2004) (on WWW, 22 December 2005, abrar.org.uk/ English/modules.php?name+News&file=article&sid=618).

133. Abdo, *No God But God,* 149.

134. Ahmed, *Women and Gender in Islam,* 152.

135. Ibid., 165.

136. Bunting, "Can Islam Liberate Women?" 1.

137. Abdo, *No God But God,* 158.

138. Ibid., 142.

139. Ibid., 158.

140. Ahmed, *Women and Gender in Islam,* 223.

141. Abdo, *No God But God,* 145.

142. Marlise Simons, "Muslim Women in Europe Claim Rights and Keep Faith," *The New York Times,* 28 December 2005.

143. Riffat Hassan, "Muslim Women and Post-Patriarchal Islam," in Cooey, Eakin, and McDaniel, *After Patriarchy*, 42.

144. Amina Wadud-Muhsin, *Qur'an and Woman* (Malayasia: Penerbit Fajar Bakti Sdn. Bhd. 1992), iv, vi.

145. Ibid., 7.

146. Hassan, "An Islamic Perspective," 116.

147. Hassan, "Muslim Women," 53-54.

148. Ibid., 60-61.

149. Fatima Mernissi, *The Veil and the Male Elite,* trans. Mary Jo Lakeland (Menlo Park, CA: Addison-Wesley Publishing Co., 1991), 79.

150. Ibid., 3.

151. Ahmed, *Women and Gender in Islam,* 55.

152. Mernissi, *The Veil and the Male Elite,* 81.

153. Barlas, *Believing Women in Islam,* xi.

154. Ibid., 11.

155. Ibid., 13.

156. Ibid., 17.

157. Amina Wadud, *Inside the Gender Jihad: Women's Reform in Islam* (Oxford: Oneworld Publications, 2006), 8.

158. Saleemah Abdul-Ghafur, "Introduction," in *Living Islam Out Loud: American Muslim Women Speak,* ed. Saleemah Abdul-Ghafur (Boston: Beacon Press, 2005), 6.

159. Saleemah Abdul-Ghafur, "Saleemah's Story," in Abdul-Ghafur, *Living Islam Out Loud,* 15.

160. Yousra Y. Fazili, "Fumbling toward Ecstasy," in Abdul-Ghafur, *Living Islam Out Loud*, 75.

161. Mohja Kahf, "The Muslim in the Mirror," in Abdul-Ghafur, *Living Islam Out Loud*, 133-134.

162. Khalida Saed, "On the Edge of Belonging," in Abdul-Ghafur, *Living Islam Out Loud*, 90.

163. Ibid., 92.

164. Precious Rasheeda Muhammad, "To be Young, Gifted, Black, American, Muslim, and Woman," in Abdul-Ghafur, *Living Islam Out Loud*, 45.

165. Afra Jalabi, "To Veil or not to Veil, That Is the Question." *Muslim Access* (on WWW, 14 March 2007, muslimaccess.com/articles/Women/to_veil_or _not.asp).

4. CONFLICTING VIEWPOINTS IN HINDUISM AND BUDDHISM

1. Susan Tyler Hitchcock and John L. Esposito, *Geography of Religion: Where God Lives, Where Pilgrims Walk* (Washington, DC: National Geographic Society, 2004), 121.

2. Urvashi Butalia, "Mother India," *New Internationalist Magazine* (15 November 2005) (on WWW, 19 April 2006, newint.org/issue277/mother.htm).

3. Jyotsna Chatterji, "Introduction," in *Religions and the Status of Women*, ed. Jyotsna Chatterji (New Delhi: Uppal Publishing House, 1990), 1.

4. Vishwa Hindu Parishad (UK), *Explaining Hindu Dharma: A Guide for Teachers,* 2nd ed. (Surrey: VHP, 2003), 7.

5. Sri Swami Sivananda, *The Vedas*, The Divine Life Society (18 January 2000) (on WWW, 4 May 2006, dlshq.org/religions/vedas.htm).

6. "Vedas," The Hindu Universe (on WWW, 4 May 2006, hindunet.org/vedas).

7. "The Vedas," in *Hinduism,* Internet Sacred Text Archives (on WWW, 4 May 2006, sacred_texts.com/hin/index.htm).

8. Sara S. Mitter, *Dharma's Daughters: Contemporary Indian Women and Hindu Culture* (New Brunswick, CT: Rutgers University Press, 1991), 73.

9. Vishwa Hindu Parishad, *Explaining Hindu Dharma,* 127.

10. "Ramayana," in *The Columbia Encyclopedia*, 6th ed. (2001-5) (on WWW, 6 May 2006, bartleby.com/65/ra/Ramayana.html).

11. V. Krishnan, *Utthara Ramayana* (on WWW, 6 May 2006, geocities.com/ Athens/Styx/7153/Utthara.html).

12. Mitter, *Dharma's Daughters,* 85.

13. Mary McGee, "Ritual Rights: The Gender Implications of *Adhikara*," in *Jewels of Authority*, ed. Laurie L. Patton (Oxford: Oxford University Press, 2002), 47.

14. V. SadagOpan, "Women in Sri Vaishnavam," in *Indian Culture and Philosophy* (13 April 2006) (on WWW, 4 May 2006, india-forum.com/articles/ 113/1/Women in Sri-Vaishnavam).

15. Ibid.

16. Sushila Patil and Moses Seenarine, "Letter to Gargi," *Saxakali Publications,* 15 August 1996 (on WWW, 6 May 2006, saxakali.com/Saxakali-Publications/ gargi.htm).

17. Soma Das, "Laws of Manu or 'Manava Dharma Shastra,'" in *Hinduism* (on WWW, 16 May 2006, hinduism.about.com/library/weekly/aa051303a.htm).

18. Mitter, *Dharma's Daughters*, 88.

19. Vishwa Hindu Parishad, *Explaining Hindu Dharma*, 152.

20. Mitter, *Dharma's Daughters*, 88.

21. "Laws of Manu," *Sacred Books of the East*, vol. 25, trans. George Buhler (1886), Internet Sacred Text Archive (on WWW, 15 March 2007, sacred-texts.com/hin/manu/manu03.htm).

22. Ibid.

23. Prabhati Mukherjee, *Hindu Women: Normative Models* (London: Sangam Books, 1993), 96.

24. Julia Leslie, "Suttee or Sati: Victim or Victor?" *Roles and Rituals for Hindu Women*, ed. Julia Leslie (Rutherford, NJ: Fairleigh Dickinson University Press, 1991), 184.

25. Vrushali Kene, interview with author, 1 May 2006.

26. *Valmiki Ramayana: Ayodhya Kanda*, trans. Desiraju Hanumanta Roa and K. M. K. Murthy, 2000 (on WWW, 18 May 2006, valmikiramayan.net/ayodhya/sarga29/ayodhya_29_frame.htm).

27. Raj Pruthi and Bela Rani Sharma, *Aryans and Hindu Women* (New Dilhi: Anmol Publications, 1995), 149-150.

28. Mitter, *Dharma's Daughters*, 86.

29. "Ramayana."

30. Swamini Niranjanananda, "Reinstating Women's Roles in Religion," Women's Initiative speech presented at Amritavarsham-50, 24-27 September 2003 (on WWW, 19 April 2006, amritavarsham.org/summit/women/niranjana.htm).

31. Nanditha Krishna, "The Equals of Men," *Newindpress on Sunday* (on WWW, 19 April 2006, newindpress.com/sunday/colItems.asp?ID=SEC20030803031539).

32. V. L. Manjul, "Starting Vedic Studies: Backed by Scripture, Girls Get Their Sacred Thread," *Hinduism Today* (31 December 2002), 59.

33. Pruthi and Rani Sharma, *Aryans and Hindu Women*, 49, 60.

34. Meena Khandelwal, *Women in Ochre Robes: Gendering Hindu Renunciation* (Albany: State University of New York, 2004), 36.

35. Katherine K. Young, "*Om*, the Vedas, and the Status of Women with Special Reference to Srivaisnavism," in *Jewels of Authority*, ed. Laurie L. Patton (Oxford: Oxford University Press, 2002), 89-90.

36. Sandra P. Robinson, "Hindu Paradigms of Women: Images and Values," in *Women, Religion, and Social Change*, ed. Yvonne Yazbeck Haddad and Ellison Banks Findly, 181-216 (Albany: University of New York Press, 1985), 192.

37. Mitter, *Dharma's Daughters*, 88.

38. Lina Gupta, "Ganga: Purity, Pollution, and Hinduism," *Ecofeminism and the Sacred*, ed. Carol J. Adams (New York: Continuum, 1993), 106.

39. Krishna, "The Equals of Men," 3.

40. Mitter, *Dharma's Daughters*, 90.

41. Lina Gupta, quoted in Maura O'Neill, *Women Speaking, Women Listening: Women in Interreligious Dialogue* (Maryknoll, NY: Orbis Books, 1990), 84.

42. Pruthi and Rani Sharma, *Aryans and Hindu Women*, 49.

43. Vishwa Hindu Parishad, *Explaining Hindu Dharma*, 99.

44. Robinson, "Hindu Paradigms of Women," 199.

45. June McDaniel, *Making Virtuous Daughters and Wives* (Albany: State University of New York Press, 2003), xii.

46. Paras Ramoutar, "Criticism and Acclaim Greet Trinidad's First Woman Priest," *Hinduism Today* (February 1994) (on WWW, 6 May 2006, hinduismtoday .com/archives/1994/2/1994-2-01.shtml).

47. Vasudha Narayanan, "Respected Guardians of Our Ancient Faith," *Welcome to Navya Shastra* (on WWW, 24 May 2006, shastras.org/VasudhaNarayanan .html).

48. Ramoutar, "Criticism and Acclaim," 7

49. "Women Priests for the Jet Age," *The Times of India* (23 June 2002) (on WWW, 23 May 2006, timesofindia.indiatimes.com/articleshow/13804983.cms).

50. V. L. Manjul, "Starting Vedic Studies," 2.

51. Krishna, "The Equals of Men," 5.

52. Patil and Seenarine, "Letter to Gargi," 4.

53. Madhu Kishwar, "Women's Politics," in *In Search of Answers: Indian Women's Voices from Manushi, A Selection from the First Five Years from a Feminist Magazine*, ed. Madhu Kishwar and Ruth Vanita (London: Zed Books, 1984), 245.

54. Dr. Arun Gandhi, quoted in Vikram Masson, "Hindu Group Asks Religious Leaders to End Caste Discrimination and to Save the Vedas," Navya Shastra, 27 November 2003 (on WWW, 24 May 2006, shastras.org/PressRelease3.html).

55. Soma Sablok, "Women in Vedas" (on WWW, 24 May 2006, geocities.com/ Athens/Pantheon/4789/Articles/Womenwomen_in_vedas.html?).

56. Mitter, *Dharma's Daughters*, 72.

57. Nelia Beth Scovill, "The Liberation of Women in Religious Sources," The Religious Consultation on Population, Reproductive Health, and Ethics (on WWW, 24 May 2006, religiousconsultation.org/liberation.htm#Hinduism).

58. Vashudha Narayanan, "Hinduism," in *Her Voice, Her Faith*, ed. Arvind Sharma and Katherine Young (Boulder, CO: Westview Press, 2003), 14.

59. Sri Swami Sivananda, "Hindu Law-Givers: The Hindu Law-Givers in the Hindu Scriptures," Oneness Commitment (on WWW, 18 May 2006, experiencefestival .com/a/Hindu_Law-Givers/id/22607).

60. Dr. Jaishree Gopal, quoted in Navya Shastra, "Navya Shastra Endorses Government of India Plan to Examine Laws of Manu," press release (on WWW, 24 May 2006, shastras.org/PressRelease12.html).

61. Swami Vivekananda, *The Message of Vivekananda* (Calcutta: Advaita Ashrama, 2000), 17.

62. Narayanan, "Hinduism," 57.

63. Linda Hess, "Rejecting Sita: Indian Responses to the Ideal Man's Cruel Treatment of His Ideal Wife," *Journal of the American Academy of Religion* 67 (1999): 17.

64. Ibid., 18.

65. Sukuma Azhicode, quoted in Prema Nandakumar, "Indian Epic Narrative— Alive and Vibrant" (24 April 2006) (on WWW, 28 May 2006, boloji.com/culture/ 007.htm).

66. Hess, "Rejecting Sita," 20.

67. Snehalata Reddy, *Sita*, quoted in ibid., 18.

68. "Sita, Speak," *Passages to India*, Independent Broadcasting Associates Inc., 2002 (on WWW, 27 May 2006, ibaradio.org/India/passages/passages.htm).

69. Nabaneeta Dev Sen, quoted in Hess, "Rejecting Sita," 21.

70. Nabaneeta Dev Sen, "Translating Chandrabati," Center for Women's Development Studies (2006) (on WWW, 19 April 2006, cwds.org/chandrabati/htm).

71. Nabaneeta Dev Sen, "Lady Sings the Blues: When Women Retell the Rama yana," *Manushi* 108 (on WWW, 15 March 2007, ninopaley.com/Sitayana/Manushi _LadySingstheBlues.html).

72. C. N. Sreekantan Nair and Sarah Joseph, *Retelling the Ramayana: Voices from Kerala*, trans. Vasanthi Sankaranarayanan (New Delhi: Oxford University Press, 2005), xviii.

73. Ibid., 108.

74. Ibid., 115.

75. Sowmya Aji Mehu, "Ramayana Gets a Feminist Twist," *The Times of India*, 12 August 2005 (on WWW, 27 May 2006, timesofindia.indiatimes.com/ articleshow/msid-1198690,curpg-1.cms).

76. Sakshi Juneja, "Searching for Sita," To Each His Own (17 November 2005) (on WWW, 27 May 2006, sakshijuneja.com/blog/2005/11/17/searching-for-sita).

77. One detailed summary of the Pali Canon's account of the Buddha's early life and awakening can be found in Richard H. Robinson, Willard L. Johnson, and Thanissaro Bhikkhu, *Buddhist Religions: A Historical Introduction*, 5th ed. (Belmont, CA: Wadsworth, 2005), 5-11.

78. The Dzogchen Ponlop Rinpoche, "What the Buddha Taught," *Shambala Sun* (May 2006), 42.

79. Ibid., 46.

80. Robinson, Johnson, and Bhikkhu, *Buddhist Religions*, 62.

81. Ibid., 63.

82. Burton Watson, trans., *The Lotus Sutra* (New York: Columbia University Press, 1993), xii.

83. Ibid., vix.

84. Ibid., xv.

85. Ibid.

86. Diana Y. Paul, *Women in Buddhism: Images of the Feminine in Mahayana Tradition*, 2nd ed. (Berkeley and Los Angeles: University of California Press, 1985), 221.

87. Ibid.

88. Ibid, 231.

89. Robinson, Johnson, and Bhikkhu, *Buddhist Religions*, 54.

90. Monica Lindberg Falk, "Thammacarini Witthaya: The First Buddhist School for Girls in Thailand," in *Innovative Buddhist Women: Swimming against the Stream*, ed. Karma Lekshe Tsomo (Richmond, VA: Carzon Press, 2000), 63.

91. Donald K. Swearer, *The Buddhist World of Southeast Asia* (Albany: State University of New York, 1995), 205n105.

92. Karma Lekshe Tsomo, "Mahaprajapati's Legacy: The Buddhist Women's Movement," in *Buddhist Women across Cultures*, ed. Karma Lekshe Tsomo (Albany: State University of New York Press, 1999), 26.

93. Falk, "Thammacarini Witthaya," 62.

94. Ibid., 70.

95. Tsomo, "Mahaprajapati's Legacy," 31.

96. Hiroko Kawanami, "Patterns of Renunciation: The Changing World of Burmese Nuns," in *Women's Buddhism, Buddhism's Women*, ed. Ellison Banks Findly (Somerville, MA: Wisdom Publications, 2000), 167.

97. Ranjini Obeyesekere, "Review of *Women under the Bo Tree: Buddhist Nuns in Sri Lanka* by Tessa Bartholomeusz," *The Journal for the Scientific Study of Religion* 34 (1995): 402.

98. Ibid.

99. Tessa J. Bartholomeusz, *Women under the Bo Tree: Buddhist Nuns in Sri Lanka* (Cambridge: Cambridge University Press, 1994), 152.

100. Yuchen Li, "Ordination, Legitimacy, and Sisterhood: The International Full Ordination Ceremony in Bodhgaya," in Tsomo, *Innovative Buddhist Women*, 176.

101. Ibid., 176.

102. Sandy Boucher, *Opening the Lotus: A Woman's Guide to Buddhism* (Boston: Beacon Press, 1997), 42.

103. I. B. Horner, *Women under Primitive Buddhism: Laywomen and Almswomen* (London: Routledge and Kegan Paul, 1930), xxiv.

104. Dr. (Mrs.) L. S. Dewaraja, "The Position of Women in Buddhism," in *The Wheel* 280 (Kandy: Buddhist Publication Society, 1981) (on WWW, 16 September 2006, accesstoinsight.org/lib/authors/dewaraja/wheel280,html).

105. Alan Sponberg, "Attitudes toward Women and the Feminine in Early Buddhism," in *Buddhism, Sexuality, and Gender*, ed. Jose Ignacio Cabezon (Albany: State University of New York Press, 1992), 8.

106. Ibid., 9.

107. Karen Andrews, "Women in Theravada Buddhism," Enabling Support Foundation (on WWW, 17 March 2007, enabling.org/ia/vipassana/Archive/A/Andrews.womenTheraBudAndrews.html).

108. Susan Murcott, *The First Buddhist Women: Translations and Commentaries on the Therigatha* (Berkeley, CA: Parallax Press, 1991), 3.

109. Ibid., 10.

110. Ibid., 38.

111. Bhikkhuni Kusuma, "Inaccuracies in Buddhist Women's History," in Tsomo, *Innovative Buddhist Women*, 6.

112. Lenore Friedman, *Meetings with Remarkable Women: Buddhist Teachers in America* (Boston: Shambhala, 1987), 8.

113. Ibid., 9.

114. Ibid., 10.

115. Quoted in ibid., 11.

116. Rita M. Gross, *Buddhism after Patriarchy* (Albany: State University of New York Press, 1993), 33.

117. Dewaraja, "The Position of Women in Buddhism," 6-7.

118. Sponberg, "Attitudes toward Women," 14.

119. Kusuma, "Inaccuracies in Buddhist Women's History," 8-9.

120. Amara Chayabongse, "Women in the Tipitaka," The World Fellowship of Buddhists website, 1 August 2549 [2006] (on WWW, 15 October 2006, wfb-hq.org/Articles%20and%20Analysis0004.html).

121. Mae Chu, member of Hsi Lai Temple, interview by author, Hacienda Heights, California, 15 September 2006.

122. Fu Chi-ying, *Handing Down the Light: The Biography of Venerable Master Hsing Yun*, trans. Amy Lui-Ma (Hacienda Heights, CA: Buddha's Light Publishing, 2004), 113.

123. Li, "Ordination, Legitimacy, and Sisterhood," 184.

124. Robinson, "Hindu Paradigms of Women," 216.

125. Choi Hee An, *Korean Women and God: Experiencing God in a Multi-religious Colonial Context* (Maryknoll, NY: Orbis Books, 2005), 33.

126. Paul, *Women in Buddhism*, 177.

127. Ibid., 217.

128. Hae-ju Sunim (Ho-Ryeon Jeon), "Can Women Achieve Enlightenment? A Critique of Sexual Transformation for Enlightenment," in Tsomo, *Buddhist Women across Cultures*, 138.

129. Gross, *Buddhism after Patriarchy*, 69.

130. Ibid., 77.

131. Paul, *Women in Buddhism*, 236.

132. Friedman, *Meetings with Remarkable Women*, 5.

133. Gross, *Buddhism after Patriarchy,* 39.

134. Tsomo, "Mahaprajapati's Legacy," 29.

135. Li, "Ordination, Legitimacy, and Sisterhood, 178.

136. Tsomo, "Mahaprajapati's Legacy," 31.

137. Karma Lekshe Tsomo, "Introduction," in Tsomo, *Innovative Buddhist Women*, xxiv.

138. Sarah LeVine, "At the Cutting Edge: Theravada Nuns in the Kathmandu Valley," in Tsomo, *Innovative Buddhist Women*, 13-15.

139. Ellison Banks Findly, "Women Teachers of Women: Early Nuns 'Worthy of My Confidence,'" in Findly, *Women's Buddhism, Buddhism's Women*, 139.

140. Ibid., 140-143.

141. Gross, *Buddhism after Patriarchy,* 179.

142. Ibid.

143. Karma Lekshe Tsomo, "Transforming Women's Position in Buddhism," in Tsomo, *Innovative Buddhist Women*, 327-328.

PART II: PROPOSING SOME SOLUTIONS

5. BRINGING WOMEN TOGETHER

1. "Empowering Women of Faith as Agents of Social Transformation, Introduction," World Conference of Religions for Peace (on WWW, 23 March 2007, wcrp.org/files/AR-Women'sProgram-2006.pdf).

2. Shawn Hubler, "Over the Hedge," *West Magazine,* in the *Los Angeles Times,* 4 June 2006, I.16.

3. Betsy Wiggins, "We Gather Together," *Family Circle* (25 November 2003), 10.

4. World Council of Churches, "The Consultation Statement," *Current Dialogue* 35 (July 2000) (on WWW, 9 June 2006, wcc-coe.org/wcc/what/interreligious/cd35 -17.html).

5. Hubler, "Over the Hedge," 4.

6. Sondra Thiederman, "Stop Stereotyping: Overcome Your Worst Diversity Enemy," Monster Career Advice (on WWW, 23 March 2007, content.monster.com/articles/3465/17733/1/default.aspx).

6. Methods of Women's Dialogue

1. Maggie Herzig and Laura Chasin, *Fostering Dialogue across Divides: A Nuts and Bolts Guide fromt he Public Conversation Project* (Watertown, MA: Public Conversations Project, 2006), 1.

2. Diana L. Eck, *Encountering God: A Spiritual Journey from Boseman to Banaras* (Boston: Beacon Press, 1993), 71.

3. Leonard Swidler and Ashok Gangadean,"Seven Stages of Deep Dialogue," Global Dialogue Institute (2 January 1999) (on WWW, 23 March 2007, astro.temple.edu/%7Edialogue/case,htm#SE).

4. Herzig and Chasin, *Fostering Dialogue across Divides,* 9.

5. See Maura O'Neill, *Women Speaking, Women Listening: Women in Interreligious Dialogue* (Maryknoll, NY: Orbis Books, 1990), chap. 2.

6. See Virginia Fabella and Mercy Amba Oduyoye, eds., *With Passion and Compassion: Third World Women Doing Theology* (Maryknoll, NY: Orbis Books, 1989); Choi Hee An, *Korean Women and God: Experiencing God in a Multi-religious Colonial Context* (Maryknoll, NY: Orbis Books, 2005).

7. Kay Lindahl, *The Sacred Art of Listening* (Woodstock, VT: Skylight Paths Publishing, 2002), 8.

8. Ibid., 68.

9. Ibid., 83.

10. Nelle Morton, *The Journey Is Home* (Boston: Beacon Press, 1985), 55.

7. Topics and Issues for Women's Dialogue

1. Susannah Heschel, "Judaism," in *Her Voice, Her Faith*, ed. Arvind Sharma and Katherine K. Young (Boulder, CO: Westview Press, 2003), 146.

2. Lynn Davidman, *Tradition in a Rootless World: Women Turn to Orthodox Judaism* (Berkeley and Los Angeles: University of California Press, 1991), 108.

3. "The Danvers Statement," The Council on Biblical Manhood and Womanhood, 2005 (on WWW, 8 November 2005, cbmw.org/about/danvers.php), rationales 1 and 10.

4. Diana Villa, "The Status of Women in the Halacha," *Hagshama* 11 (January 2001) (on WWW, 11 October 2005, wzo.org.il/en/resources/view.asp?id+152)

5. Paul J. Kobelski, "The Letter to the Ephesians," in *The New Jerome Biblical Commentary*, ed. Raymond Brown, Joseph A. Fitzmyer, and Roland E. Murphy (Englewood Cliffs, NJ: Prentice Hall, 1990), 890.

Bibliography

Abdo, Geneive. *No God But God: Egypt and the Triumph of Islam.* Oxford: Oxford University Press, 2000.

Abdul-Ghafur, Saleemahm, ed. *Living Islam Out Loud.* Boston: Beacon Press, 2005.

Abou-Bakr, Omaima. "A Muslim Woman's Reflections on Gender." www.crescentlife .com/thisthat/feminist%20muslims/muslim_womans_reflection _on_gender.htm

Abugideiri, Hibba. "My Faith, My Sustaining Guide." In *National Geographic Geography of Religion,* edited by Susan Tyler Hitchcock and John L. Esposito, 372-395. Washington, DC: National Geographic Society, 2004.

Ahmed, Leila. *Women and Gender in Islam.* New Haven, CT: Yale University Press, 1992.

Al-Faruqi, Dr. Lois Lamya. "Islamic Traditions and the Feminist Movement: Confrontation or Co-operation?" (20 October 2004). www.crescentlife .com/thisthat/feminist%20muslims/islam_and_feminist_movement.htm.

———. "Women in Qur'anic Society." (20 October 2004). www.crescentlife.com/ thisthat/feminist%20muslims/women-in-quranic-society.htm.

Amsellem, Wendy. "Living within My Era." Drisha Institute for Jewish Education. www.drisha.org/viewpoints_archives/wendyamsellem.htm.

An, Choi Hee. *Korean Women and God: Experiencing God in a Multi-religious Colonial Context.* Maryknoll, NY: Orbis Books, 2005.

Andrews, Karen. "Women in Theravada Buddhism." Enabling Support Foundation. www.enabling.org/ia/vipassana/Archive/A/Andrews/womenTheraBudAndrews .html.

Aylon, Helene. "Jewish Women and the Feminist Revolution." Jewish Women's Archive. www.jwa.org/feminism/_html/JWA002.htm.

Bangee, Marya. "The Flight of Our Rights: Zaynab al-Ghazali." *Alkalima* (October 2005). www.alkalima.com/?page=Archives&vol=8&issue=1&id=90.

Barlas, Asma. *Believing Women in Islam.* Austin: University of Texas Press, 2002.

Bartholomeusz, Tessa J. *Women under the Bo Tree: Buddhist Nuns in Sri Lanka.* Cambridge: Cambridge University Press, 1994.

Becher, Jeanne, ed. *Women, Religion, and Sexuality: Studies on the Impact of Religious Teachings on Women.* Philadelphia: Trinity Press International, 1990.

Berkowitz, Adena. "An Orthodox Feminist Speaks—In Response to Our Critics." *JOFA Journal* (Winter 1999–Shevat 5759). www.jofa.org/pdf/JofaWinter1999 .pdf.

Berner, Leila Gal. "Hearing Hannah's Voice." In *Daughters of Abraham,* edited by Yvonne Yazbeck Haddad and John L. Esposito, 35-49. Gainesville: University Press of Florida, 2001.

Blair, Sheila S., and Jonathan M. Bloom. "Art and Architecture; Themes and Variations." In *The Oxford History of Islam*, edited by John L. Esposito. Oxford: Oxford University Press, 1999.

Boucher, Sandy. *Opening the Lotus: A Woman's Guide to Buddhism*. Boston: Beacon Press, 1997.

Broner, E. M. "Jewish Women and the Feminist Revolution." Jewish Women's Archive. www.jwa.org/feminism/_html/JWA006.htm.

Butalia, Urvashi. "Mother India." *New Internationalist Magazine* (15 November 2005). www.newint.org/issue277/mother.htm.

Carlson-Thies, Christiane. "Man and Woman at Creation: A Critique of Complementarian Interpretations." *Priscilla Papers* (Fall 2004). www .cbeinternational.org/new/free_articles/ManandWomanatCreation.pdf.

Chatterji, Jyotsna, ed. *Religions and the Status of Women*. New Delhi: Uppal Publishing House, 1990.

Chayabongse, Amara. "Women in the Tipitaka." The World Fellowship of Buddhists website. 1 August 2549 [2006]. www.wfb-hq.org/Articles %20and%20 Analysis0004.html.

Chittister, Joan. "Calling the Power of Women." *Spirituality and Health* (October 2005).

Chi-ying, Fu. *Handing Down the Light: The Biography of Venerable Master Hsing Yun*. Translated by Amy Lui-Ma. Hacienda Heights, CA: Buddha's Light Publishing, 2004.

Christians for Biblical Equality, "Men, Women, and Biblical Equality." www.cbeinternational.org/new/about/biblical_equality.shtml.

Cochran, Pamela D. H. *Evangelical Feminism*. New York: New York University Press, 2005.

Cooey, Paula M., William R. Eakin, and Jay B. McDaniel, eds. *After Patriarchy: Feminist Transformations of the World Religions*, Maryknoll, NY: Orbis Books, 1991.

Council on Biblical Manhood and Womanhood. "The Danvers Statement." www.cbmw.org/about/danvers.php.

Crollius, Arij A. Roest. "Interreligious Dialogue: Can It Be Sincere?" *SEDOS Bulletin on Net* (20 July 2000). www.sedos.org/english/Crollius.html

Das, Soma. "Laws of Manu or 'Manava Dharma Shastra." In *Hinduism*. www.hinduism.about.com/library/weekly/aa051303a.htm.

Davidman, Lynn. *Tradition in a Rootless World: Women Turn to Orthodox Judaism*. Berkeley and Los Angeles: University of California Press, 1991.

Davison, Anne. "Learning to Live in a Europe of Many Religions: A Curriculum for Interfaith Learning for Women." World Council of Churches. 2000. www.wcc-coe.org/wcc/what/interreligious/cd35-18.html.

Dev Sen, Nabaneeta. "Lady Sings the Blues: When Women Retell the Ramayana." *Manushi 108*. www.ninopaley.com/Sitayana/Manushi_LadySingstheBlues .html.

———. "Translating Chandrabati." Center for Women's Development Studies (2006). www.cwds.org/chandrabati.htm.

Dewaraja, Dr. (Mrs.) L. S. "The Position of Women in Buddhism." In *The Wheel* 280. Kandy: Buddhist Publication Society, 1981. www.accestoinsight.org/ lib/authors/dewaraja/wheel280.html.

Eck, Diana L. *Encountering God: A Spiritual Journey from Boseman to Banaras.* Boston: Beacon Press, 1993.

Eggebroten, Anne. "On Being Evangelical and Ecumenical." *EEWC Update* (Summer 2003). www.eewc.com/Update/Summer2003OnBing.htm.

Egnell, Helene. "Dialogue for Life: Feminist Approaches to Interfaith Dialogue." In *Theology and the Religions: A Dialogue,* edited by Viggo Mortensen, 249-256. Grand Rapids, MI: Eerdmans, 2003.

"Empowering Women of Faith as Agents of Social Transformation." World Conference of Religions for Peace. www.wcrp.org/files/AR-Women'sProgram-2006.pdf.

Ezzat, Heba Raouf. "Rethinking Secularism . . . Rethinking Feminism" (7 January 2002). www.islamonline.net/English/contemporary/2002/07/Article01.shtml).

———. "Women and the Interpretation of Islamic Sources" (October 1999). www.crescentlife.com/thisthat/feminist%20muslims/women-and-interpretation-of-islamic-sources.htm.

Fabella, Virginia, and Mercy Amba Oduyoye, eds. *With Passion and Compassion: Third World Women Doing Theology.* Maryknoll, NY: Orbis Books, 1989.

Falk, Monica Lindberg. "Thammacarini Witthaya: The First Buddhist School for Girls in Thailand." In Tsomo, *Innovative Buddhist Women,* 61-71.

Fazili, Yousra Y. "Fumbling toward Ecstasy." In Abdul-Ghafur, *Living Islam Out Loud,* 75-85.

Findly, Ellison Banks. "Women Teachers of Women: Early Nuns 'Worthy of My Confidence.'" In *Women's Buddhism, Buddhism's Women,* edited by Ellison Banks Findly, 133-55. Boston: Wisdom Publications, 2000.

Fine, Wendy Wolfe. "Modern Orthodox Judaism as an Option for Professional Women." *Journal of Jewish Communal Service* (Winter/Spring 1995): 153-164.

Fisher, Michael M. J., and Mehdi Abedi. *Debating Muslims: Cultural Dialogues in Postmodernity and Tradition.* Madison: University of Wisconsin Press, 1990.

Franzmann, Majella. *Women and Religion.* New York: Oxford University Press, 2000.

Friedman, Lenore. *Meetings with Remarkable Women: Buddhist Teachers in America.* Boston: Shambhala, 1987.

Furstenberg, Rochelle. "The Flourishing of Higher Jewish Learning for Women." *Jerusalem Letter* (26 Nisan 5760/1 May 2000). www.jcpa.org/jl/jl429.htm.

Gopal, Dr. Jaishree. In "Navya Shastra Endorses Government of India Plan to Examine Laws of Manu: Commends Hindu Leaders for Initiating Anti-Untouchability Campaign." Press release (5 July 2005). www.shastras.org/PressRelease12.html.

Greifenhagen, F. Volker. "Islamic Fundamentalism(s): More Than a Pejorative Epithet?" In Schick, Jaffe, and Watkinson, *Contesting Fundamentalisms,* 63-75.

Greenberg, Blu. "Orthodox, Feminist, and Proud of It." Beliefnet, Inc. 2004. www.beliefnet.com/story/47/story_4714.html.

Groothuis, Rebecca Merrill, and Ronald W. Pierce. "Introduction." In Pierce and Groothuis, *Discovering Biblical Equality*, 13-20.

Gross, Rita M. *Buddhism after Patriarchy: A Feminist History, Analysis, and Reconstruction of Buddhism*. Albany: State University of New York Press, 1993.

Gupta, Lina. "Kali, the Savior." In Cooey, Eakin, and McDaniel, *After Patriarchy*, 15-38.

———. "Ganga: Purity, Pollution, and Hinduism." In *Ecofeminism and the Sacred*, edited by Carol J. Adams, 99-116. New York: Continuum, 1993.

Hassan, Riffat. "An Islamic Perspective." In Becher, *Women, Religion, and Sexuality*, 93-128.

———. "Muslim Women and Post-Patriarchal Islam." In Cooey, Eakin, and McDaniel, *After Patriarchy*, 39-64.

Hassey, Janet "Evangelical Women in Ministry a Century Ago." In Pierce and Groothuis, *Discovering Biblical Equality*, 39-57.

Hauptman, Judith. "The Challenge Facing the Conservative Movement." *The Jewish Week* (8 July 2005). www.thejewishweek.com/top/editletcontent/php3?artid+4295&print+yes

Herzig, Maggie, and Laura Chasin. *Fostering Dialogue across Divides: A Nuts and Bolts Guide from the Public Conversations Project*. Watertown, MA: Public Conversations Project, 2006.

Heschel, Susannah. "Judaism." In *Her Voice, Her Faith: Women Speak on World Religions*, edited by Arvind Sharma and Katherine K. Young, 145-167. Boulder, CO: Westview Press, 2003.

Hess, Linda. "Rejecting Sita: Indian Responses to the Ideal Man's Cruel Treatment of His Ideal Wife." *Journal of the American Academy of Religion* 67 (1999): 1-32.

"Historian: Women's Place in Methodism Inconsistent." United Methodist News Service (20 August 2003). www.archives.unc.org/interior_print.asp?mid=1021.

Hitchcock, Susan Tyler, and John L. Esposito. *Geography of Religion: Where God Lives, Where Pilgrims Walk*. Washington, DC: National Geographic Society, 2004.

Horner, I. B. *Women under Primitive Buddhism: Laywomen and Almswomen*. London: Routledge and Kegan Paul, 1930.

Huff, Peter A. "The Challenge of Fundamentalism for Interreligious Dialogue." *Cross Currents* 50, no. 1-2 (Spring-Summer 2000). www.crosscurrents.org/Huff.htm.

Hunt, Mary. "Different Voices Different Choices: Feminist Perspectives on Ministry— A Contribution from the United States." Talk presented at WOW conference, 23 July 2005. www.cnwe.org/DifferentVoicesMaryHuntWOWtal.doc

Ingersoll, Julie. *Evangelical Christian Women: War Stories in Gender Battles*. New York: New York University Press, 2003.

Institute for Interreligious Dialogue, 2001-2003. "Introduction." www.iid.org.ir/IIDE/AboutUs.asp?Menu=2

Jalabi, Afra. "To Veil or Not to Veil, That Is the Question" (14 March 2007). www.muslimaccess.com/articles/Women/to_veil_or_not.asp.

JOFA: Jewish Orthodox Feminist Alliance. www.jofa.org/about.php/about.

John Paul II. *Familiaris Consortio.* Rome: Libreria Editrice Vaticana, 1981).

———. *Mulieris Dignitatem* (1988). ww.wf-f.org/MulierDig.html.

———. *Ordinatio Sacerdotalis* (May 1994). www.wf-f.org/OrdSac.html.

Johnson, Dr. Judith, "Ordinations on the St.Lawrence." *New Women, New Church* (Winter 2004-2005). Women's Ordination Conference. www.womensordination .org/pages/art_pages/art_2005Ord.

Jones, Rebecca. "Does Christianity Squash Women?" Speech at Bryn Mawr, April 2000. www.cbmw.org/resources/articles/christianityandwomen.pdf.

Judaism 101: A Glossary of Basic Jewish Terms and Concepts. A project of the Union of Orthodox Jewish Congregations of America. 12 October 2005. www.ou.org/about/judaism/m.htm.

Juneja, Sakshi. "Searching for Sita." To Each His Own (17 November 2005). www.sakshijuneja.com/blog/2005/11/17searching-for-sita/.

Kahf, Mohja. "The Muslim in the Mirror." In Abdul-Ghafur, *Living Islam Out Loud,* 130-138.

Kamali, Mohammad Hashim. "Law and Society: The Interplay of Revelation and Reason in the Shariah." In *The Oxford History of Islam,* edited by John L. Esposito, 107-153. Oxford: Oxford University Press, 1999.

Katz, Lisa. "All about Judaism/Branches of Judaism." About Religion and Spirituality website. www.judaism.about.com/od/conservativejudaism/ Conservative_Judaism.htm.

Kawanami, Hiroko. "Patterns of Renunciation: The Changing World of Burmese Nuns." In *Women's Buddhism, Buddhism's Women,* edited by Ellison Banks Findly, 159-171. Somerville, MA: Wisdom Publications, 2000.

Khandelwal, Meena. *Women in Ochre Robes: Gendering Hindu Renunciation.* Albany: State University of New York Press, 2004.

Kimball, Charles A. "Absolute Truth Claims." In *War or Words,* edited by Donald W. Musser and D. Dixon Sutherland, 105-123. Cleveland: The Pilgrim Press, 2005.

King, Ursula. "Christianity and Feminism: Do They Need Each Other?" *International Journal for the Study of the Christian Church* (October 2004): 194-206.

———. "Hinduism and Women: Uses and Abuses of Religious Freedom." In *Facilitating Freedom of Religion or Belief: A Deskbook,* edited by Tore Lindholm, W. Cole Durham, and Bahia G. Tahzib-Lie, 523-543. Netherlands: Koninklijke Brill NV, 2004.

Kishwar, Madhu. "We Shall Re-Examine Everything." *Manushi* January 1979. In *In Search of Answers,* edited by Madhu Kishwar and Ruth Vanita, 242-245. London: Zed Books, 1984.

———. "Women's Politics." In *In Search of Answers: Indian Women's Voices from Manushi, A Selection from the First Five Years from a Feminist Magazine,* edited by Kishwar Madhu and Ruth Vanita. London: Zed Books, 1984.

Kobelski, Paul J. "The Letter to the Ephesians." In *The New Jerome Biblical Commentary,* edited by Raymond Brown, Joseph A. Fitzmyer, and Roland E. Murphy. Englewood Cliffs, NJ: Prentice Hall, 1990.

Krishna, Nanditha. "The Equals of Men." *Newindpress on Sunday.* www.newindpress .com/sunday/colItems.asp?ID=SEC20030803031539.

Krishnan, V. *Utthara Ramayana.* www.geocities.com/Athens/Styx/ 7153/ Utthara.html.

Kroeger, Catherine Clark. "Does Belief in Women's Equality Lead to an Acceptance of Homosexual Practice?" *Prisicilla Papers* (Spring 2004).

Kuikman, Jackie. "Jewish Fundamentalisms and a Critical Politics of Identity: The Makings of a Post-Zionist Discourse." In Schick, Jaffe, and Watkinson, *Contesting Fundmentalisms*, 48-62.

Küng, Hans. "Replacing Clashes with Dialogue among Religions and Nations." In *War or Words,* edited by Donald W. Musser and D. Dixon Sutherland, 7-21. Cleveland: The Pilgrim Press, 2005.

Kusuma, Bhikkhuni. "Inaccuracies in Buddhist Women's History." In Tsomo, *Innovative Buddhist Women*, 5-12.

Lande, Aasulv. "Creative Dialogue." In *Theology and the Religions: A Dialogue*, edited by Viggo Mortensen, 403-408. Grand Rapids, MI: Eerdmans, 2003.

"Laws of Manu." *Sacred Books of the East.* Vol. 25. Translated by George Buhler (1886). Internet Sacred Text Archive. www.sacred-texts.com/hin/manu/manu03.htm.

Lerner, Dr. Anne Lapidus. "On the Rabbinic Ordination of Women." JTS: The Rabbinical School. www.jtsa.edu/rabbinical/women/excerpts.shtml.

Leslie, Julia. "Suttee or Sati: Victim or Victor?" In *Roles and Rituals for Hindu Women,* edited by Julia Leslie, 175-190. Rutherford, NJ: Fairleigh Dickinson University Press, 1991.

LeVine, Sarah. "At the Cutting Edge: Theravada Nuns in the Kathmandu Valley." In Tsomo, *Innovative Buddhist Women*, 13-29.

Levinson, Pnina Nave. "Women and Sexuality: Traditions and Progress." In Becher, *Women, Religion, and Sexuality*, 45-63.

Li, Yuchen. "Ordination, Legitimacy, and Sisterhood: The International Full Ordination Ceremony in Bodhgaya." In Tsomo, *Innovative Buddhist Women*, 168-199.

Lindahl, Kay. *The Sacred Art of Listening.* Woodstock, VT: Skylight Paths Publishing, 2002.

Manji, Irshad. *The Trouble with Islam: A Muslim's Call for Reform in Her Faith.* New York: St. Martin's Press, 2003.

Manjul, V. L. "Starting Vedic Studies: Backed by Scripture, Girls Get Their Sacred Thread." *Hinduism Today* (October/November/December 2002). www.proquest.umi.com/pqdweb?did=581432441&Fmt=3&clientId =42799&RqT=309&VName=PQD.

Marcotte, Roxanne D. "Egyptian Islamists and the Status of Muslim Women Question." *Journal for the Study of Religions and Ideologies* (Summer 2005). jsri.ro/old/html%20version/index/no_11/roxannedmarcotte-articol .htm.

Masson, Vikram. "Hindu Group Asks Religious Leaders to End Caste Discrimination and to Save the Vedas." Navya Shastra (27 November 2003). www.shastras.org/PressRelease3.html.

McCulley, Carolyn. "Liberated from Feminism: the Personal Testimony of Carolyn McCulley." The Council on Biblical Manhood and Womanhood (2005). www.cbmw.org/resources/articles/mcculley.php.

McDaniel, June. *Making Virtuous Daughters and Wives*. Albany: SUNY Press, 2003.

McGee, Mary. "Ritual Rights: The Gender Implications of *Adhikara*." In *Jewels of Authority*, edited by Laurie L. Patton, 32-50. Oxford: Oxford University Press, 2002.

Mernissi, Fatima. *The Veil and the Male Elite*. Translated by Mary Jo Lakeland. Menlo Park, CA: Addison-Wesley Publishing Co., 1991.

Michael-Rush, Peggy. "A Reluctant Feminist." *EEWC Update* (Spring 2004). www.eewc.com?Update/Spring2004Reluctant.htm.

Mitter, Sara S. *Dharma's Daughters*. New Brunswick, CT: Rutgers University Press, 1991.

Mollenkott, Virginia Ramey. "Feminism and Evangelicalism." *EEWC Update* (Spring 2005). www.eewc.com/Update/Spring2005Feminism.htm.

Moore, Rev. Joy J. "Women in Ministry." United Methodist Communications. United Methodist Church (2 December 2005).

Morton, Nelle. *The Journey Is Home*. Boston: Beacon Press, 1985.

Muhammad, Precious Rasheeda. "To Be Young, Gifted, Black, American, Muslim, and Woman." In Abdul-Ghafur, *Living Islam Out Loud*, 36-49.

Mukherjee, Prabhati. *Hindu Women: Normative Models*. London: Sangam Books, 1993.

Murcott, Susan. *The First Buddhist Women: Translations and Commentary on the Therigatha*. Berkeley, CA: Parallax Press, 1991.

Nair, C. N. Sreekantan and Sarah Joseph. *Retelling the Ramayana: Voices from Kerala*. Translated by Vasanthi Sankaranarayanan. New Delhi: Oxford University Press, 2005.

Nandakumar, Dr. Prema. "Indian Epic Narrative—Alive and Vibrant" (24 April 2005). www.boloji.com/culture/007.htm.

Nannas, Shoshana. "Feminism within Ultra Orthodoxy." *The Jewish Observer* (October 1998).

Narayanan, Vasudha. "Hinduism." In *Her Voice, Her Faith: Women Speak on World Religions,* edited by Arvind Sharma and Katherine K. Young, 11-57. Boulder, CO: Westview Press, 2003.

———. "Respected Guardians of Our Ancient Faith." *Welcome to Navya Shastra*. www.shastras.org/VasudhaNarayanan.html.

Nesbitt, Rev. Paula D. "Women's Ordination: Problems and Possibilities." WOC 2000 Plenary Talks. Women's Ordination Conference. www .womensordination.org/pages/art_pages/Nesbitt.htm.

Niranjanananda, Swamini. "Reinstating Women's Roles in Religion." Speech presented at Amritavarsham-50, 24-27 September 2003. www.amritavarsham .org/summit/women/niranjana.htm.

Nunes-Harwitt, Melissa. "Masekhet Sukkah." Drisha Institute for Jewish Education. www.drisha.org/viewpoints_archive/melissa_nunesharwitt.htm.

Nunley, Jan. "Two Southern California Parishes Vote Alignment with Uganda Diocese," Episcopal News Service (17 August 2004). www.episcopalchurch .org/3577_48614_ENG_HTM.htm.

Obeyesekere, Ranjini. "Review of *Women under the Bo Tree: Buddhist Nuns in Sri Lanka* by Tessa Bartholomeusz." *The Journal for the Scientific Study of Religion* 34 (1995): 402-403.

Olsen, Ted, "Weblog: Methodist Court Acquits Homosexual Minister." *Christianity Today* (22 March 2004) www.christianitytoday.com/ct/2004/112/11.0.html.

O'Neill, Maura. *Women Speaking, Women Listening: Women in Interreligious Dialogue.* Maryknoll, NY: Orbis Books, 1990.

Patil, Sushila, and Moses Seenarine. "Letter to Gargi." *Saxakali Publications* (15 August 1996). www.saxakali.com/Saxakali-Publications/gargi.htm.

Paul, Diana Y. *Women in Buddhism: Images of the Feminine in Mahayana Tradition.* 2nd edition. Berkeley and Los Angeles: University of California Press, 1985.

Patterson, Dorothy. "The High Calling of Wife and Mother in Biblical Perspective." In *Recovering Biblical Manhood and Womanhood: A Response to Evangelical Feminism,* edited by John Piper and Wayne Grudem. Wheaton, IL: Crossway Books, 1991.

Pennington, Kim. "Resources for Women." The Council on Biblical Manhood and Womanhood. www.cbmw.org/resources/women-intro.php.

Pierce, Ronald W. "Contemporary Evangelicals for Gender Equality." in Pierce and Groothuis, *Discovering Biblical Equality,* 58-77.

Pierce, Ronald W., and Rebecca Merrill Groothuis, eds. *Discovering Biblical Equality: Complementarity without Hierarch.* Downers Grove, IL: InterVarsity Press, 2004.

Plaskow, Judith. "Transforming the Nature of Community: Toward a Feminist People of Israel." In Cooey, Eakin, and McDaniel, *After Patriarchy,* 87-105.

Porcile-Santiso, Maria-Teresa. "Roman Catholic Teachings on Female Sexuality." In Becher, *Women, Religion, and Sexuality,* 192-220.

Pruthi, Raj, and Bela Rani Sharma. *Aryans and Hindu Women.* New Delhi: Anmol Publications, 1995.

Qureshi, Emran, and Heba Raouf Ezzat. "Are Sharia Laws and Human Rights Compatible?" Qantara.de: Dialogue with the Islamic World (11 December 2004). www.qantara.de/webcom/show_article.php/_c-373/nr-6/i.html2.

"Ramayana." *The Columbia Encyclopedia.* 6th edition (2001-5). www.bartleby.com/65/ra/Ramayana.html.

Ramoutar, Paras. "Criticism and Acclaim Greet Trinidad's First Woman Priest." *Hinduism Today* (February 1994). www.hinduismtoday.com/archives/1994/2/1994-2-01.shtml.

Ratzinger, Joseph Cardinal. "Letter to Bishops of the Catholic Church on the Collaboration of Men and Women in the Church and in the World," 31 July 2004. www.vatican.va/roman_curia/congregations/cfaith/documents/rc_con_cfaith_doc_20040731_collaboration_en.html.

Rinpoche, The Dzogchen Ponlop. "What the Buddha Taught." *Shambala Sun* (May 2005). 41-47.

Robinson, Richard H., Willard L. Johnson, and Thanissaro Bhikkhu. *Buddhist Religions: A Historical Introduction.* 5th edition. Belmont: Wadsworth, 2005.

Robinson, Sandra P. "Hindu Paradigms of Women: Images and Values." In *Women, Religion, and Social Change,* edited by Yvonne Yazbeck Haddad and Ellison Banks Findly, 181-216. Albany: University of New York Press, 1985.

Rouse, Carolyn Moxley. *Engaged Surrender.* Berkeley and Los Angeles: University of California Press, 2004.

Ruether, Rosemary Radford. "Catholicism, Women, Body, and Sexuality: A Response." In Becher, *Women, Religion, and Sexuality,* 221-232.

———. "Christian Feminist Theology." In *Daughters of Abraham,* edited by Yvonne Yazbeck Haddad and John L. Esposito. Gainesville: University Press of Florida, 2001.

———. "The Church as Liberation Community from Patriarchy: The Praxis of Ministry as Discipleship of Equals." Catholic Network for Women's Equality (5 August 2005). www.cnwe.org/wowtalk.doc.

———. *Sexism and God-Talk: Toward a Feminist Theology.* Boston: Beacon Press, 1983.

Ruthven, Malise. *Fundamentalism: The Search for Meaning.* Oxford: Oxford University Press, 2004.

Saarinen, Risto. "After Rescher: Pluralism as Preferentialism." In *Theology and Religions: A Dialogue,* edited by Viggo Mortensen, 409-413. Grand Rapids, MI: Eerdmans, 2003.

Sablok, Soma. "Women in Vedas." www.geocities.com/Athens/Pantheon/47889/Articles/Women/women_in_vedas.html?

SadagOpan, V. "Women in Sri Vaishnavam." In *Indian Culture and Philosophy* (13 April 2006). www.india-forum.com/articles/113/1Women-in-Sri-Vaishnavam.

Saed, Khalida. "On the Edge of Belonging." In Abdul-Ghafur, *Living Islam Out Loud,* 86-94.

Salgodo, Nirmala. "Religious Identities of Buddhist Nuns: Training Precepts, Renunciant Attire, and Nomenclature in Theravada Buddhism." *Journal of the American Academy of Religion* (December 2004): 935-953.

Sanneh, Lamin. "Secular Values in the Midst of Faith: A Critical Discourse on Dialogue and Difference." In *Theology and Religions: A Dialogue,* edited by Viggo Mortensen, 137-152. Grand Rapids, MI: Eerdmans, 2003.

Schafer, Ingrid, ed. "Power and Promise of Deep Dialogue." Global Dialogue Institute. 7 March 1998. www.astro.temple.edu/~dialogue/case.htm.

Schick, Carol, JoAnn Jaffe, and Ailsa M. Watkinson, "Considering Fundamentalism." In Schick, Jaffe, and Watkinson, *Contesting Fundamentalisms.*

Schick, Carol, JoAnn Jaffe, Ailsa M. Watkinson, eds. *Contesting Fundamentalisms.* Halifax: Fernwood Publishing, 2004.

Schuenemeyer, Rev. Mike. "About Our Lesbian, Gay, Bisexual, and Transgender [LGBT] Ministries." United Church of Christ. www.ucc.org/lgbt/about.htm.

Schüssler Fiorenza, Elisabeth. *In Memory of Her.* New York: Crossroads, 1983.

———. "We Are Church—A Kingdom of Priests." 22 July 2005. Catholic Network of Women's Equality. www.cnwe.org/WOW-AKindom-ElisabethSFtalk.doc.

——. *Wisdom Ways.* Maryknoll, NY: Orbis Books, 2005.

Scovill, Nelia Beth. "The Liberation of Women in Religious Sources." The Religious Consultation on Population, Reproductive Health, and Ethics. www.religiousconsultation.org/liberation.htm#Hinduism.

"Sita, Speak." *Passages to India.* Independent Broadcasting Associates (2002). www.ibaradio.org/India/passages/passages.htm.

Sivananda, Sri Swami. "Hindu Law-Givers: The Hindu Law-Givers in the Hindu Scriptures." The Global Oneness Commitment. www.experiencefestival .com/a/Hindu_Law-Givers/id/22607.

———. "The Vedas." The Divine Life Society (18 January 2000). www.dlshq.org/ religions/vedas.htm.

Sponberg, Alan. "Attitudes toward Women and the Feminine in Early Buddhism." In *Buddhism, Sexuality, and Gender*, edited by Jose Ignacio Cabezon, 3-33. Albany: State University of New York Press, 1992.

Sunim, Hae-ju. (Ho-Ryeon Jeon). "Can Women Achieve Enlightenment?" In *Buddhist Women across Cultures*, edited by Karma Lekshe Tsomo. Albany: State University of New York Press, 1999.

Swearer, Donald K. *The Buddhist World of Southeast Asia*. Albany: State University of New York Press, 1995.

Swidler, Leonard, and Ashok Gangadean. "Seven Stages of Deep Dialogue." Global Dialogue Institute. 2 January 1999. www.astro.temple.edu/%7Edialogue/ case.htm#SE.

Syed, Mohammad Ali. *The Position of Women in Islam: A Progressive View*. Albany: State University of New York Press, 2004.

Teubal, Savina. "Jewish Women and the Feminist Revolution." Jewish Women's Archive. www.jwo.org/feminism/_html/JSA070.htm.

Thelle, Notto R. "Interreligious Dialogue: Theory and Experience." In *Theology and Religions: A Dialogue*, edited by Viggo Mortensen, 129-136. Grand Rapids, MI: Eerdmans, 2003.

Thiederman, Sondra. "Stop Stereotyping: Overcome Your Worst Diversity Enemy." Monster Career Advice. www.content.monster.com/articles/3465/17733/ 1/default.aspx.

Thomas, Linda E. "Womanist Theology, Epistemology, and a New Anthropological Paradigm." *Cross Currents* (Summer 1998). www.crosscurrents.org/ thomas.htm.

Track, Joachim. "Theology of Religions: A Challenge for the Churches." In *Theology and Religions: A Dialogue*, edited by Viggo Mortensen, 355-386. Grand Rapids, MI: Eerdmans, 2003.

Tsomo, Karma Lekshe. "Mahaprajapati's Legacy." In *Buddhist Women across Cultures*, edited by Karma Lekshe Tsomo, 1-45. Albany: State University of New York Press, 1999.

———. "Transforming Women's Position in Buddhism: Strategies." In Tsomo, *Innovative Buddhist Women*, 326-329.

Tsomo, Karma Lekshe, ed. *Innovative Buddhist Women: Swimming against the Stream*. Richmond, VA: Curzon Press, 2000.

"The United Church of Christ: A Family of Faith for a Global Community." www.ucc.org/aboutus/family.htm.

United Methodist Church. "Equal Rights Regardless of Sexual Orientation." In *The Book of Discipline of the United Methodist Church, 2004*. Nashville, TN: United Methodist Publishing House, 2004.

———. "Status of Women." *The Book of Resolutions of the United Methodist Church, 2004*. Nashville, TN: United Methodist Publishing House, 2004.

———. "Women and Men." In *The Book of Discipline of the United Methodist Church, 2004*. Nashville, TN: United Methodist Publishing House, 2004.

United States Conference of Catholic Bishops. *Follow the Way of Love: A Pastoral Message to Families* (1994). www.usccb.org/laity/follow.shtml.

Valmiki Ramayana: Ayodhya Kanda. Translated by Desiraju Hanumanta Roa and K. M. K. Murthy (1998-2006). www.valmikiramayan.net/ayodhya/sarga29/ayodhya_29_frame.htm.

"Vedas." The Hindu Universe. www.hindunet.org/vedas/.

"Vedas." In *Hinduism.* Internet Sacred Text Archives. www.sacred_texts.com/hin/index.htm.

Villa, Diana. "The Status of Women in the Halacha." *Hagshama* (11 January 2001). www.wzo.org.il/en/resources/view/asp?id=152.

Vishwa Hindu Parishad (UK). *Explaining Hindu Dharma: A Guide for Teachers,* 2nd ed. Surrey: VHP, 2003.

Vivekananda, Swami. *The Message of Vivekananda.* Calcutta: Advaita Ashrama, 2000.

Wadud, Amina. "A'ishah's Legacy." *New Internationalist* 345 (May 2002). www.newint.org/issue345/legacy.htm.

———. *Inside the Gender Jihad: Women's Reform in Islam.* Oxford: Oneworld Publications, 2006.

Wadud-Muhsin, Amina. *Qur'an and Woman.* Malayasia: Penerbit Fajar Bakti Sdn. Bhd., 1992.

Watson, Burton, trans. *The Lotus Sutra,* New York: Columbia University Press, 1993.

Webb, William J. "Gender Equality and Homosexuality." In Pierce and Groothuis, *Discovering Biblical Equality,* 401-13.

Wegener, David. "Southern Baptists Lead the Way: CBMW Interview with SBC Committee member Dr. Dorothy Patterson. *Journal for Biblical Manhood and Womanhood* (Summer 1998).

Welch, Sharon D. *After Empire: The Art and Ethos of Enduring Peace.* Minneapolis: Fortress Press, 2004.

Wiggins, Betsy. "We Gather Together." *Family Circle* (25 November 2003).

Women for Faith and Family. "Affirmation for Catholic Women" (2005). www.wf-f.org/EngAff.html.

World Council of Churches. "The Consultation Statement." *Current Dialogue* 24 (July 2000). www.wcc-coe.org/wcc/what/interreligious/cd35-17.html.

WOC (Women's Ordination Conference). "Introduction." www.womensordination.org/intro.html.

———. "Why Ordination?" www.womensordination.org/why.html.

Young, Katherine K. "*Om,* the Vedas, and the Status of Women with Special Reference to Srivaisnavism." In *Jewels of Authority,* edited by Laurie L. Patton, 84-121. Oxford University Press, 2002.

Index

Imagining the Sacred, Vernon Ruland, S.J.

Christian-Muslim Relations, Ovey N. Mohammed, S.J.

John Paul II and Interreligious Dialogue, Byron L. Sherwin and Harold Kasimow, Editors

Transforming Christianity and the World, John B. Cobb, Jr.

The Divine Deli, John H. Berthrong

Experiencing Scripture in World Religions, Harold Coward, Editor

The Meeting of Religions and the Trinity, Gavin D'Costa

Subverting Hatred: The Challenge of Nonviolence in Religious Traditions, Daniel L. Smith-Christopher, Editor

Christianity and Buddhism: A Multi-Cultural History of Their Dialogue, Whalen Lai and Michael von Brück

Islam, Christianity, and the West: A Troubled History, Rollin Armour, Sr.

Many Mansions? Multiple Religious Belonging, Catherine Cornille, Editor

No God But God: A Path to Muslim-Christian Dialogue on the Nature of God, A. Christian van Gorder

Understanding Other Religious Worlds: A Guide for Interreligious Education, Judith Berling

Buddhists and Christians: Toward Solidarity through Comparative Theology, James L. Fredericks

Christophany: The Fullness of Man, Raimon Panikkar

Experiencing Buddhism: Ways of Wisdom and Compassion, Ruben L. F. Habito

Gandhi's Hope: Learning from Others as a Way to Peace, Jay B. McDaniel

Still Believing: Muslim, Christian, and Jewish Women Affirm Their Faith, Victoria Erickson and Susan A. Farrell, Editors

The Concept of God in Global Dialogue, Werner G. Jeanrond and Aasulv Lande, Editors

The Myth of Religious Superiority: A Multifaith Exploration, Paul F. Knitter, Editor.

A Muslim Looks at Christianity: Essays by Mahmoud Ayoub, Irfan Omar, Editor.